Souls
On Fire

Souls On Fire

Portraits and Legends of Hasidic Masters

Elie Wiesel

Translated from the French
by Marion Wiesel

VINTAGE BOOKS

A Division of Random House, New York

FIRST VINTAGE BOOKS EDITION, February 1973

Copyright © 1972 by Elie Wiesel

All rights reserved under International
and Pan-American Copyright Conventions.
Published in the United States
by Random House, Inc., New York,
and simultaneously in Canada
by Random House of Canada Limited, Toronto.
Originally published in France
as *Célébration Hassidique*
by Editions du Seuil, Paris.
This edition originally published by
Random House, Inc., in February 1972.

Library of Congress Cataloging in Publication Data
Wiesel, Eliezer.
  Souls on fire.
  Translation of Célébration hassidique.
  1. Hasidism—History. 2. Tales, Hasidic.
I. Title
[BM198.W513 1973]   296.8'33   72-8056
ISBN 0-394-71870-4

Manufactured in the United States of America

CONTENTS

Israel Baal Shem Tov, 3

Disciples I, 40

The Maggid of Mezeritch, 53

Disciples II, 82

Levi-Yitzhak of Berditchev, 89

Elimelekh of Lizensk, 113

Disciples III, 131

Israel of Rizhin, 140

Disciples IV, 164

Nahman of Bratzlav, 169

The School of Pshiskhe, 203

Menahem-Mendl of Kotzk, 228

Background Notes, 260

Synchronology, 269

Souls
On Fire

My father, an enlightened spirit, believed
in man.
My grandfather, a fervent Hasid, believed
in God.
The one taught me to speak, the other to sing.
Both loved stories.
And when I tell mine, I hear their voices.
Whispering from beyond the silenced storm,
they are what links the survivor to their memory.

ISRAEL
BAAL SHEM TOV

AND IT CAME TO PASS that the
great Rebbe Israel Baal Shem Tov, Master of the Good Name,
known for his powers in heaven as well as on earth, decided to
try once more to force his Creator's hand.

He had tried many times before—and failed. Burning with
impatience, he wanted to end the ordeals of exile forcibly; and
this time he was but one step away from success. The gates
were ajar; the Messiah was about to appear and console the
children and old men awaiting him, awaiting no one else but
him. The Diaspora had lasted long enough; now men everywhere would gather and rejoice.

The heavens were in an uproar. The angels were dancing.
Red with anger, outraged, Satan demanded an audience with
God. Brought before Him, he protested, invoking laws and
precedents, history and reason. Look at man's impudence, he
said, how dare he take things in his own hands? Does the world
deserve redemption? And the conditions to warrant the Messiah's coming, have they been met?

God listened. And had to recognize the validity of Satan's
arguments: *Lo ikhshar dara,* the Rebbe's gesture was judged
premature; his generation was not yet ready for a miracle of

such magnitude. Moreover, since the order of creation may not be disturbed with impunity, he and his faithful scribe Reb Tzvi-Hersh Soifer were deported to a distant uncharted island. Where they were promptly taken prisoners by a band of pirates.

Never had the Master been so submissive, so resigned.

"Master," the scribe pleaded, "do something, say something!"

"I can't," said the Baal Shem Tov, "my powers are gone."

"What about your secret knowledge, your divine gifts: your *yikhudim?* What happened to them?"

"Forgotten," said the Master. "Disappeared, vanished. All my knowledge has been taken away; I remember nothing."

But when he saw Hersh Soifer's despair, he was moved to pity. "Don't give up," he said, "we still have one chance. You are here, and that is good. For you can save us. There must be one thing I taught you that you remember. Anything—a parable, a prayer. Anything will do."

Unfortunately, the scribe too had forgotten everything. Like his Master, he was a man without memory.

"You really remember nothing," the Master asked again, "nothing at all?"

"Nothing, Master. Except . . ."

". . . except what?"

". . . the *aleph, beith.*"

"Then what are you waiting for?" shouted the Master, suddenly excited. "Start reciting! Right now!"

Obedient as always, the scribe proceeded to recite slowly, painfully, the first of the sacred letters which together contain all the mysteries of the entire universe: *"Aleph, beith, gimmel, daleth . . ."*

And the Master, impatiently, repeated after him: "*Aleph, beith, gimmel, daleth ...*".

Then they started all over again, from the beginning. And their voices became stronger and clearer: *aleph, beith, gimmel, daleth* ... until the Baal Shem became so entranced that he forgot who and where he was. When the Baal Shem was in such ecstasy, nothing could resist him, that is well known. Oblivious to the world, he transcended the laws of time and geography. He broke the chains and revoked the curse: Master and scribe found themselves back home, unharmed, richer, wiser and more nostalgic than ever before.

The Messiah had not come.

This tale is characteristic because it contains most of the basic elements of Hasidism. The fervent waiting, the longing for redemption; the erratic wanderings over untraveled roads; the link between man and his Creator, between the individual act and its repercussions in the celestial spheres; the importance of ordinary words; the accent on fervor and on friendship too; the concept of miracles performed by man for man. It is also characteristic because it may well ... not be true.

Like most of the stories about the Baal Shem—or the Besht, as he is called in Hasidic tradition—it describes events that may or may not have happened, and if they did, may or may not have happened in quite the way they are told. Viewed from the outside, all of these tales are incomprehensible; one must enter them, for their truth may be measured only from the inside. Whether accurately retold or invented outright by his admiring contemporaries, they must be passed on exactly as the narrator received them in his childhood. Clearly, it is to relive that childhood that he is telling them in his turn.

I would listen to them as night fell—between the prayers of Minha and Maariv—in the House of Study filled with the flickering shadows of yellow candles. The Elders spoke of the great Masters as though they had known them personally. Each had his favorite Rebbe and a legend he liked above all others. I came to feel that I was forever listening to the same story about the same Rebbe. Only the names of people and places changed. Motives, deeds, responses and outcomes hardly varied; just as there was always a person in need, there was always someone to lend him a hand. This apparent repetition troubled me, and so one day I discussed this with my grandfather: "I don't understand. Is it possible there really was only one Rebbe?"—"Yes," said my grandfather, "it is possible, and even probable. Every Rebbe has but one Hasid and every Hasid has but one Rebbe. One could not exist without the other."—"Isn't this a sign of weakness?" I asked.—"No," replied my grandfather, "it is their very strength."

In fact, he was that Hasid. Every Shabbat and every Holy Day, he would leave his village to come and celebrate with us. I would remain with him until he went back home. I accompanied him to the mikvah, the ritual bath; to services; to the Rebbe. He would sing and I sang with him; he would speak and I thrilled to every one of his words. He would say: "A Hasid must know how to listen. To listen is to receive. The Jew who does not know how or does not wish to receive is not Jewish. Our people is what it is because it knew how to listen and receive the Law, right? Yet, though the Torah was given only once, each one of us must receive it every day."

In his presence, the others in the House of Study kept respectfully silent. A fabulous storyteller, he knew how to captivate an audience. He would say: "Listen attentively, and above all, remember that true tales are meant to be transmitted —to keep them to oneself is to betray them." He knew how intently I listened; he must have known that I would remember, but he had no way of knowing how closely I would follow his advice. My very first Hasidic tales I heard from him. He made me enter the universe of the Baal Shem and his disciples, where facts became subservient to imagination and beauty. What difference did it make that events and chronological dates no longer matched? I surely didn't care. What mattered to me was not that two and two are four, but that God is one. Better still: that man and God are one.

I can still hear my grandfather's voice: "There will, of course, always be someone to tell you that a certain tale cannot, could not, be objectively true. That is of no importance; an objective Hasid is not a Hasid."

He was right. The Baal Shem's call was a call to subjectivity, to passionate involvement; the tales he told and those told about him appeal to the imagination rather than to reason. They try to prove that man is more than he appears to be and that he is capable of giving more than he appears to possess. To dissect them, therefore, is to diminish them. To judge them is to detach oneself and taint their candor—in so doing, one loses more than one could gain.

And so it is not surprising that the Baal Shem should have fared so poorly with the lay historians, who were, after all, "outsiders." He eludes them. Historically speaking, the character barely emerges, his outlines blurred by contradictions.

7

Nothing about him can be said with certainty. Those who claim to have known him, to have come close to him or loved him, seem incapable of referring to him in terms other than poetic. He has made them dream so much that they describe him as in a dream. That is at least part of the reason why so many rationalists study him with thinly veiled hostility. By becoming a legend, his life has slipped from their grasp.

There were scholars who made him the target of unrestrained animosity, an animosity which went beyond any ideological stance. He simply disturbed them in their roles of historians. They dismiss him as a charlatan, a vulgar drunkard, an ignorant and greedy quack, because they resent him.

Unable to draw a line—any line—between mythical and real being, between fiction and testimony, they are embarrassed. Particularly since their subject is a man who, in a comparatively recent past, shook the very foundations of Judaism, by revolutionizing its thoughts, its perceptions, its way of life. A man who almost single-handedly opened the soul of his people to a new creativity, a creativity heretofore unexplored, of man come to grips with what crushes or lifts him toward infinity.

The man who left his mark on so many survivors of so many massacres in Central and Eastern Europe, the leader who not only made survival imperative but possible, the Master who gave song to despairing communities, managed—we shall never know how—to disappear without leaving the professional seekers even a fragment of valid autobiographical material. Obsessed by eternity, he neglected history and let himself be carried by legend.

The works attributed to him—*Shivkhei ha-Besht, Keter Shem Tov, Tzvaat ha-Ribash*—really belong to others. His apocryphal letters—to his children, his disciples—have been questioned more than once. There remains of him no portrait, no document, no signature constituting irrefutable evidence that behind the legend there was a man, a face, a consciousness. Perhaps this was but another way for him to emphasize his contempt for things written. To the disciple who had transposed his verbal teachings to paper, the Master said: "There is nothing of me in your pages; you thought you heard what I didn't say." Also: "I said one thing, you heard another, and you wrote a third." For the Baal Shem, imagination gains in impact with each passing moment. Until finally its power is perhaps greater than that of any testimony. The real and the imagined, one like the other, are part of history; one is its shell, the other its core. Not to recognize this is to deny art—any form of art—the right to exist.

Yet it is precisely on the imagination that the Baal-Shem plays—even after his death. Each of his disciples saw him differently; to each he represented something else. Their attitudes toward him, as they emerge from their recollections, throw more light on themselves than on him. This explains the countless contradictory tales relating to him.

The historians may have been troubled, but not the Hasidim. Hasidism does not fear contradictions; Hasidism teaches humility and pride, the fear of God and the love of God, the at once sacred and puerile dimension of life, the Master's role of intermediary between man and God, a role that can and must be disregarded in their I-and-Thou relationship. What does it prove? Only that contradictions are an intrinsic part of man.

But not of historians. Frustrated by his elusiveness, they fight him. Some go so far as to deny his very existence. They would like us to believe that he was—quite simply—invented by his disciples, whose own existence they fortunately do not doubt. Others, to restore the balance, claim that . . . there were actually two Baal Shem Tovs and that the Hasidic movement was founded . . . by the other.

Controversies, confusion of places and dates, paradoxes, the Baal Shem's legend abounds with them. He who had the talent to clarify ideas and concepts appears to have done his utmost to obscure the trails leading to his person.

The exact date of his birth has not been established: 1698 according to some, 1700 according to others—as though it made any difference. There seems to be no disagreement as to the place of his birth: a small village—a fortress perhaps—named Okop. Still, the scholars have some difficulty in agreeing on its precise location. Dubnov believes it to be near Kamenetz, Balaban moves it to the banks of the Dniepr, whereas Schechter prefers to see it in Bukovina. As for Mahler, he simply annexes it to Galicia. Evidently the Baal Shem succeeded in turning even geography into a mystery.

Mystery again in all references to his childhood, his education, his family life, his travels, his wanderings across mountains and valleys to come to the aid of anyone in need of help or love.

His parents—Eliezer and Sarah—were rich and generous, according to some; poor but generous, according to others. Their son—Israel—was given to them as a reward when they were almost one hundred years old. They had shown themselves hospitable and indulgent toward the Prophet Elijah, according to one version, and toward Satan, according to another. Their son was to be a symbol of promise and consolation, a guiding light to a people in distress.

Eliezer, the father, was so kind, so generous a man, says legend, that it had been decided in heaven to put him to a test.

And so, one Friday eve, a stranger dressed in rags, leaning on a staff, a bundle on his back, knocked at the old couple's door just as they were sitting down to celebrate the first meal of Shabbat. Without even the slightest hint of disapproval in their countenance, they warmly received the visitor, though he had transgressed the law. And because they neither offended nor embarrassed the poor prophet, he told them the news: the following year they would no longer be alone.

Another tale describes Eliezer as a victim turned hero. Captured and carried off by barbarians, he makes a career in the royal palace, counseling the sovereign and helping him plan and win his wars. Though the king showers him with honors, Eliezer privately continues to carry out the duties of a good Jew, obeying the laws of Torah. Of course, the king becomes so fond of him that he offers him his daughter in marriage. The marriage takes place, but to the princess' great chagrin, is not consummated. Pleading for her forgiveness, he confesses not only that he is married, but that he is a Jew. Reassured about her charms, she magnanimously helps him leave the kingdom. And because of his faithfulness to his people and to his wife, a son was born to him blessed with all gifts and vested with all powers.

At his death, Eliezer told his heir: "I leave before I can make you into a man who fears God and loves those who fear Him. Remember one thing: God is at your side and He alone is to be feared." Later the Baal Shem was to add: "God sees, God watches. He is in every life, in every thing. The world hinges on His will. It is He who decides how many times the leaf will turn in the dust before the wind blows it away."

Orphaned and destitute, without a friend, he practiced all trades: tutor, beadle, ritual slaughterer. Somewhat clumsy and absent-minded, eccentric, he lived on a meager subsidy from the community. He was still very young when the community took the first opportunity to get him married. But soon after the marriage, his wife died and he reverted to his former marginal, introspective existence, and waited for a sign.

There are countless legends concerning the life he led before his revelation. Some say that he saved schoolboys from werewolves and warlocks. Others, that he could bring mountains together. And that during his walks through the forests, he spun dreams in which ends found their beginnings and the world's song reverberated in God's.

Some sources claim he was a saint who fled the limelight; others describe him as a harmless dunce; still others endow him with enough wisdom and learning to make him into a judge of the rabbinical court: a *Dayan,* an arbiter of the community. It is as such that he is said to have made the acquaintance of Reb Abraham—or is it Ephraim?—Kitiver, who wished to arrange a suitable match for his daughter Hannah. Her age at the time? A few months, according to some texts, much more —since she was already divorced—according to others. No matter, the engagement contract was signed, showing the boy's name as Israel, son of Eliezer, and mentioning no title whatever. Shortly thereafter Hannah's father died.

Years went by, until one day the "bridegroom," dressed in peasant clothes, appeared in Brodi to see Reb Gershon Kitiver, Hannah's brother, who took him for a beggar and offered him alms. "No," said the visitor, "that won't do. There's something I want to say to you alone." Then he added roughly: "I want my wife, give me my wife."

Reb Gershon, one of the town's notables, did not take the jest lightly. Even after he had been shown the agreement signed by his father, he advised his sister against marrying this primitive, clumsy peasant. Hannah chose to obey her late father's wish and a date was set for the wedding. Before the ceremony, the Baal Shem drew Hannah aside and told her: "I am not who you think I am, but you must tell no one." He then described the road he had chosen and predicted the difficulties they would encounter, the obstacles still left to overcome. Hannah declared herself ready to confront them at his side.

Then followed hard, unrewarding days. Reb Gershon was ashamed of his brother-in-law and therefore persuaded the couple to go away, as far away as possible. He bought them an inn with a tavern, and then a horse and cart. Isolated in the Carpathian Mountains, Israel and Hannah lived in misery. They dug the soil and eked out a bare subsistence selling lime in the villages.

One day he was summoned by the local rabbi, who undertook to give him a lesson in Judaism. The Baal Shem, in quick succession, put on and removed his simpleton's mask. The rabbi was perplexed: how could the expression on a face change so rapidly? Stunned, he demanded his visitor tell him the truth.

"So be it," said the Baal Shem. "But you must keep what I tell you to yourself. For the moment."

However, there lived in Brodi a woman who was mad. She saw through all men's masks. Brought face to face with the Baal Shem, she said: "I know who you are and I am not afraid of you. I know that you possess certain powers; I also know that you may not use them before the age of thirty-six."

"Be quiet," he answered, "otherwise I shall convene a court to evict the Dybbuk inside you."

The frightened woman held her tongue—but she knew. The others found out much later. Seven lonely and ascetic years

2 3

went by before the Baal Shem received the order to reveal himself and assume his destiny.

On that particular Saturday, a pupil of Reb Gershon interrupted a journey to spend Shabbat with Israel and Hannah. It was midnight when he awoke trembling with fright: a huge flame was rising from the hearth. Thinking to prevent a fire, he ran to extinguish it. When, instead, he saw his host flooded in light, he fainted. As he regained consciousness, he heard the Baal Shem scolding him: "One does not look where one should not." After Shabbat, the traveler hurried back to Brodi, where he stormed into the House of Study, shouting the great news: "There is a new source of light close by." The men rushed to the edge of the forest and there built a throne with branches and leaves. The Besht took his seat. "I shall open a new way," he declared.

He was thirty-six.

The madwoman had seen right. She had known before anyone else. Strange: more than any of the town's devout and erudite men, she spoke the language of the young saint in the forest.

Strange, too, the Baal Shem's pilgrimage to the Holy Land. What had moved him to undertake it? Vague desire or well-defined project? One legend tells that bandits somewhere in the Carpathians revealed to him the existence of a tunnel leading to Jerusalem. Another legend claims that he reached the Holy Land by way of Istanbul, accompanied by his scribe Tzvi-Hersh Soifer or—alternately—by his daughter Udil. To simplify matters, a third version insists that he brought both—or then again, that maybe he made the trip ... twice. A fourth version: his project came to naught; he never went at all.

More enigmas: did he or did he not participate in a public

debate with Jacob Frank's followers in Lemberg? Did he or did he not practice healing, distribute amulets to influence fate and drive out demons? Opinions are divided. Even the date of his death is controversial. Some say he died the first day of Shavuot, others affirm it was the second.

Remember: all this confusion centers around a man who lived not in the Middle Ages, but in the eighteenth century. This contemporary of Voltaire and Kant, of Lessing and Diderot, built his empire not in a still far removed and backward Africa, but in the heart of Europe, where man in his quest for enlightenment had begun to reduce history to a human scale. People were striving to learn, to travel, to explore and experience. The word everywhere was becoming challenge, instrument of rebellion, heralding revolutionary changes. Men used it to smash idols and altars—and wanted to make certain that the rest of the world knew. Yet politicians and philanthropists, adventurers and preachers, conquerors and dreamers, all made their way into the chronicles, if not the history, of their times—all except the Baal Shem.

There remains of him nothing but legend, a legend whose profound and lasting reverberations paradoxically gained in strength with time. More than any other Jewish historical figure, with the exception of the Prophet Elijah, the Besht was present in joy as well as in despair; every *shtibel* reflected his light, his warmth. Every Hasid had two Masters: his own and the Baal Shem—each drew his strength from the other. The first was needed to live, the second to believe. Whoever disclaimed kinship with the Baal Shem found himself relegated outside the mainstream of the Hasidic community. The most hauntingly beautiful legends are those in which the Baal Shem is the central—or at least a major—character.

Perhaps then we should say that he was the sum of all tales that were—and still are—told about him and his work. More precisely: that he *is* his legend.

Yet the son of Sarah and Eliezer was not the first Baal Shem. There had been other Masters of the Name before him. Joel Baal Shem, Eliahu Baal Shem, Binyamin Baal Shem: wandering miracle-makers all, covering the countryside, visiting towns and villages, sometimes pushing as far as Worms and London. And then there was the mysterious Adam Baal Shem, considered the forerunner of Hasidism; he is the one rumored to have entrusted his esoteric writings to his son for transmission to the Master of the Good Name. Saints or picturesque healers, depending on one's point of view, they were more or less proficient in their art; one came to see them to exorcise evil, chase away demons and make sterile women bear children. To distinguish the Baal Shem from the others, the word *Tov* was added to his name. Thus he became the Master of the *Good* Name, and all others receded into the background, if not oblivion. He remained alone, unchallenged.

Nor was he the first Hasid. Without going back as far as the Hasidim of the Talmud or of the twelfth century, there existed during the period immediately preceding the Baal Shem's appearance, Hasidic brotherhoods of a sort in Brodi, Bar, Kitev and Medzebozh. They brought together Kabbalists and noted scholars, among them Gershon Kitiver, Nahman of Horodenko, Nahman of Kossov, Wolfe Kitzes, Yitzhak of Drohobitch, Shabtai Rashkover. Theirs were closed circles—they wished to remain an elite. To discourage potential new members, they evolved rules for admission that required every candidate not only to display superior knowledge in Talmud and Kabbala, but also to pledge himself to the rigorous practice of asceticism and to "abstain from indulging in prophecy." It is said that the Besht himself tried to become one of them. He was refused, his knowledge being considered insufficient. Thus, there were Hasidim before the Besht, but Hasidism such as we know it was created—or re-created—by him. He gave an existing term new content and form.

It was not an easy task. Some of these early Hasidim were his worst adversaries before rallying around him as friends, companions and disciples. In the beginning they reproached him with having thrown open the gates too wide: they were weary of the masses. With a few exceptions, all submitted to his authority in the end, the small Hasidic brotherhoods absorbed by the new movement. Reb Nahman of Kossov was one of the exceptions; he refused even to meet the Baal Shem. Only after long and insistent urging by his disciples did he accept a face-to-face meeting. He started with a challenge: "They say you can read other men's thoughts, is that true?" — "Yes," replied the Baal Shem. — "Prove it. Tell me what I am thinking of this very moment." — "God, of course," said the Baal Shem, taking no chances, since God must be present in every thought of every devout Jew. — "Too easy," was his guest's not unexpected comment. — "True," replied the Baal Shem, "it is easy because in fact all men think of God. What varies is their way. If you like, I'll tell you yours." Whether he did, no one knows. Though Reb Nahman did not become a Hasid, he thereafter forbade others to criticize the Baal Shem in his presence. He would say: "This is an argument which concerns only him and me. It started before us; it has opposed David to Saul, Hillel to Shammai. I forbid you to become involved."

The Baal Shem was more successful with other spiritual leaders of the region, such as Pinhas of Koretz, Yaakov-

Yosseph of Polnoye and Dov-Ber of Mezeritch. The first he conquered with the intensity of his gaze; the second, with his tales; the third, with his fire.

To enlarge his following, the Baal Shem spared neither time nor strength. He was constantly on the roads, making sudden appearances here and there, in forests and in marketplaces; accosting strangers, rich or poor, learned or ignorant, making followers of them all. If someone caught his particular interest, he did not rest until he met him and, if possible, drew him into his intimate circle. To please Nahman of Kossov, he once subjected himself to the hardships of a long journey, proving thereby what little importance he attributed to distances if he could give pleasure to a friend. More than once did he travel night and day only to celebrate Shabbat with Yaakov-Yosseph of Polnoye.

For those he esteemed, he was generosity personified: kind, obliging, considerate. Learning that one of his followers was indulging in the mortification of his body, he took the time to write him a long letter, pleading with him to consider his health and even giving him a few practical suggestions, such as what to eat and what to drink and when.

Only when it came to the official rabbis did the Besht show himself merciless. "One day they will be so many, they will prevent the coming of the Messiah!" Nor did he like physicians: "They think they must explain everything, and yet they see nothing but the surface of man's ills." His disciples, mostly simple and devoted men, he loved like a father or an older brother, showing interest in the activities of each, to the smallest detail. He wanted to know everything, understand everything. Each one of his disciples was convinced that the Master saw no one but him and gave to no one but him. One day, says legend, his disciples understood that in his eyes they were all equal—and "they remained silent a long time."

Still, even though he focused his attention on his followers, the Master was careful not to neglect those outside his immediate circle.

His frequent journeys through the fifty towns and villages mentioned in the *Shivkhei ha-Besht* were intended primarily to recruit followers, apostles as it were, destined to become community leaders He gave of himself generously and without reservations to all who needed him, without any thought as to the future usefulness of the recipients; every human being deserved his attention. He simply appeared wherever he, or someone like him, was necessary, wherever utterly alone men and women, on the brink of despair, needed a sign, a messenger.

A man of contagious intensity, he changed all who approached him. The most mediocre of men vibrated at his contact; an encounter with him was the event of a lifetime.

To have his gaze rest on you meant feeling his fire run through you. An old peasant protects him from the cold—in return, the peasant will become rich and live for a hundred years. A boy recites his lesson with fervor—he will reap glory among his peers. A thief has the misfortune to cross his path. Discovered, he turns to the Master and says: "Since you know how to look, why don't you rather try to see the good?" And so, even the thief enters the enchanted garden of Hasidic legend.

I can still hear my grandfather telling me: "In the Besht's universe, no one felt left out." That was true for his disciples as well. For Hasidim, no man is a stranger; for the Rebbe, no Hasid is unwanted. A Hasid who no longer practices remains a Hasid nevertheless; he will be saved in the end. By his companions who feel responsible for his fate. Beshtian Hasidism is founded on solidarity.

Unlike the Rebbes of succeeding generations, the Baal Shem had no permanent residence, maintained no court, kept neither servant nor secretary to screen visitors and act as a shield between himself and his solicitors. He wished to remain accessible to all who came to him to share their worries, their anguish. And he not only received them, he met them halfway. Always in motion, he granted himself no respite. Traveling sometimes with his coachman Alexei, sometimes with his scribe Tzvi-Hersh Soifer, he tried to be everywhere at once; what he wanted was to end all waiting, personify all hope. If one believes his legend, he succeeded. He belonged to all.

He addressed himself to men and women, some say more frequently to women than men, in synagogues and streets, at fairs and in taverns, at all hours, day or night. He needed to touch as many people as possible. No place was too far, no man too unworthy: "As long as the branch is not cut from the tree every hope is justified," he said. And also: "To pull another out of the mud, man must step into the mud himself." He is also supposed to have said: "Small Tzaddikim like small sinners, a great Tzaddik likes a great sinner." No wonder that, according to popular tradition, he tried to come to the aid of Shabtai-Tzvi's and Jacob Frank's damned souls. Not to judge others was one of the Baal Shem's principles; his function was to help, not to condemn.

And so it was with total unconcern that he moved in and out of suspect—not to say ill-famed—circles; he felt more useful there than among the just. Robbers sought him out to be their arbiter; criminals and outlaws asked for his blessing; and drunkards chose him as their confessor. He considered it an art and a virtue to listen to others.

One day he saw a man who had had too much to drink; he was stammering and singing sad songs. The Baal Shem listened attentively, and remarked: "When a man confesses himself, the way he chooses to do it doesn't matter. One may not turn away."

He loved to observe the peasants and ruffians who crowded the taverns drinking and singing their songs at the top of their lungs. He once introduced a young Jewish student to them: "He sings better than you," said he. Moments later they were all dancing to a new tune. Years passed, and a group of high-waymen were getting ready to kill a Jew, when suddenly their chief looked at him closely, and asked: "Can you sing?" — "Yes." — "Then sing!" And the Jew, too, remembered their encounter of long ago. He sang, and so was spared.

It is only natural that the Baal Shem was much talked about. People praised his powers and quoted his maxims. The Jewish world was in an uproar; it followed his astounding as-cent with fear or hope, or both. To remain indifferent was impossible; one took a stand for or against this extraordinary personality who seemed to be everywhere at once, come and gone in a flash, leaving behind him a trail of wonder or anger. Both the traditional rabbinical and the rationalist emancipatory circles were in ferment. The first considered him too revolu-tionary; the second, too orthodox. All tried to find quick and efficient methods of fighting him before it was too late. It was already too late. The legend of the Baal Shem had fired Jewish imagination with such violence and in so many places, nobody could stop or even brake his momentum. He answered a need.

For the eighteenth century was not very kind toward these Jews who lived in the most ravaged parts of Central and Eastern Europe. They remained unaffected by the great liberating currents. The struggle against despotism and social injustice that was under way was not intended to alleviate *their* suffering. The Jews, mostly those from Poland and the Ukraine, were left to their own devices.

They had no rights whatever. They had to buy protection. Their freedom, their life hinged on the good will of local squires who exploited their commercial talents. Let the innkeeper or the superintendent present himself at week's end with a purse that was too light, and he would end up in jail savagely beaten. With no one to bail him out. This situation prevailed particularly in the small villages and isolated towns; none was to be pitied more than the Jew who lived in an out-of-the-way hamlet; he felt forgotten, forsaken by his brethren.

The larger communities had other kinds of problems; they were too divided. There were barriers between those with learning and those without, between the rich and the poor, the leaders and the craftsmen, the notables and the average citizens; the different classes watched each other with distrust, bitterness and rancor. At the top of the social ladder: the secular leaders (usually well-off if not rich), the rabbis named by them, the Talmudists, the devout, the teachers. Whoever possessed neither title nor fortune was ignored. Whoever showed neither knowledge nor piety belonged to the oppressed class and was doomed to impotence.

On a spiritual plane, Judaism went through a crisis that was no less serious: the existing rabbinical institutions were too rigid, too cloistered and inflexible. They allowed no digression, they tolerated no individual endeavor. Traumatized by the nightmare of false Messiahs of the seventeenth century, the rabbis looked askance at anything that seemed new, anything that was obscure. Whoever strayed from the strict interpretation of the Law or made too many promises was immediately suspected of heresy. They believed that Judaism had suffered too much at the hands of inspired visionaries and demagogues. And so, to protect tradition, they surrounded it with fences and obstacles; whoever tried to overturn them left himself open to fanatic, merciless repression.

The Jew, who has only his memory, remembers the dreams awakened and trampled by a Shabtai-Tzvi and his disciples. He knows that for man in exile, hope can become the most excruciating of tortures, the most cruel of dangers. To remain steadfast, one must know how to wait, how to be patient; to last, one must bend and follow the narrow but familiar paths and reject the call of the unknown.

But man cannot live indefinitely without a dream and without a legend. Therefore, if someone appears who brings them both—it is enough. He will impose himself and reign.

And yet the Baal Shem himself is said to have considered fame unworthy. The night he had the vision, and learned that the time had come for him to leave the mountain, to throw away his mask and assume the role and destiny of Israel's shepherd, his heart came close to breaking. In his anguish he fasted three days and three nights, praying to have the command revoked. He was thirty-six.

One day he sent his disciples to a distant village to meet a *Lamed Vavnik*, a Just Man, one of the thirty-six without whom the world could not survive. The Baal Shem told the disciples: "This man resembles me like a brother, we are of the same age, we share the same origins, the same virtues and the same knowledge. Before coming down to earth, we decided jointly that we would, at the very first opportunity, observe the first commandment: that of *Kibud Em*, to honor our mothers. How? We would not cry. So as not to worry them. We kept our word. I never cried in my mother's presence, though as soon as she left the house to go to market or services, I could not hold back my tears. When the neighbors remarked on her apparent insensitivity, she naturally could not understand, and naturally she suffered. As for my friend, he controlled himself even when his mother was away. And that is why it was decided above that as a reward he would be allowed to remain a hidden Just Man, whereas I was condemned to fame."

His admirers defended him against himself. Beneath the revealed Baal Shem, said they, there was another, hidden Baal Shem who was as great as he was intangible. They did not hesitate to rank him on a par with Moses. According to them, everything pertaining to him was bathed in holiness: his master was the Prophet Ahia of Shilo, the very same that David had as his instructor; Rabbi Yitzhak Lurie and Shimon Bar-Yohai— the most prestigious pillars in the history of Kabbala—were his peers; in his ascensions to the higher spheres, he would sometimes win victories over these distant forerunners and participate in study sessions at the patriarch's side; then, too, he frequently had occasion to converse with the Messiah.

In a letter to his brother-in-law, Reb Gershon Kitiver, the Baal Shem gives this account of one of these dialogues. To the question: "But when, when will you come?" the Messiah answered: "When your spring will run over, when your teaching will cover the land." He even conversed with the Angel of Death, asking him: "Why do you massacre so many innocent and helpless Jews?" — "I do it for the sake of heaven, for the love of God and for His glory," answered the Angel with disquieting humor.

Legend attributes his privileges to the "root of his soul," to his so-called ancestral merits. Even so, the Baal Shem seems to have chosen to project the image of a man who cannot count on inherited gifts but must work hard for every victory. His charisma was of his own making. This is one of the appealing characteristics of Hasidism: everything is offered, yet everything remains to be done. Though powers may be given by God, it is for man to take them from Him.

The Baal Shem was a man of the people in the true sense of the word. He could not claim a notable ancestry, nor did he occupy an exalted social position; nothing linked him to the ruling class. He had no official titles, no influential friends, no powerful protectors. He had neither material possessions nor wealthy admirers. He could not even lay claim to vast Talmudic learning. On the contrary, he enjoyed playing the ignorant analphabet who stammers a few basic prayers unwillingly and with great difficulty.

This partly explains his immediate success among the less fortunate—they identified with him. Had he been a rabbi's son, or an *ilui,* a prodigy, he would have made less impact on people's imagination. His humble origins made it easier for the poor to approach him. In a way, he represented their sublimated selves. He told them what they wanted to hear: that every one of them existed in God's memory, that every one of them played a part in his people's destiny, each in his way and according to his means.

He assured them that a simple but sincere prayer has as much merit as a mystical incantation, that the fervor born in a pure heart is greater than the one born of a complex and unfathomable thought. He said: "The coachman who kisses the holy scrolls of the Torah pleases God more than the angels who praise Him and do nothing else." He warned them to be suspicious of anyone claiming to have all the answers: "You want to know if a particular Rebbe is genuine? Go and ask his advice. Ask him if he knows a way to chase impure thoughts from your mind; if he says yes, you'll know he is a fake." He told them that pride derived from knowledge is worse than ignorance, that to seek is better than to find. The greatness of man, he taught them, lies in his capacity for humility. Let him start by submitting to God: he will grow and he will be free. He taught them that sometimes it must be enough to *believe* there is a secret. And also that man requires little to elevate and fulfill himself, as long as that is what he longs for, longs for with all his heart.

He explained to them that abstract erudition is not the sole vessel of truth or the sole path leading to saintliness. And that saintliness is not the only link between man and the eternity he carries inside him. Song is more precious than words, intention more important than formulas. And since it is given to every man to acquire all the powers, why despair? Why give up the fight? One tear, one prayer can change the course of events; one fragment of melody can contain all the joy in the world, and by letting it go free, influence fate. And no elite has a monopoly on song or tears; God listens to the shepherd playing his flute as readily as He listens to the saint renouncing his earthly attachments. The prisoner's craving equals the wise man's: the one, like the other, has a bearing on the essence of man.

He taught them to fight sadness with joy. "The man who looks only at himself cannot but sink into despair, yet as soon as he opens his eyes to the creation around him, he will know joy." And this joy leads to the absolute, to redemption, to God; that was the new truth as defined by the Baal Shem. And Jews by the thousands let themselves be carried by this call, they needed it to live and to survive. Thanks to it, there was joy —following pain—and it brought together the dispersed and

26

exiled. The joy of man no longer alone, the joy of the old sage waiting for the upheaval of time, the joy of a father wanting to talk and of children eager to listen. The Baal Shem was a moment of rapture and exaltation in times of mute lamentation. When he died in 1760, twenty-four years after his revelation, there remained in Central and Eastern Europe not a single Jewish town that was left unaffected. He had been the spark without which thousands of families would have succumbed to gloom and hopelessness—and the spark had fanned itself into a huge flame that tore into the darkness.

One day he promised his disciples to show them the Prophet Elijah. "Open your eyes wide," he said.

A few days later they saw a beggar enter the House of Study and emerge clutching a book under his arm. Shortly thereafter they watched him leaving a ceremony, taking along a silver spoon. The third time he appeared to them disguised as a soldier on a horse, asking them to light his pipe.

"It was he," said the Baal Shem, "The secret is in the eyes."

His disciple Rebbe David Leikes tells: "After the last meal of Shabbat, our Master turned to me and asked me for a coin to buy a drink. Naturally, I had no money on me, but how could I disobey? I put my hand in my pocket, and when I brought out a coin—I was not surprised."

In a dream, the Baal Shem glimpsed his future neighbor in paradise. Upon awakening, he decided to pay him a visit. He found a robust and earthy man. How well he disguises himself, thought the Baal Shem, and asked to be sheltered for a few days.

The Besht was convinced his host was leading a double life;

that he was getting up at night to accomplish God knows what worthy deeds. Wrong: the man slept deeply and until the next morning, when he rose early, hastily said his prayers and gulped down a copious breakfast. At lunch he ate even more, and three times as much at dinner. And so it went for several days.

Let us wait for Shabbat, thought the Baal Shem. Perhaps his saintliness coincides with that of the seventh day. Wrong again: his host ate and slept even more than during the week. Unable to contain himself any longer, the Baal Shem spoke to him: "When I came here, I had a question to ask you. I shall not ask it. But now I have another: why do you eat so much?"

"I'll tell you," answered the man. "It has to do with my father. Who was a good Jew, gentle and frail, aspiring only to please the Lord; nothing else interested him. Neither money nor honors, not even health. He lived only for and by the Torah. One day he was on his way to services when he was grabbed by bandits who tied him to a tree and ordered him to kiss a cross. He refused, of course. They beat him mercilessly; still he refused. They then poured kerosene over him and set him on fire. And because my father was so weak and thin, he burned only a moment; almost as soon as he was lit, he was burned out. And I, who saw him, who saw it all, swore that if ever I was put to the same test, I would not let them get away so easily. I would show them that a Jew does not go out like a miserable skinny candle. No. When I burn, I shall burn so long that they will burst with anger. That is why I eat so much; all my energy, all my passion is devoted to eating. Not that I am hungry, you understand . . ."

"Yes, I understand," said the Baal Shem, smiling. "Go on, continue; you must. What you are doing, you are doing well." And, after a moment's silence: "We'll talk about it again."

28

One morning, accompanied by his disciples, he was walking through an uninhabited region.

"I am thirsty," complained one of the young men, "I am burning, I am dying of thirst."

No sign of water anywhere. The countryside was like a desert.

"Don't worry," said the Baal Shem, "when God created the world, He foresaw your thirst as well as its remedy."

Shortly thereafter they came upon a peasant balancing two pails of water on his shoulders.

"My lord has gone mad," grumbled the peasant, "this morning he sent me here to walk back and forth with this load of water; just like that, for no reason at all."

"You see," said the Baal Shem to the thirsty student, "when He created the world, He arranged this madness solely so that you might quench your thirst."

It happened during the High Holy Days. The Baal Shem had conducted New Year services with special fervor, concentrating on the prayers relating to redemption. Out of a common impulse, his disciples hurried to their secret retreat at the edge of the forest as soon as services were over—to wait together. Suddenly the youngest, who had stayed behind, had a frightening thought: the Messiah was about to come—and there would be no one to welcome him!

He ran to warn his companions. Out of breath, he burst open the door and saw them sitting around the table in solemn silence. He understood that they, too, were convinced that the so anxiously awaited savior was on his way and that soon they would hear the pounding of his staff, announcing his presence.

The wait lasted late into the night. Then they went back to town, dejected. It is said that had the youth not interrupted their silent vigil, the awaited one would have appeared.

"Imagine a palace with an infinite number of doors," said the Baal Shem to his disciples. "In front of every door the visitor finds a treasure. Satisfied, he feels no urge to continue. Yet, at the end of the hallways, the king is waiting to receive those among his subjects who think of him rather than of the treasure."

One morning he prayed longer than usual. Weary, the disciples left. Later, the Master commented sadly: "Imagine a rare bird at the top of a tree. To reach it, men form a human ladder, thus allowing one of them to climb to the very top. But those at the bottom cannot see the bird and therefore lose patience and go home. The ladder falls apart, and up there the rare bird has flown away."

During Simhat·Torah the Baal Shem warned his followers that they were about to witness a peculiar service: "Promise me you will not laugh!"

They promised.

And during the services the Master invited the Seven Shepherds of the world, including Adam, Abraham and David, to ascend the bimah and read from the Torah. At the end, he invited the Messiah. That proved too much for some of the disciples. They began to laugh. A shadow clouded the Master's face and—for what seemed an infinity—he refused to look at them.

"Do you want to know what Hasidism is? Do you know the story of the ironmonger who wanted to become independent? He bought an anvil, a hammer and bellows and went to work. Nothing happened—the forge remained inert. Then an old ironmonger, whose advice he sought, told him: 'You have everything you need except the spark.' That is what Hasidism is: the spark."

30

●　　●　　●

What was Hasidism at its inception? A man. The Baal Shem. His was a powerful appeal to consolation, to unity. His Hasidism was neither philosophical doctrine nor system of social ethics and certainly not a new theosophy sprinkled with folklore and rebellion. Yet it was a combination of all of these; a desire to arrive at a synthesis. An acceptance of the fact that one may be a Jew in many different ways. For all paths lead somewhere, provided that God is present at the start.

This Hasidism has been erroneously compared to Spinoza's Pantheism. For the Baal Shem's followers, God is not neutral. Nor is He an abstraction. He is at once ally and judge of man inside creation. The bond between them is irreplaceable, it is love. God himself needs love. Whoever loves God will be loved in turn, loved by man and loved by God. It is in man that God must be loved, because the love of God goes through the love of man. Whoever loves God exclusively, namely, excluding man, reduces his love and his God to the level of abstraction. Beshtian Hasidism denies all abstraction.

"God is the shadow of man" was commented upon by the Baal Shem as follows: just as a shadow follows the gestures and motions of the body, God follows those of the soul. If man is charitable, God will be charitable too. The name of man's secret is God, and the name of God's secret is none other than the one invented by man: love. Who loves, loves God.

It is in this sense that in Beshtian Hasidism, God is present even in evil, even in sin. He takes part in creation and chooses the side of man. For whoever creates affirms that the creative act has meaning, a meaning which transcends the act itself. And what is love if not a creative act, in which two beings fuse into a single consciousness scarred and healed a thousand times? Love's mystery resides in oneness, and so does God's. "Whatever is above is also down below." Between the present concrete world and the other, the one to come, there is a link as between source and reflection. God does not oppose humanity, and man, though vulnerable and ephemeral, can attain immortality in the passing moment. In man's universe, everything is connected because nothing is without meaning.

Thence the tolerance the Baal Shem exhibited toward sinners. He refused to give them up as lost. If need be, he could understand—though not accept—evil in others. But evil without consciousness of evil he deemed inadmissible.

That is why he never tried to convert non-Jews to Judaism. He preferred to "convert" Jews to Hasidism, or in a wider sense, to Judaism.

To realize himself, the Baal Shem's Hasidism teaches us, man must first of all remain faithful to his most intimate, truest self; he cannot help others if he negates himself. Any man who loves God while hating or despising His creation, will in the end hate God. A Jew who rejects his origins, his brothers, to make a so-called contribution to mankind, will in the end betray mankind. That is true for all men.

"Beware, your coachman is dangerous and wicked," said the Baal Shem to one of his followers. "I saw him walk by the church without crossing himself. If he does not love his God, why then would he love you?"

The entire Hasidic concept is contained in this anecdote. The Baal Shem was concerned with people rather than theories. Theories could wait. His disciples—the Maggid of Mezeritch, Shneur-Zalmen of Ladi, Nahman of Bratzlav—could formulate them later. For the moment, what mattered was to communicate experience rather than scholarship, intuition rather than logic.

The Baal Shem's major concern was to create links at every level. To him, everything that brought people together and consolidated the community was good; everything that sowed discord was bad.

And so he turned a poetic image, the mystical concept of *likut nitzotzot,* the in-gathering of dispersed sparks, into concrete action. Man's role is to mitigate solitude; whoever opts for solitude chooses the side of death.

That is why, in all his tales, wandering nameless beggars play such a particular and important role. They too make people dream, they too are links between men. Every woodcutter may be a prophet in disguise, every shoemaker a Just Man, every unknown the Baal Shem. What is man if not a link between Adam and the Messiah, representing more than his own span, heralding more than he could wish to receive? A shepherd plays a tune—the Baal Shem relates him to King David. A stranger in rags provokes laughter—the Master refers to him as Abraham.

If the Baal Shem could have met Rabbi Haim Ben-Atar, who was awaiting him in the Holy Land, together the two men would have hastened the coming of the Messiah, or so says Hasidic tradition, with the stress on encounter. Every encounter quickens the steps of the Redeemer; let two beings become one and the world is no longer the same; let two human creatures accept one another and creation will have meaning, the meaning they will have imposed upon it. That is the new idea introduced into Jewish life by Hasidism. The individual is not a cog in a monstrous machine; it is within his power to modify the very laws which imprison him and the very relationship maintained by the Judge with the accused and witnesses. If it is true, as the Baal Shem says, that it is possible for man to hide the light of dawn emanating from the forest simply by shielding his eyes with his hands, still it is no less true that he can rediscover it by merely moving his hands. That is precisely what the Baal Shem accomplished. Thanks to him, thanks to this simple motion of a hand, the Hasid had discovered the world in all its awesome majesty and beauty.

And now let us speak of the miracles the Baal Shem is said to have performed in his lifetime and even after his death. The narrator did not evoke them earlier because, he readily admits, they trouble him; they flout his reason, his taste for rationality. Are we to believe that this awkward, retiring man, once having reached the prime of life, sought to amuse himself by rearranging the order of the universe? It is claimed that he brought learning to some, deprived others of their memory, recovered misplaced objects and horses that had lost their way. It is said that he earned total allegiance from men and beasts alike, and even from the angels up above; if an angel was not to his taste, he was replaced. It is said that he healed the sick—by gorging them with chicken soup—and that he prescribed a remedy against snoring. And . . . that he tried to persuade a priest that he should break his celibacy.

Naïve and childish, these tales are bound to make us smile. Written and transmitted without any literary purpose, could it be that they were meant to test our reason or our faith or perhaps our imagination? To prove that the Baal Shem is above and beyond anything man can even begin to imagine in his dreams? Did the Master encourage them? To his servant Reb Yaakov he entrusted the mission to travel and make his fortune by telling stories—about the Besht, of course. But did he wish Reb Yaakov or any of the others to add and embellish as they chose? Those exaggerations—did they originate with him?

And to what end? To impress admirers who were already bound to him with their entire being? He who was so great and genuine in so many areas, why should he have felt the need to show his hold on the occult by resorting to miracles?

Perhaps he wanted to show the link—one more—between man's experiences and man's dreams, and how one may transcend the first with the help of the latter. We may contemplate such a hypothesis. We may even go one step further and say that while the Baal Shem indeed did not need miracles, his future followers did—they needed them to persevere, to take hold. They needed to believe that God took an interest in His creation, that He listened to all the voices; they needed to believe that miracles were still possible, even for them. That may be why he performed them.

All his prodigious deeds seem to spring from a desire to unite the people by offering it song and legend as refuge and shield. The Jewish people, dispersed and decimated, needed new vigor —so the Master promised children to childless couples. If he moved with the "speed of lightning," it was because he was freeing some innkeeper rotting in a dungeon—there was forever a Jewish innkeeper somewhere whom the prince had put in jail for not paying dues, for not doing well enough or, on the contrary, for doing too well. Was an enemy concocting a plan of persecution? The Master knew what prayer to recite, and where, in order to foil the plot. Was someone stumbling in the dark? With a mere look the Baal Shem set him back on the right road. The main theme remains constant: man owes it to himself to reject despair; better to rely on miracles than opt for resignation. By changing himself, man can change the world.

Thus it is possible for man to accept his contradictions. And to discover humility within pride, simplicity within generosity, charity within justice. There is no alternative: one must impose a meaning on what perhaps has none and draw ecstasy from nameless, faceless pain.

Certainly, by agreeing to follow the Baal Shem outside time, to the limit of perception, we run the risk of finding ourselves in a world which is not real. The Baal Shem himself had to pay the price. Toward the end of his life particularly, he displayed increasing signs of irritation and depression, expressing himself in ways "defying the laws of language." He who had worked so hard to make himself understood, no longer succeeded. Faces, words and incidents were forgotten; he was losing touch with his surroundings. He could be seen knocking his head against a tree or following what seemed to be a strange choreography with his body. He expressed regret at having used his powers; he was no longer himself.

One day he spoke longer than ever, and his words were more enticing than ever. His disciples were entranced, conscious of living privileged moments. Suddenly he stopped. And forgot what he had said. And forgot even that he had spoken.

Another time, during the same period, he felt himself sinking. One of his disciples saw him sway, and called out: "Master!" and this outcry brought him back to the surface.

He had lived too fast and had made too many promises that God did not keep.

At the age of sixty he became ill; his insides were tearing him apart. It was Passover. Deviating from habit, he celebrated the Holy Day far from other people, plunged into silent and uninterrupted meditation.

Seven weeks later, during Shavuot, feeling the end approaching, he gave his intimates detailed instructions for his burial. He requested them to sing at his bedside and invited a *minyan* for the last service. "I have two hours to chat with God," he said. Seeing tears on the faces of his faithful, he added: "Why do you cry? I am leaving by one door only to enter by another."

Rebbe Pinhas of Koretz began to pray, pleading on his behalf. "Too late," the Master told him, "what is done is done; what is done will not be undone."

When he died, the two clocks in his house stopped.

Symbolic break, dividing time and the fate of Hasidism. The end of an era. And the birth of another: the movement was to continue its work, expand its reign, go from conquest to conquest, from triumph to triumph, bring fresh air into stifling huts, surprise into routine lives, accompany the sick into their very anguish and the condemned into their resigned or questioning silence.

In the course of the next two centuries, his legend surfaced in many trials his followers endured: it helped people stay alive and sometimes to prepare for death. It appeared even in the kingdom of night. In the vision of a Jewish poet, the Baal Shem visits Jews massacred somewhere in the East. Their corpses fill the trenches to the very top. Suddenly their arms stretch up toward their illustrious visitor and a cry is heard: "Welcome, Rebbe Israel Baal Shem Tov, thank you for your miracles, Rebbe Israel, son of Eliezer."

And so, in the kingdom of Hasidic legend, the Baal Shem follows his disciples to the end of night. Another miracle? Certainly not. Death negates miracles, the death of one million children negates more than miracles.

What cannot help but astound us is that Hasidim remained Hasidim inside the ghetto walls, inside the death camps. In the shadow of the executioner, they celebrated life. Startled Germans whispered to each other of Jews dancing in the cattle cars rolling toward Birkenau: Hasidim ushering in Simhat Torah. And there were those who in Block 57 at Auschwitz tried to make me join in their fervent singing. Were these miracles? Some of those that failed? Perhaps.

Yet there is something else. There is the spark lit in the Carpathian Mountains which has refused to go out. On the contrary, it rekindles our own wavering flame. Consolidated in Jerusalem, Hasidism reappears in the Diaspora everywhere. It would be difficult to imagine a more curious phenomenon: with almost the totality of its followers lost in the Holocaust, Hasidism today is throbbing with newly found vigor. At the Lubavitcher court in Brooklyn, you can see hundreds of youths from every corner of the land. I met Hasidim in Leningrad, Kiev and Moscow, and I was deeply moved by their hidden faith.

And all of them define themselves in relation to the old Masters long dead. They live in America but they belong to Lizensk, Mezeritch or Rizhin. There are no more Jews in Wizsnitz, but there are Wizsnitzer Hasidim on both sides of the ocean. The same is true for the other Hasidic branches or dynasties. Ger, Kossov, Sadigor, Karlin—these kingdoms have but transferred their capitals. Lubavitch is everywhere except in Lubavitch; Sighet and Satmar are no longer in Transylvania but wherever Satmarer and Sigheter Hasidim live and remember. And then there are the tales the Besht has left us, for us to relive as though they were our own. That is the most striking, the most moving of his miracles.

Are we worthy of these tales and legends? It all depends.

Are we still able to repeat them without impairing their innocence? It all depends. Are we still able to recite, with fervor and gratitude: *aleph, beith, gimmel, daleth,* the way he once did, a long time ago, to free us from exile by the word? Are we still capable of beginning all over again?

DISCIPLES I

THIS IS HOW Rabbi Yaakov-Yosseph of Polnoye found his way into the Hasidic fold:

One morning he arrived at the Sharogrod synagogue and
found it empty.

"Where are the faithful?" he asked the beadle.

"At the market."

"All of them? At this hour, when they should be praying?"

"Well, you see, there is this stranger there, telling stories.
And when he speaks, one doesn't want to leave."

"What impudence! Go and bring him here at once!"

The beadle had no choice, he obeyed as was his duty. He
ran to the market, made his way through the crowd and transmitted the order to the storyteller.

"Fine," the stranger said calmly, "I am coming."

The rabbi did not get up to receive him: "Who are you
and how dare you divert this community from the ways of the
Lord?"

"Don't get angry," said the visitor, "a rabbi like you ought
never to give in to anger. Instead, listen to a story."

"What! More stories! Your insolence seems to have no
limits! You'll pay for this!"

40

"Anger is something one must learn to control," the visitor said gently. "Listen to me . . ."

And there was in his voice a certain quality that troubled the rabbi and he fell silent. He could not keep himself from listening, never before had he felt such a need to listen.

"This is a story that happened to me," said the Baal Shem. "I was riding in a coach drawn by three horses, each of a different color, and not one of them was neighing. I could not understand why. Until the day we crossed a peasant on the road who shouted at me to loosen the reins. And all at once, the three horses began to neigh."

·In one blinding flash the rabbi of Sharogrod understood the meaning of the parable. For the soul to vibrate and cry out, it must be freed; too many restrictions will stifle it.

And he began to cry. He cried as he had never cried before: freely, spontaneously, without apparent reason. What happened later is well known: Rebbe Yaakov-Yosseph became one of the pillars of the new movement.

"Man is not alone," said the Baal Shem to his companion Rebbe Pinhas of Koretz. "The past is heavy with meaning; it fills our solitude. You and I, all of us must be aware of it. Long ago, in Egypt, every one of us strove for the preservation of the holy language, the names of our ancestors and the memory of the Covenant. Every one of us was at the prophets' feet to receive their teachings. Every one of us followed Yohanan Ben-Zakkai into exile and every one of us heard the terrifying words of Shimon Bar-Yohai. And that is why we must stay together."

And they stayed together.

* * *

Brilliant and humble but a fierce individualist, Rebbe Pinhas of Koretz was intent on finding his own path rather than following a Master—any Master. That is what kept him from declaring himself the Baal Shem's disciple, though he was and remained his friend.

A Hasidic tradition says that Rebbe Pinhas of Koretz learned three things from the Baal Shem; it does not say what they were. It adds that, in exchange, Rebbe Pinhas taught the Baal Shem three things; perhaps they were the same.

He regretted not having a voice. "If I could sing," he said, "I would force God to live among men."

He had no use for honors and riches. Though he was poor, he would say: "I have never yearned for anything I did not already have."

When he became a Master—against his will—he said: "Everything I know I learned before, sitting in the last row near the hearth, out of sight. And now, here I am, occupying the place of honor—and I don't understand."

His many admirers disturbed him so much that he asked God to make him repulsive in the eyes of the people. His wish was granted. Thereafter he was shunned. But the resulting solitude weighed heavily on his wife. Later it affected even him. So he begged God to restore his gifts to him, confessing: man must not try to be what he is not.

His passion: to bring back into the fold the Jewish converts to Christianity. His discussions with them were open; he never tried to evade issues. He would explain the merits and possibilities of repentance and then appeal to them to recite the *Sh'ma Israel* with him, saying: "It doesn't cost you anything!" To please him, some consented.

42

One day, having been told that a group of atheists was demanding proof of God's existence, he rushed to the synagogue, opened the Holy Ark, seized the scrolls of the Torah and shouted: "I swear that God exists, isn't that proof enough? What more do they want?"

Truth to him was the highest virtue of all. He said: "If all men spoke the truth, there would be no further need to wait for the Messiah; he would have come long ago."

During the preparations for his journey to the Holy Land, Rebbe Pinhas of Koretz became ill. Trembling with fever, delirious, he spoke only of death. Never had his faithful seen him so dejected, so anguished. Over and over he called for his friend Rebbe Haim of Krasna, begging him not to leave him: "If you stay, I shall be less afraid of the Angel of Death."

When the end came, Rebbe Haim was in a neighboring village and it was Shabbat. A rabbinical council, convened in emergency session, authorized the dispatch of a messenger to summon him. Reb Haim arrived the next day. Too late.

Though he was rich, learned and covered with honors, Rebbe Nahman of Kossov nevertheless belonged to a Hasidic brotherhood practicing asceticism.

His was a rebellious spirit; he opposed everybody. To the Hasidim, he represented the anti-Hasid; to the enemies of the Baal Shem, he was his supporter.

When people drew his attention to the fact that the Hasidim, contrary to ancestral tradition, had adopted a new version of the prayer book, he became vexed: "Why do you care? What makes you so sure that all our ancestors reached paradise?"

From the very beginning of their friendship, the relationship between Rebbe Nahman of Kossov and the Baal Shem was ambiguous, and so it remained to the end. Once the Baal Shem let slip a rather strange statement: "Rebbe Nahman of Kossov seeks to catch me, nay, kill me; but he won't succeed."

"Do you know who rescinded the celestial decree that would have unleashed catastrophe unto our people?" the Baal Shem asked Rebbe Nahman of Horodenko. "I'll tell you. Neither I nor you, nor the sages, nor the great spiritual leaders. Our litanies, our fasting were all in vain. We were saved by a woman, a woman of our people. This is how it happened: She came to the synagogue, tears running down her face, and addressed the Almighty: 'Master of the Universe, are You or are You not our Father? Why won't You listen to Your children imploring You? You see, I am a mother. Children I have plenty of: five. And every time they shed a tear, it breaks my heart. But You, Father, You have so many more. Every man is Your child, and every one of them is weeping and weeping. Even if Your heart is made of stone, how can You remain indifferent?' And," the Baal Shem concluded, "God decided she was right."

Rebbe David Kitzes was an enthusiastic traveler. On a faraway island he met a man dressed in oriental clothes who questioned him at great length about the situation of the Jews in Central Europe.

"They're all right," answered Rebbe David. "Thanks to God."

"Wretch," the Baal Shem later reprimanded him, "you should have told him of our suffering! You should have cried out our distress! Do you have any idea *who* was asking you all those questions?"

44

•   •   •

Rebbe David Leikes cried only one time in his life: the day the Baal Shem died.

Rebbe David was known and liked for his exuberant, contagious joy. Prayer sent him into rapture; he turned even the lamentations into song.

He outlived his wife, four sons and three daughters. At seventy-three he was alone and in mourning. Yet he did not give in to sadness. To praise God, one must live, he said, and to live, one must enjoy life; one must enjoy life in spite of life.

And he remarried. An innkeeper, who bore him three sons and a daughter. He lived on contentedly to become president of the local rabbinical court, and remained lucid to the end. He was one hundred years old and on his deathbed when, hearing the court deliberating in the next room, he complained: "Why do you leave me out? All my life I was God's associate in His work down here; is this the time to push me aside?"

And so he listened to witnesses, noted contradictory depositions and pronounced his verdict. A moment later his countenance was serene: "Here I am, leaving one court for another," he whispered.

His last words.

Rebbe Leib, surnamed the Grandfather of Shpole, was fond of saying: "If I had seen the Baal Shem Tov a second time, I would have become somebody."

He was somebody.

Known for his kindness, simplicity and warmth, his surname suited him perfectly. He played with children and he loved stories. He had a talent for making people happy. He was also

45

the first Rebbe to turn dance into a ritual. Watching him sway and turn, the son of the Great Maggid of Mezeritch exclaimed: "Your dancing counts for more than my prayers."

Like most Hasidic Masters of his generation, he had led a turbulent existence before he made himself known.

He had been a member of a troupe of wandering beggars, roaming from village to village, provoking laughter or anger, earning applause or lashes for doing the very same thing, just barely managing to escape whenever an established Tzaddik came close to uncovering his true identity.

His adventurous past even included a two-month stay in prison. Before escaping from it, he succeeded in coaxing a horse thief into repenting. And it became a joint escape. Only when the future Rebbe became a beadle, did he and his accomplice part ways.

"Before I was born," he said, "I refused life. What's the good of toiling among mortals who are prey to their own weaknesses? To entice me into accepting, I was permitted to set certain conditions. I made four: that I would never forget anything; never be sick; beget only children who would become honest and simple Jews; and one more condition which I have neither the wish nor the right to divulge."

This story has a sequel:

"Do you know who finally made me change my mind? A peasant with a shovel in his hands who accosted me as though I were an old acquaintance. 'Hey, you,' he said, 'take a good look: I work without respite to give a little joy, a little rest to people who sorely need it, and what do you do? You lie around here as if creation had no human purpose. Why do you refuse to help me?' You see," added the Grandfather of Shpole, "I could resist the angels but not him. Because, well . . . Do you know who he was? Yes, it was the Baal Shem himself."

46

Rebbe Leib was on the side of man, defending him even against God:

"Lord, You are unjust. You filled books with hell and hearts with desire; is it surprising then that man permits himself to be seduced by evil? Now, if it were the other way around . . ."

Another time: "If You think You can bring Your people back into the fold by making them suffer, then I, Leib, son of Rachel, swear to You that You will not succeed. So why try? Save Your children by giving them joy, by delivering them. By doing it that way, You have nothing to lose and everything to gain."

And again: "Lord, save Your people before it is too late. Otherwise there may be no one left to save."

Famine was devastating the country. The Grandfather of Shpole convened a tribunal of ten Talmudic scholars: "I need you to sit in judgment. I am accusing Him who kills His children."

And he quoted texts and commentaries, decrees and decisions as evidence that God was in the wrong; that He was not fulfilling His duties toward man.

The trial lasted three days. Isolated from the outside world, the court deliberated without fear or prejudice, examining the problem from all angles, weighing all arguments, and finally reached a verdict: "Whereas the Father of all creatures is responsible for their sustenance, let Him put an end to the famine."

During New Year services, it was the Grandfather of 'Shpole's custom to retire to his room for an hour or two before

47

the blowing of the shofar. Why? To speak to God in a language which is not that of prayer books:

"Don't think of man's sins, I beg of You. Think rather of his good deeds. They are fewer, I agree. But You must admit, they are more precious. Believe me, it isn't easy to be good in this world. And if I didn't see with my own two eyes that man, in spite of all obstacles, is capable of kindness, I would not believe it. And so I ask of You: don't be harsh with Your children; rare as it may be, it is their kindness that should surprise You."

When Rebbe Nahum of Tchernobil came to see the Baal Shem, the latter said to his wife: "Hannah, look at this man; he is a thief."

"A thief, he? He is a saint!"

"A thief, I tell you. He wants paradise all to himself."

To a guest he said: "You want me to take you with me? Very well. On one condition: tell me what distinguishes the nocturnal litanies referred to as *Tikun Leah* from the ones called *Tikun Rachel?*"

Rachel and Leah: Jacob's two wives. Their prayers are recited at midnight, and it is also at midnight that one laments the destruction of the Temple and the exile of the Shekhina.

"I think I know the difference between them," whispered Rebbe Nahum. "What Leah accomplished with tears, Rachel, who was more beautiful and happier too, accomplished with joy."

Why must the Just Man concern himself with earthly matters, with men of every station?

"Imagine a man on a roof," explains Rebbe Nahum. "He

48

sees a pearl lying in the dust. Were he not to come down from his roof, how would he pick it up?"

One day he stopped abruptly in the midst of a sermon: "Brothers, listen to my words, even if you don't understand them. A day will come when the Messiah will speak to you, and you will not understand him either. You may as well get used to it."

He also said: "I am much more afraid of my good deeds that please me than of my bad deeds that repel me."

He led a humble and austere life: "I like poverty," he said. "It is God's gift to man, a treasure."

Rebbe Mikhal of Zlotchev was asked an embarrassing question: "You are poor, Rebbe. And yet every day you thank God for taking care of your needs. Isn't that a lie?"
"Not at all. You see, for me poverty is a need."

He said: "Man's consciousness is in perpetual motion. Mine follows great men in their rise and attracts the lowly, to lift them up with me."

And also: "Saintliness is sometimes nothing but impure temptation."

One of his prayers: "I have but one request; may I never use my reason against truth."

Before Rebbe Mikhal's revelation in Yampol, where he shared a miserable hut with his family, people thought him mad. Mad because he habitually prayed knocking his head against the wall until he drew blood.
The Baal Shem had to persuade him to accept a post of

preacher-rabbi. People were afraid of him. They claimed that he could see through them. He needed only to look at a man's forehead to guess his sins. One day the faithful appeared at the synagogue with their caps pulled way down to their eyebrows. His wry comment: "You really believe that a garment can prevent my eyes from seeing?"

Like all of the Baal Shem's disciples, he dreaded pride. He said: "When I shall meet my Maker, I will be asked why I did not learn all that man can and must learn during his passage on earth. I shall reply: Don't blame me, I wasn't intelligent enough, that is hardly my fault." — "Then why didn't you give up earthly pleasures and devote yourself to serving the Lord?" — "You mustn't blame me, I shall say, I lacked the physical strength for that. Then the court will examine my humanitarian activities and I shall be forced to admit that here too I failed to do my duty. My excuse? That I myself led a destitute existence. In the end, I can foresee it, one of the judges, unable to restrain his anger, will cry out: 'One thing I cannot understand. You neither lived nor prayed as you should have, why then are you so proud?' And to that," said Rebbe Mikhal, "to that argument I shall have no answer."

Infinitely naïve and pious, Rebbe Wolfe of Zbaraj repeated every night before going to bed: "I revoke my rights on all I possess; whatever belongs to me is no longer mine. In this way, no matter what thieves may carry away, they will not have violated the law."

One day his wife quarreled with their servant in his presence. Seeing the two women leave for the rabbinical court, he got up, put on his Shabbat clothes and followed them there.

"Why did you take the trouble?" asked his wife. "I don't need your help."

"You don't, but the servant does. You, they know; but she is a poor orphan. No one will help her, no one will plead her cause."

To his coachman, he said: "Please throw away your whip. Even if a horse does deserve punishment, what makes you think it is up to you to inflict it?"

People came to him to denounce some Jews who were playing cards late into the night.

"And you want me to condemn them?" he cried out. "Why me? And in the name of what? And for what crime? They stay up late? It's a good thing to resist sleep! They concentrate on the game. That is good too! Sooner or later they will give up card-playing—what will remain is a discipline of body and mind. And this time they will place it in the service of God! Why then should I condemn them?"

He was attending a circumcision. Stepping outside for a moment, he noticed the coachman shivering with cold:

"Inside it is warm," he told him. "Go in, warm yourself, have a drink and something to eat."

"Who will watch the horses?"

"I will."

The coachman did as the Master wished. Several hours later people saw Rebbe Wolfe, half frozen in the snow, jumping from one foot to the other, at a loss to understand why the guests were making such a fuss.

Rebbe Hersh, son of the Baal Shem, is depicted by legend as a shy, rather insignificant man. While his father lay dying, he was asleep. He had to be awakened and taken to the sick Master's bedside—who spoke to him, but Rebbe Hersh did not understand.

Called upon to take over the movement, he was found lacking in authority.

He withdrew into himself, and in the end, spoke only to his dead father. In his dreams, he asked him: "How can I serve God?"

The Baal Shem climbed a high mountain and threw himself into the abyss. "Like this," he answered.

Another time the Baal Shem appeared to him as a mountain on fire, erupting into a thousand flaming fragments: "And like this as well."

THE MAGGID
OF MEZERITCH

"WHY ARE YOU CRYING, *Mother? Because the house is burning?*" — "*Yes.*" — "*We shall build another, I promise you.*" — "*It's not the house, son. If I cry, it is because a precious document is being destroyed before our eyes.*" — "*What document?*" — "*Our family tree; it is illustrious, you know.*" — "*Don't cry. I'll give you another. I'll start anew, I promise you.*"

At the time, Dov-Ber was five.

Born in Volhynia in 1710, ten years after the Baal Shem, the future Maggid of Mezeritch came from a poor family. He was a brilliant student, and like the Baal Shem, married young and earned a meager living first as a teacher of children and later as a wandering preacher. He was respected throughout the region, and known to be honest, severe and demanding. Destitute, he found shelter in an abandoned hut, and that is where he and his wife lived in utter misery and also where their son, Avraham, was born.

A story is told that, exasperated by his wife's complaints,

one day Dov-Ber cried out: "So be it, I shall curse my people, since they could but will not help us." Then he went outside, and staring at heaven, continued: "May Your people know happiness, peace and wealth." And after a sigh, he added: "But its money, the money it is refusing me, may it be thrown to the stones and into the brambles."

Though he remained poor, he never complained of it again. On the contrary, he turned his poverty into a virtue. Like most early Masters, he had at first been a fervent adversary of Hasidism. Both as a Talmudic scholar and a mystic believing in self-mortification, he did not approve of the Baal Shem's way. Dov-Ber's way was to make life harder, not easier. He himself led a sober, inward-directed existence, sometimes fasting from one Saturday to the next. He inflicted pain on his body until it became unbearable and he fell gravely ill. Physicians were consulted, but all confessed their helplessness. Then someone suggested he see the Baal Shem, the visionary-healer everyone was talking about. He went. Out of medical necessity rather than intellectual curiosity. But he went. Expecting some relief or perhaps even a cure, but certainly not a sign powerful enough to make him deviate from his set path.

We know that their first meeting was a failure. Even though the visitor had expected little, it was worse than a disappointment; it was nothing. The Baal Shem told him a bizarre story about coachmen and horses (similar to the one he told Yaakov-Yosseph of Polnoye), and that was all. The sick and anxious Maggid countered the Master's small talk with gruff silence. I didn't come from so far away to listen to stories about horses, he thought. Unable to communicate, the two men seemed to have nothing in common.

Bitter at having wasted his time, the Maggid returned to the inn and prepared himself for the journey home. The horses were harnessed, the carriage waiting, when a messenger arrived summoning him to the Baal Shem. He agreed to go back. Why? Perhaps he felt that having come this far, he might as well give the healer a second chance. It was midnight when they met again. The Baal Shem handed him the Book of Splendor, the Zohar: "Can you read?" — "Yes." — "Well then, read!" The Maggid obeyed. "That is not the way one reads," the Baal Shem interrupted. "I can see that you know how to decipher the signs, but your knowledge lacks soul."

That was the turning point. The room filled with light. The Maggid stood at Sinai again; he saw the fire and understood how much he lacked. He also understood that the Besht was the only man capable of helping him reach the heights. He became his disciple, his witness, his foremost apostle. Later, while spreading the Master's teachings, he went so far as to authenticate the most incredible stories by stating: "I was there."

Example: "When the Baal Shem ate, an angel came down, seized his food and turned it into an offering of fire. I saw it, I was there."

Did he believe his own stories? Probably. He loved to repeat them. He told stories about his Master but only rarely quoted him. Maxims, parables, key ideas of the Baal Shem, one finds in the work of others. The Maggid leaves us nothing but tales heavy with miraculous deeds. No doubt that was his way of conveying his personal concept of the Rebbe—the Master vested with almost unlimited powers—and also of accentuating the exclusive intimacy that characterized his relationship with the Baal Shem. As though he alone had been privileged to see what the Master had hidden from others.

•   •   •

"What did you learn in Mezeritch?" Rebbe Aharon of Karlin was asked. — "Nothing at all." — "What do you mean?" — "Yes," he said, "in Mezeritch, I learned that I am nothing at all."

"And you?" Rebbe Levi-Yitzhak of Berditchev was asked. "What did you discover at the Great Maggid's school?" — "I discovered that God exists, that He is of this world, of all worlds." — "But, Rebbe, everybody knows that!" — "No," answered the illustrious Rebbe of Berditchev. "They say it everywhere, but in Mezeritch they know it."

A third Hasidic Master, Rebbe Shmelke of Nikolsburg, testified in his own way: "A long time ago, in the blindness of my youth, I mortified my body so it would tolerate my soul. Since Mezeritch, I know that cannot be right. Body and soul must and can live in harmony."

These three stories are characteristic. They show the quality of the pilgrims attracted by Mezeritch and also the diversity of knowledge they drew from it.

"After the death of our Master Israel Baal Shem Tov, the Shekhina herself shouldered her bundle and stick and moved from Medzebozh to Mezeritch," legend tells us by way of several renowned disciples. Authentic or apocryphal, no matter. It illustrates a fact: it was the Maggid who took over. From that moment on he was undisputed head of the rapidly expanding movement, and its center, therefore, shifted elsewhere. Briefly contested at first, his authority soon went unchallenged. Moral guide, teacher, experienced tactician, seasoned organizer and outstanding visionary combined in one person, Rebbe Dov-Ber of Mezeritch counted three hundred disciples, or so they say, of which thirty-nine became leaders and founders of dynasties in their own right.

With him, Hasidism underwent its first structural if not ideological mutation: from the realm of legend to that of history. Even those historians who, for reasons best known to themselves, questioned the physical existence of the Baal Shem, never denied that the Maggid of Mezeritch was his successor.

We know only what we are permitted to know about this spiritual leader who shrouded himself in mystery. While he himself put nothing down on paper, his disciples transcribed his commentaries on Torah and Talmud, his interpretation of Zohar, his words of advice and parables, and quoted them abundantly in their own works. Levi-Yitzhak of Berditchev carried his zeal to extremes; he recorded the Master's most trivial remarks. Another disciple, Rebbe Zusia of Onipol, went further yet: he devoted his entire life to scrupulously repeating everything he had heard in Mezeritch.

Thus we know many facts about his origins, his childhood, his life before and after his decisive encounter with the Baal Shem. We know, for example, that in his youth he liked to rise at dawn and walk beside the streams and lakes; he was learning the art of listening. We know that he was nearsighted. That he limped. That he was constantly afflicted by obscure pains. That he trembled before speaking in public. We also know that he ate and slept as little as possible; that under his severe exterior hid a generous man and tender father. But above all, we know his incomparable, unequaled role in the development of Hasidism and the enrichment of the exalted universe that is its own.

In Mezeritch, new center of learning, talented men abounded. Among them were Elimelekh of Lizensk, Zusia of Onipol, Shneur-Zalmen of Ladi, Israel of Kozhenitz, Yaakov-Yosseph of Lublin. One could even meet some of the Baal

Shem's companions, such as Pinhas of Koretz or Yaakov-Yos-seph of Polnoye. Together and individually, they acknowledged the Maggid as their guide. Each of his disciples received from him whatever he needed to take root and fulfill himself accord-ing to his own truth. To some the Maggid taught *Nigla*, the revealed science, to others *Nistar*, the esoteric science reserved for the select few. At the same time, and with equal conviction, he showed the simple uneducated people that merely by reciting the prayer *Sh'ma Israel*, they could be worthy of redemption. For each he found the right word, the needed gesture. In his presence, people realized how much was still to be learned. They suddenly became aware of depths within themselves never recognized before. And that to achieve total awareness, they needed his help. Those who indulged in mortification, he taught that the body is sacred as long as it is alive and that to mutilate it is an offense to God. Those too comfortably en-sconced in their existence and neglecting the virtue of fear, he showed what fear could be.

Many whose lives had been transformed by the Baal Shem, and many others who wanted to change theirs, flocked to Mez-eritch. The Maggid knew whom to attract and encourage and whom to turn away. His intuition was such that he gave meaning to all waiting and corrected all shortcomings. If we are to believe his admirers, he, like his Master, could accurately describe people simply by looking at an object of their making.

All testimonies concur: the Maggid had mastered the art of winning the absolute loyalty of men by upsetting their equilib-rium. His methods relied on surprise and shock. His pronounce-ments were as unexpected as his silences. To one visitor he made a single comment: "The horse who knows he is a horse, is not. Man's major task is to learn that he is not a horse." To another he said: "Just as there is light and darkness in the world, there is light and darkness in man's mind." On his lips, ordinary sentences took on the weight of confessions. "When the sick Maggid told a simple story," according to Israel of Rizhin, "the bed he rested on would shake violently, and so would the privileged few present." The Baal Shem made people dream, the Maggid made them tremble.

A man, a mystic, came to see him. The visitor had given up food and sleep and was seeking total renunciation. The Maggid first directed his son, Rebbe Avraham, to feed him by force. Then he ordered him to repeat after him, word by word, the ritual confession, the *Vidui: Ashamnu, bagadnu, gazalnu*— We have sinned, we have betrayed, we have stolen. The man fainted. When he came to, the Maggid sent him away, ordering him never to let it happen again: some words are as important as deeds—some words *are* deeds.

Another visitor, a Hasid and noted Talmudic scholar, came to seek his advice. He was afraid he was losing his faith. The Maggid did not engage the man in lengthy philosophical discussions, but instead asked him to repeat with him, over and over again, the very first prayer every Jewish child learns by heart. And that was all.

"One day," Rebbe Wolfe of Zhitomir tells us, "we were all sitting around the table in the House of Study. It was a Friday afternoon. We could hear the Maggid, in his study next door, reading the Sidra, the weekly portion of Scripture customarily read on Shabbat. Suddenly he stopped, the door opened, and there he was, standing motionless in the doorway, staring at us, or perhaps at someone beyond us. His whole being was on fire, but most of all, his face, most of all, his eyes. Seized with panic, Rebbe Pinhas, Rebbe Shmelke, Rebbe Elimelekh and Rebbe Zusia ran into the street. Rebbe Levi-Yitzhak hid under the table. As for me, gripped by a strange exultation, I began to applaud with all my strength—and to this day I regret it."

And do you know how Rebbe Avraham Kalisker came to attach himself to the Maggid's court? For years he had lived in seclusion, refusing to meet people so as not to take time away from Torah. One day he heard a Hasid quote the Maggid's interpretation of *Umala haaretz kinyanekha,* the earth is full of things that permit man to acquire a partnership with God. Rebbe Avraham Kalisker needed no more: he climbed out the nearest window and hurried to Mezeritch. Later he told the famous Gaon of Vilna: "What *I* learned in Mezeritch? One simple truth: *vehai bahem,* Torah is given to man so he may celebrate life and everything that makes life a source of celebration."

The Holy Seer of Lublin testifies: "Once I heard the Maggid say *Ein Ke'elokhenu,* no God is like our God, the last prayer of the service. At that very moment the skies parted and I saw the words coming alive before my eyes: I *saw* that there is no God like our God."

One day the Maggid invited Rebbe Wolfe of Zhitomir to say grace after the Shabbat meal. Afterward he asked him: "What did you feel?" — "Two hands on my head," said the astonished disciple. — "That was the Prophet Elijah ordaining you a rabbi," said the Maggid.

As for Shneur-Zalmen, the illustrious author of the *Tanya* and founder of the school of Lubavitch, he praised the Maggid's vast erudition. Not his supernatural powers. He would say: "Miracles? In Mezeritch? Who had the time to notice them all?" As for himself, Shneur-Zalmen, he was impressed only by the prodigiously acute and prolific mind of the Maggid. Himself a noted scholar and philosopher, he stated without the slightest hesitation: "Whatever I know is nothing compared with what he knows."

On the other hand, we have the testimony of another great Hasidic figure, the mysterious Leib, son of Sarah, who proclaimed to anyone willing to listen: "I came to the Maggid not to listen to discourses, nor to learn from his wisdom; I came to watch him tie his shoelaces."

In Hasidic vocabulary, the Great Maggid means the one from Mezeritch. What made him great? We shall enlarge on this later; for the moment let us say that the impact of certain Masters must be measured by evaluating the men they inspire. Those who made up the Maggid's "court" were personalities of the first rank. That they chose him to be their leader proves that they, who were known as his peers, believed in his superiority.

For he acceded to leadership by means of a formal election. There are three versions describing the event.

Here is the first: It happened on the second day of Shavuot, also the first anniversary of the Baal Shem's death. The *Havraya Kadisha,* the entire holy assemblage made up of his disciples, was gathered around a table presided over by Rebbe Hersh, the late Master's son. Suddenly Rebbe Hersh rose, removed his white kaftan, and wrapping it around the Maggid's shoulders, wished him *mazel tov, mazel tov,* congratulations. After a moment of surprised silence, all those present joined in approvingly: *Mazel tov, mazel tov,* may the good star accompany our new leader.

Second version: Just before he died, the Baal Shem told his disciples that the one among them who would teach them how to overcome pride would be his successor. The problem was put to each of them; the Maggid happened to be called first. His answer: Since pride is one of God's attributes, man cannot uproot it entirely, all at once; it must be fought every day and at every moment. This reply was so favorably received, no one else was questioned.

The third version is the most poetic. It excludes the direct participation of the Baal Shem and leaves the decision entirely in his disciples' hands. They are said to have agreed that the one among them who would reveal something new about the late Master's life, his work or his teaching, would become his successor. And each told all he knew. Stories and quotations followed one another. When the Maggid's turn came, he related that every Friday, before Shabbat, the Baal Shem Tov would leave his body and exchange it for a new one. "I saw him do it with my own eyes," said the Maggid. He was the only one to see it.

Later, of course, more legends were created emphasizing the Maggid's superiority over his companions, for he had been the Master's favorite disciple. Once the Master is believed to have told him: "I need you. Whether a source is blessed or not depends on the person drawing from it."

Another time the Besht was overheard saying: "If only Dov-Ber could go to the *mikvah,* he would bring the Messiah." But being too sick, always, he couldn't go to the ritual baths. So close was the relationship between Master and disciple— still according to Hasidic legend—that after giving him his blessing, the Baal Shem asked the Maggid to bless him in return.

Hasidism's historians tell us that the two men met around

1752, eight years before the Baal Shem's death. There are those who claim that the Maggid visited the Baal Shem only twice, the second—and longest—time for six months. How did the two men become so close so quickly? No one knows. Master and disciple both possessed the secret of *kfitzat haderekh,* of juggling time. But whether the Baal Shem really saw the Maggid as his heir has never been established.

Actually, the Baal Shem had at least two other disciples comparable in importance to the Maggid: Pinhas of Koretz and Yaakov-Yosseph of Polnoye. The first is remembered as the sage, or "brain," of Hasidism; the second, as its first chronicler and historian.

Rebbe Pinhas, a profoundly humble man, never aspired to the throne; Rebbe Yaakov-Yosseph did. It seems that at first Rebbe Pinhas even supported him. Against the Maggid.

Yaakov-Yosseph was well known for his loyalty to the Baal Shem. In fact, he almost never left him, content to live in his shadow. His works on Hasidism are the first of their kind. He spent thirty years compiling them, and the Baal Shem's name is mentioned in them 280 times. He considered himself the Master's favorite scribe—and favored he was. The Master had a special liking for him, that is certain. One day he cried out, and there were witnesses: "Master of the Universe, when I die I shall not ask to be rewarded for my good deeds, but only for having brought You my Yossele."

Why then wasn't Yaakov-Yosseph chosen? It isn't clear. Perhaps because he was too rigid and not sociable enough. His relationships with people, especially leaders, were awkward. Jealous by nature, he probably lost his temper with anyone who approached or claimed to have come close to the Master, feeling perhaps that no one else could understand the Master. And then, of course, he was too intellectual for the majority.

Their attitude was: let the makers-of-words remain with their solitary studies and refrain from involvement in community affairs, where deeds have priority over thoughts.

Yaakov-Yosseph took his defeat badly. He felt bitter, rejected by his colleagues, misunderstood, a victim of injustice. His friend Pinhas of Koretz did his best to comfort him with a parable: "When the king retires at night, his crown rests on a nail fastened to the wall. Why on a nail, which is nothing but a common object? Why not on a minister's head? Because the minister might take himself seriously and believe he is the king. No such danger with a nail." Yaakov-Yosseph must have been lacking in humor; he was not to be consoled. His relations with the Maggid and his followers deteriorated until he refused even to partake of their Shabbat meals. He would stay home and eat there by himself. His bitterness became unbearable when he realized that . . . his books did not sell. The story goes that when on a visit to Berditchev not a single buyer appeared, he flew into a rage and threatened to curse the whole town. To appease him, Rebbe Wolfe of Zhitomir urgently dispatched an anonymous messenger to purchase one hundred copies. And the town was saved.

Fact or anecdote, it reflects the individual fate of the man and not his work. From the very beginning, his work added an indispensable foundation to the movement. Perhaps the Maggid was chosen over him because Hasidism even then preferred the spoken word to the written one, experience to knowledge and people to books. Yaakov-Yosseph taught; the Maggid inspired. Yet the Maggid's aim was not merely to inspire his disciples, but to train leaders. During the Baal Shem's lifetime Hasidism had been one man; the time had come to make it into a movement. A centralized, coherent and structured movement with objectives and rules, disciplines and prerogatives.

Both excellent strategist and administrator, the Maggid succeeded in a few short years, twelve to be exact, in establishing and firmly implanting a Hasidic network spanning all of Eastern Europe. Thanks to the Maggid, the flame kindled by the Baal Shem made its way into thousands of widely dispersed communities, small and large. He knew precisely whom to send where to carry out what mission; nothing escaped him, he left nothing to chance.

He had his own reasons for sending Aharon of Karlin to Lithuania and Elimelekh of Lizensk to Galicia. Each could succeed only in the place he was sent; they were not interchangeable.

Dividing Central Europe into more or less well-defined regions, he assigned a Rebbe to each whose task it was to lay the groundwork. What were the means at their disposal? A few tales, a few melodies and an unshakable faith in the Baal Shem's way. And everywhere they found people willing to listen, and willing to join. These Rebbes, these emissaries knew no borders. They crossed the highest mountains and the deepest valleys; nothing could stop them; they never left feeling they had sown in the wind.

Rebbe Menahem-Mendl of Vitebsk was asked what he had accomplished in Vitebsk. His answer: "When I arrived there, I found torn clothes and whole hearts; now it is the opposite."

Elsewhere, among the poverty-stricken tribes of Galicia, the task of the Maggid's emissaries was to bring hope and consolation to people living in despair and humiliation. To upset the established order, rock the institutions, tear down the barriers separating poor and rich, scholar and craftsman, peasant and townsman. And above all, to show that to be Jewish could be a link, a faith in new beginnings.

Conceived by the Baal Shem, the Hasidic idea owes the Maggid its adaptation, its practical application. Before him, it was impulsive, vague, fragmentary. Idealized in the extreme, it was vulnerable. Its core needed to be protected and strengthened, it needed a supporting framework and the external marks of an expanding movement. And most of all it needed to be anchored in reality.

The instrument? The Tzaddik, the Rebbe. The Master, the Just Man. Here again the Maggid turned a vague concept of the Baal Shem's into a viable doctrine. As he saw it, the Tzaddik had to combine the virtues and gifts, as well as fulfill the roles and obligations, of saint, guide and sage. Spokesman for God in His dealings with man, intercessor for man in his dealings with God. Required to be almost a superman, he was expected to accept pride without becoming proud; to incite anger without succumbing to it; to strive for goals beyond his reach, assuming full responsibility for possible consequences and contradictions. The Tzaddik had to know the art of speaking, the better to remain silent, and the art of silence, the better to speak.

By placing the emphasis on the Tzaddik, by setting almost unattainable standards for him, the Maggid, contrary to his predecessor, focused his attention on the elite, on his immediate circle, rather than on the average Hasid. His circle of intimates was exclusive. To want and seek admission meant nothing. To deserve it meant little. The Maggid chose his disciples personally, according to criteria known only to himself. A thinker like Shneur-Zalmen and a primitive soul like Leib, son of Sarah, seemingly moved in two entirely distinct worlds. Yet each in his own sphere had attained a kind of perfection and glory. The same could be said of all the others; each occupied a well-defined place in the Maggid's hierarchy. Legend tells us of one exception. One particularly talented follower is said to have gained admittance into the inner circle, and having tasted too many secret fruits too soon, took to drinking and later, to everyone's amazement, to raving and ranting; saying things, wild things . . . Hasidic chronicles mention him only rarely and with reticence; they evidently find it embarrassing to admit that one of the Great Maggid's most brilliant students could have turned out so badly. The other disciples—all of them— did the Master honor by becoming zealous missionaries, tireless preachers, bearers of dreams and Hasidic exultation, wandering from country to country, from village to village, from congregation to congregation, creating a kingdom whose prince was the teller of tales who sang and made others sing.

This made it necessary for the Tzaddik to lead a deliberately ambiguous existence, ambiguous on two levels: he had to be an example one admired but did not emulate, and remain open to the world while retaining his link to a universe both secret and inaccessible.

The reason is clear. For the simple man to experience and survive disasters past and present, for the simple mind to absorb, however unwillingly and unwittingly, enigma and pain and contend with the daily tedium and worries of an opaque existence; for the expatriate going through life as a suspect and undesirable stranger, what was needed was a messenger familiar enough to understand, yet unfamiliar enough to suggest the unknown, mystery, escape. What was required, above all, were men who inspired confidence; there had to be hope even if one could not solve one's problem alone. And since the

Tzaddik, by definition, knows the answer, it means there is an answer. Trials and misfortunes, therefore, do have a meaning and do not dissolve into nothingness; they leave their imprint in a collective memory assured of survival. That is another of the Tzaddik's roles; he must encourage the Hasid by teaching him never to consider himself useless, abandoned, negated by a universe he does not understand.

Thus, the Maggid was the answer to a need that was particularly acute in a multitude of obscure regions of Poland, the Ukraine, Rumania, Hungary, Austria and White Russia. His school provided these isolated communities with leaders. Thanks to him, the Jew had someone to turn to in his anguish: his Tzaddik. Who had to be conscious of the almost unlimited powers vested in him both in the visible and the invisible present to carry out his mission. His own soul needed to be sovereign, or else how could he presume to influence another's? And if his own destiny eluded him, how could he even try to affect another's? The Maggid interpreted the Talmudic saying *Veda ma lemala mimkha* as follows: *veda,* know, that *ma lemala,* what occurs up above, *mimkha,* derives from you as well. Whatever the event, *you* are its origin; it is through *you,* through *your* will, that God manifests Himself.

It is said that one day the Maggid decided that the time had come to bring man's exile to an end. The decision caused alarm in heaven. He was asked: "Who do you think you are to dare tampering with the celestial order?" — "I am the *Tzaddik hador,* this generation's Just Man," he replied. — "You? Prove it." — "Very well, my disciples will furnish you the proof." Gathered hurriedly, they were asked point-blank: "Am I or am

I not this generation's Just Man?" Thunder-struck, the disciples remained silent. The Maggid repeated his question; nobody said a word. He tried a third time and again was met by silence, always the same silence. It was a strange refusal, one that has remained unexplained to this day. One wonders why these blindly devoted men refused, at the critical moment, to support their Master. What is known is that, contrary to his predecessor, he never tried again. It was written that the Messiah still had to stay with the angels for a long time to come. Man would have to wait.

His former opponent, Rebbe Pinhas of Koretz, seems to have reacted to this episode when he declared: "If I wanted, I could make the Messiah come as easily as I lift a straw, but I prefer to rely on God."

Yet the Maggid wished his disciples to develop confidence in their own powers; failing that, they could not adequately discharge themselves of their rabbinical functions. Flagrant display of pride? Perhaps. But since man and especially Just Man is created in God's image, he may and must, under certain circumstances, assume one or another of His attributes. *Umilbashto anava,* God's cloak is humility, was interpreted in Mezeritch as meaning: humility should be like a cloak; one must know how to take it off sometimes.

And yet, to offset the danger inherent in such a concept of the Just Man, the Maggid frequently stressed the importance of humility as a cardinal virtue. Only a humble man can afford ambitious impulses approaching vanity. The line between pride and vanity is thin and the stakes are high. He said: "You may observe every commandment of Torah, you may purify and perfect yourself by obeying every law, and yet, if at the last moment your consciousness is tainted by a single vain thought, then all has been in vain. And you can wrap all your good deeds, all your worthy intentions into a bundle and throw it into hell."

The struggle against pride evidently was a major problem for the Maggid and his school. Everybody spoke about it so much and so often, one wonders if anything else really mattered.

A notorious Mitnagged—opponent of the movement—discussing the subject with Rebbe Wolfe of Zhitomir, voiced his astonishment. He complained: "I have troubles with my son-in-law. Since his Mezeritch adventure, all he ever talks about is his fight against pride. I don't understand: what does he have to be so proud of? He does nothing, has nothing, knows nothing. I, on the other hand, studied with the Gaon of Vilna, know half the Talmud by heart, am generous with the needy, attend services three times a day and lead a saintly life. And yet, look at me: do I look like I must fight pride?"

Dialogue between Elimelekh of Lizensk and his brother Zusia of Onipol:

"Where and how should man begin to serve God?"

"Simple," said Elimelekh, "if he begins by seeing how small and insignificant he is, he will appreciate the greatness of God."

"What!" said Zusia. "Let man begin with himself? How arrogant! Let him instead look up at the Lord's greatness and then he cannot but realize how very small he is."

Since neither convinced the other, they sought the Maggid's counsel. His comment: "Actually, you are both right; both your attitudes are correct. Still, it is safer for man to start his quest aware of his limitations, namely, with himself. He who lies on the ground cannot fall down."

On another occasion the Maggid said: "Let him who wants fervor not seek it on the mountain peaks—there he will find only storms; rather let him stoop and search among the ashes."

He undoubtedly had common sense. His teachings include practical advice and admonitions that could be published under the title: the education of a Rebbe. He was a thorough teacher; he even taught his disciples the art of speaking in public. His advice: "Whenever you deliver an address stop before the end, before you have said it all." And also: "Remember that a good speaker must become one, not with his audience, but with his words; the moment he hears himself speak, he must conclude."

To Rebbe Zusia, he gave the following advice:
"Listen, I cannot teach you the ten cardinal rules governing the conduct of man wishing to serve his Creator. However, there are three things you can learn from a child and seven you can learn from a thief. From an infant learn how to laugh, how to cry and how to keep constantly busy. From the thief? First of all: that whatever he does, he does secretly. Two: that whatever he does not obtain today, he will try to obtain tomorrow. Three: he is loyal to his accomplices. Four: he is ready to sacrifice himself for the object of his desire, even though it may have no value to others. Five: once the desired object becomes his own, he loses interest. Six: he is not afraid of hardship. Seven: nothing on earth could make him change trades, in other words, he does not want to be anyone but himself."

Though the Maggid had flashes of humor, they were few. Earnest to the point of solemnity, concerned with the image he projected, he did not encourage informality and certainly not distractions. In his eyes, only the essential was permissible. People came from far away to hear him utter a single word, which then sufficed to feed a lengthy meditation, or they came simply to spend Shabbat under his roof.

Among the pilgrims: Solomon Maimon, famous philosopher, friend of Kant and Mendelssohn. He came for a specific reason of his own: he wanted to see the Maggid and evaluate him. The Maggid refused to receive him, and the offended philosopher was kept waiting until the end of the week before he was admitted. He tells us: "Came the first meal of Shabbat . . . There was white everywhere . . . The Maggid was dressed in white . . . Even his snuffbox was white . . . Around the table, the disciples were singing. The Maggid asked each of them to recite a verse of the Biblical passage to be read the following day. Then he took all the quotations and wove them into a discourse. And every one of his followers was certain that the Master was speaking to him alone."

In Mezeritch the climate was one of tension and stress. People lived on the brink of nervous exhaustion; the very idea of diversion was sacrilegious. The Maggid was feared, and that was how he wanted it.

One Yom Kippur, legend tells us, it happened that the Maggid, who then still resided in Medzebozh, inadvertently touched a fringe of the ritual shawl covering the Baal Shem. He was seized by uncontrollable trembling. And when he leaned against the table, the table, too, began to tremble.

His disciples did not need to touch him to start trembling. It was enough for them to see him—even from afar.

No, he never laughed. But sometimes he smiled.

A very pious and very wealthy Jew wanted to impress him with a description of the austerity to which he subjected himself. "Tell me what you eat every day," the Maggid inquired. — "Oh, almost nothing. Bread and salt." — "That's bad," said the Maggid, "that's very bad. I order you to eat white bread and cake, and also to drink sweet wine." — "But, Rebbe, why?" cried the astounded Hasid. — "I shall tell you why. You see: if you are content with black bread and water, you will come to the conclusion that the poor can subsist on stones and spring water. If you eat cake, you will give them bread."

Another anecdote: A famous physician, attached to the royal court of Prussia, offered him a bargain: "I shall heal your body if you will heal my soul." — "Agreed," said the Maggid, "let's see which one of us will succeed." If one is to believe legend, the physician became a Hasid while the Maggid remained incurably ill.

And still another story: A farmer and his wife pleaded with him to intercede on their behalf: "We are childless; we want a son." — "Very well," said the Maggid. "That will be fifty-two rubles [fifty-two being the numerical value of *Ben*, the Hebrew word for son]." The couple bargained, offered half. To no avail. The Maggid would not budge: "You want me to pray for you? Then you must pay the price." Finally the peasant became angry, and turning to his wife, he said: "Let's go home, we'll manage without him, we'll say our own prayers and God will help us without charge!" "So be it," the Maggid said, and smiled.

The Baal Shem's words had been: "Sometimes God seems very removed from man—why? It is the father's duty to teach his son to walk. To accomplish this he moves forward

73

and backward without warning, at the risk of letting the child stumble and fall."

Dov-Ber had his own comment: "God, in His infinite love, restrains His powers to enlighten, so that man may receive step by step, stage by stage, the revelation of what lies beyond his limits: that is the way of a father teaching his son to walk."

But wherein lay the greatness of the Great Maggid of Mezeritch? And why is he still referred to in that way today? He left no work of Talmudic scholarship, no ethical system, no new philosophy. Whatever we know about his towering personality—his charisma, insight and complexity—we know from his followers; we must take their word for it. Moreover, a close analysis of ideas attributed to him leads to the conclusion that primarily he tried—and succeeded—to perpetuate the Baal Shem's theories; the so-called Beshtian Hasidism. His views on *Tzimtzum haelokut,* the stricture of divinity to permit the birth and growth of the world, are taken from the Baal Shem, who had taken them from the Lurianic Kabbala. The same applies to his concept of the Shekhina's omnipresence, even in evil and misfortune. *Let atar panui minei,* the Baal Shem had proclaimed, God dwells in all things—even in sin, and assuredly in the sinner.

It must be said: the more he learns, the more the child in me is disconcerted by the Great Maggid. The Maggid's contribution as a theoretician does not seem fundamental. His attempts at resolving metaphysical problems—relationships between man and God, man and man, man and himself—indicate no breakthrough, no revolutionary approach. Whatever he said, the Baal Shem had said before, directly or indirectly. The victim's cry and the executioner's laughter, the injustice inherent in the weakness of the poor and the arrogance of the rich, understanding pushed to its limits by its fascination with infinity, man's solitude as opposed to God's, the link between Good and Evil, the presence between the vision of death and the vision of death's Victor. These questions had troubled the Baal Shem as they had troubled those whose heritage he claimed. Even the role the Maggid ascribes to the Master inside the community can be traced to the Baal Shem. In general, the importance of his work lies in its continuity rather than its innovations.

In fact, not only did his Master's greatness exceed the Maggid's, even his disciples often surpassed him, each in his particular domain. Shneur-Zalmen eclipsed him in matters of Halakah and speculative philosophy; Levi-Yitzhak of Berditchev, in his love for the people of Israel and its every member; Shmelke of Nikolsburg, in Talmudic scholarship; Zusia of Onipol, in humility; and Aharon of Karlin, in rhetoric. The Maggid must have been aware of it. Often he would muse aloud: "What sin did I commit that I became a Rebbe? And a famous one at that?" Sometimes he would add: "I wish it on the wicked." How is one to explain his impact on peers and disciples alike? A result of his versatility? Of his infirmity? Or of the impression he created of possessing more than one key to more than one gate? Or simply because he wore the glorious crown of the first Master?

It probably had to do more with his followers than with him, and one must look to them for the signs and reasons of the Maggid's greatness. They needed a guide, a Rebbe to overcome

their doubts, their solitude. Mezeritch was for them what Medzebozh had been for the Maggid: refuge, stability, presence.
After Mezeritch, they knew that the road started elsewhere and
ended elsewhere. The same motivations that had driven the
Maggid to the Baal Shem bound his own disciples to the Maggid. The greater they were, the deeper their inner solitude
and their need for someone to lean on, someone to shield them
against excessive pride and exaggerated humility. They came
to Mezeritch seeking human contact as much as knowledge.
They needed to belong, to be a part of a spiritual fraternity.
They needed to feel that others shared their thirst, even if their
ways of quenching it were not always the same. And also they
craved confirmation that they were partners in a beautiful, ex-
hilarating adventure that would bring them closer together. To
be in Mezeritch meant not only to be with the Maggid, but also
to live with comrades, friends and allies.

They felt that self-perfection could be attained only through
others, an idea that is basic to Hasidism. From the moment
they realized that the road to God leads through man, and that
man is God's only link to His creation and the key to its mystery, their paths had to lead through Mezeritch. The Maggid
then became the symbol of their individual and collective quest.
He himself remarked about his disciples: "I found light locked
in a closet; all I did was open the door."

Was this his sole merit? His only claim to greatness? Surely
not.

He was great because he *dared* succeed the Baal Shem. He
must have known that inevitably comparisons would be drawn
and that inevitably he would be the loser.

He was great because he understood the importance of *transmitting* teachings and new discoveries. He accepted his role as
vessel of communication; of executor rather than innovator. In-

stead of trying to found a new movement, he used his talents to consolidate the one he had inherited.

And then, too, he was great because he foresaw the need to train spiritual leaders for the many isolated and neglected communities; perhaps he intuitively knew that European Jewry was embarking on a long and bloody journey, and that it would need all the help and support it could get.

Another thing, both rare and perhaps more revealing than any other: once his disciples became leaders in their own right, the Maggid did not begrudge them their fame and accomplishments. Nor did he ever reproach them for seeking new ways; he wanted them to be different. His thirty-nine disciples did not resemble him, nor did they resemble one another. Each went on to establish his own dynasty, a school bearing his own seal, expressing his own views about man's destiny in general and the people of Israel's in particular. Rather than keeping them dependent on him, he wanted them to reign as sovereigns and in his name. He, the Maggid of Mezeritch, heir of the Baal Shem, was the bond between them.

Yet he was not like the Baal Shem, and therein lies another clue to the Maggid's greatness. Succeeding the Master, he sought neither to emulate nor to resemble him. He had his own style of living, his own kind of relationship with people. No one else would have dared deviate so completely from the Master's path. Most would probably have striven to achieve total identification with the movement's founder by following in his footsteps and by adhering as closely as possible to his established ways. Had the Maggid done this, he would have become another Baal Shem, a small, more or less successful imitation.

The Maggid rejected easy answers and chose a different road. That was his way of paying homage to the Master's work. He understood that to remain faithful to his teacher, he needed the strange mixture of courage and devotion required to stray from the Master's course. His "deviationism" was a synthesis of continuity and innovation, yet he never became a dissident. The Maggid owed it to himself, *not* to the Baal Shem, to keep alive the Baal Shem's image, his legend and his heritage.

And so Mezeritch did not become another Medzebozh. Unlike the Baal Shem, the Great Maggid rarely left Mezeritch and avoided crowds. The Baal Shem had been constantly on the move, showing interest in men of many backgrounds, everywhere; the Maggid addressed himself to a select few. The Baal Shem had told stories; the Maggid made speeches. The Baal Shem celebrated services with the crowd, and the larger it was, the happier he was; the Maggid prayed alone, and only at the end of services were nine privileged disciples invited to join him in a *minyan*.

The Baal Shem had been accessible and always ready to be of service. Anyone could come and see him without having to go through intermediaries. Not so the Maggid. He was the first to appoint a *gabbe* or *shamash* (secretary, servant, guard) to keep intruders away.

More than his Master, the Maggid seems to have had an affinity for drama and staging. The Baal Shem had wandered around dressed alternately as a coachman or a peasant, a woodcutter or a vagabond. The Maggid had a different vision of himself. He assumed the role of high priest and habitually donned the white flowing robes of that office. He inspired respect. The Baal Shem had inspired love.

Toward the end of his life, the Maggid used crutches, which made his already impressive appearance even more awesome. His sickness became one more barrier erected between himself and the outside world.

• • •

And then a strange thing happened: the Maggid decided, unexpectedly and without explanation, to move from Mezeritch to Onipol. Why? The reasons are not clear. Not much is said about the move in Hasidic literature. Was it caused by the increasingly virulent attacks of the opposition, the Mitnagdim? Possibly. But if that is the answer, it is not complete. For the move does not seem to have resolved the conflict, which continued more savagely than ever; geography had little to do with the war between the fanatic Hasidim and their equally fanatic opponents.

(Besides, the attacks were directed more against his apostles than against the Maggid himself. These followers of his, accomplished missionaries though they were, did not have an easy task. Clerical and secular leaders alike treated them as reformers if not outright heretics. They were subjected to many humiliations, especially in the important centers of the Ukraine and White Russia. But the more persecuted they were, the more support they gathered.)

How then is one to explain the Maggid's precipitate departure? Perhaps he felt his work was done; his disciples, influential Rebbes and known Tzaddikim all, no longer needed him. Disillusioned, desperately ill, he may have felt left out and useless.

Or perhaps he longed for privacy and solitude. Having devoted his entire life to others, he may have wished to withdraw into himself to better evaluate the changes that had taken place inside him while he was engaged in changing the image so many Jews had of their place in society.

Another possibility. Perhaps this highly intuitive man had a premonition of disillusionments to come: conceived as a movement of opposition, Hasidism was on its way to becoming just another establishment.

Whatever the motives, the move which occurred in 1772 seems not to have profoundly affected the Hasidic world. True, more dramatic events marked that particular year. Poland was dissected and divided between Germany, Austria and Russia, bringing more suffering for more Jews. When nations fought among themselves, more often than not, the Jews were the ones to pay the price.

That year also saw the first Hasidic book, the *Toldot,* by Rebbe Yaakov-Yosseph of Polnoye, published and—publicly —burned. It was the year the Mitnagdim prevailed upon the prestigious Eliahu, Gaon of Vilna, to excommunicate the Hasidim. Hasidic leaders considered launching a counteroffensive, imposing a counterban. The Maggid withheld his approval; he wished to prevent a deepening of the rift. Better to endure and wait. But the anti-Hasidic measures multiplied and became unbearable, particularly in Lithuania. The Hasidim were persecuted as though they were outside the law. And so, one memorable night, ten of the Maggid's followers assembled in the House of Study, and by the eerie light of black candles, pronounced the solemn and awesome incantation which, according to tradition, banishes foes from the living community of Israel. Suddenly, in the midst of the ceremony, the familiar sound of crutches was heard approaching: the Maggid. He was sad and angry: "You have lost your head" was all he said. And there they remained, unable to move, stricken with remorse, having grasped the full meaning of his words uttered like a verdict; they had lost him as their head, he was going to leave them. Forever. Soon thereafter he consoled them: "I promise you that whenever Hasidim and Mitnagdim will quarrel, the Hasidim will win."

When he died a few months later it was snowing. A storm was blowing furiously over the village as if to sweep it away. Wrapped in his ritual shawl, his phylacteries on his forehead and left arm, he was surrounded by his intimates. His last words: "Keep together, stay united, always."

They did not, though, not really, not for long, yet his tales remain intact, and through them we feel close to the Maggid's disciples, and through them, to the Maggid himself, and to the Baal Shem. And through all of them we are linked to the most fervent moments of Jewish imagination and Jewish soul; without them our history would be poorer, much poorer, for it would be a dreamless history, devoid of nostalgic legend.

DISCIPLES II

"ONLY YOU, LORD, know why sometimes I rank myself ahead, and other times after, others," Rebbe Barukh of Medzebozh exclaimed one day.

A proud man, prone to fits of anger and depression, this grandson of the Baal Shem's, brought up by the Maggid of Mezeritch and educated by Rebbe Pinhas of Koretz, claimed to be different from the other Hasidic Masters of his generation, and he was. He believed that everything was due him, for he saw himself as heir, not to his father, who went almost unnoticed, but to his grandfather. Did he truly believe that he alone was the Baal Shem's legitimate successor? Possibly. The fact is that to him every Rebbe was a potential rival and usurper. He declared himself superior to all of them.

This open arrogance could not fail to cause him trouble and provoke hostilities. His own brothers-in-law complained about his whims and frivolities and went so far as to denounce him to the Great Maggid. Whose grandson was to say later: "Rebbe Barukh of Medzebozh tried to ascend to heaven by stepping on the heads of other Tzaddikim."

He was forever dissatisfied, distrustful, suspicious; his grudges were universal in scope. Yet people forgave him his excessive language, his abrupt changes of mood. His visitors were blessed, even as he insulted them, even as he cursed them. To a child who had surprised him in a domestic quarrel, he said: "You don't understand; what you have just witnessed was a discussion between God and the Shekhina." Legend has absolved him. And more: it has granted him a place of honor. He is the only one to be called "Rebbe Reb" Barukh.

At the time of the Baal Shem's death he was only three, yet he remained obsessed by him. He wanted to resemble him, equal him. Sensing his failure, he often gave in to bleak anxiety and gloom. Though he fought as hard as he could, he was plagued by self-doubt. How was he to know whether the Hasidim's admiration was intended for him or his grandfather? To bring some diversion and cheer into his life, he retained the services of a famous jester: Hershele Ostropoler. This Hershele, devoted but brazenly impudent, became the only person to stand up to him and tell him the truth openly.

A story: One evening Hershele lights a candle. Reb Barukh reprimands him: the room is still too dark. The next evening Hershele lights a dozen candles. And Reb Barukh scolds him again: "Are you trying to blind me?" — "I don't understand you," says Hershele. "Yesterday you were angry with darkness, today you are annoyed with light . . ." Whereupon Reb Barukh bursts out laughing: "*You* want to teach *me* when and how I should unleash my wrath upon the world?"

"This world," he said, "is filled with light for whoever knows it, and covered with darkness for whoever loses his way . . . As for myself, I live in it as a stranger. So does God. Thus our relationship is that of two strangers in a hostile land."

Another time: "Imagine two children playing hide-and-seek; one hides but the other does not look for him. God is hiding and man is not seeking. Imagine His distress.

"The greatest merit of the Prophet Elijah," he said, "is that when he fought the kings and crushed the idols, the people did not react as to a miracle but instead cried: God is our God."

Another time: "To attain truth, man must pass forty-nine gates, each opening onto a new question. Only to arrive finally before the last gate, the last question, beyond which he could not live without faith."

He died at fifty-four. At his bedside, the Zohar was open at the page where there is mentioned a certain "wrath blessed from above and from below," and whose name is: Barukh.

Menahem-Mendl of Vitebsk was the only true disciple of the Maggid of Mezeritch to have met the Baal Shem; the Maggid himself had introduced him. Menahem-Mendl was eleven years old at the time and already known as a brilliant Talmudist.

Surrounded by his faithful, the Baal Shem looked at the boy searchingly and began to tell him a story that some of those present forgot immediately and whose hidden meaning eluded the others; only he, little Menahem-Mendl, remembered the tale in all its details and understood its significance: it was his life's story, from its first to its last day. The honors, the duties, the responsibilities, the illnesses, the disappointments, the journeys to the Holy Land: it was all there.

Later, whenever his health worried his friends, he would reassure them: "I still have one half, or one quarter, of the way to go."

This is how he became Rebbe:

The Maggid of Mezeritch, receiving a delegation of his followers from Vitebsk, entrusted them with his belt and cane. They were to be delivered to a certain Rebbe Menahem-Mendl, who lived in their town.

When the travelers returned home, they began looking for the fortunate man in their midst. In vain. There was no Rebbe Menahem-Mendl in Vitebsk. In their zeal to find him, they questioned even the passers-by on the streets. So doing, they came across a shabbily dressed woman, who told them: "I know one Mendl, only one, my son-in-law." They rushed to his house and without a word handed him the Maggid's cane and belt. Menahem-Mendl accepted them, and at that very moment his visitors realized that he had become another.

"My mission on earth," he said, "is to recognize the void—inside and outside me—and fill it."

Considerate, discreet, he was well liked by people of all backgrounds, and at all the courts. The Maggid publicly displayed his affection for him, appointing him to blow the shofar on Rosh Hashana. When Menahem-Mendl left for the Holy Land, the honor went to Levi-Yitzhak of Berditchev, who, overcome by emotion, clasped the shofar and fainted. "His predecessor, Menahem-Mendl, saw further and did not succumb to fear," the Maggid commented.

To friends expressing their admiration, he said: "Far from me the idea of rejecting your praise. I shall need it. And the day I shall face the heavenly tribunal, I shall request your appearance as my witnesses. Each of you will then justify my life by praising me, by stating what he thinks of me just as he does now. And I shall be happy, sure of having won my case. But then, at the last moment, one member of the court will ask me: "And you, Menahem-Mendl, what do *you* think of yourself? And I shall become humble and silent again."

"To fear punishment is nothing," he said. "What we must fear is sin."

Like all Hasidic Masters, he lived wholly in his expectation of the Messiah's coming. Mornings he would go to the window, look outside and sadly remark: "He has not yet come, for the world is still the same."

His most beautiful words: "Man is the language of God."

Enthusiastic, filled with ardor and exultation, Rebbe Aharon of Karlin was Hasidism's emissary to Lithuania and Russia. Tirelessly he made the rounds of towns and villages, braving and challenging adversaries, establishing networks— small but numerous—wherever he set foot. By continuously giving of himself, body and soul, this child of well-to-do parents, raised in comfort, fell prey to an obscure ailment which carried him away in three days; he was thirty-six. In Mezeritch, the Maggid mourned for him, comparing him to the High Priest Aaron, brother of Moses.

Here is Rebbe Aharon's commentary on Jacob's ladder, represented in the Bible as standing on earth, its tip touching the sky: "Let man stand erect, his feet solidly planted on the ground, and his head will touch the sky."

"If I were given a chance to change places with Abraham, I would refuse," he told a Hasidic audience. "You see, God needs men like Abraham, not fools like me."

One day he was heard crying: "There are two possibilities. Either God is king of the world and I am not doing enough to serve Him, or He is not, and then it is my fault."

A friend, on his way home from Mezeritch, where he had spent a few years, knocked on Rebbe Aharon's door. It was late at night.

"Who is it?" asked Reb Aharon.

"It is I," the visitor replied innocently, sure of being recognized.

"God alone has a right to say *I*. Earth is too small to contain two *I*'s. Haven't you learned that where you come from?"

His friend understood that he still had much to learn and returned to Mezeritch that very night.

Aharon of Karlin taught his followers not to hate life and not to renounce its wealth. Sadness turns into sin, he told them, because it dulls the mind; eventually it becomes hate, self-hate. And whoever hates himself will in the end hate others.

He also said: "He who does not strive upward, falls; he who does not better himself, loses ground."

Disciple of the Maggid, Rebbe Wolfe of Zhitomir chose to remain preacher, rather than be crowned Master. Thence his concern with language.

"Thought is essentially infinite," he said. "What confines it is the spoken word. Then why does man try to express himself? I'll tell you why: the spoken word's function is to humanize thought."

He said: "I fail to understand the so-called enlightened people who demand answers, endless answers in matters of faith.

For the believer, there is no question; for the non-believer, there is no answer."

Before his death, Rebbe Wolfe told his servant: "I can see ... A day will come, and it fills me with fear. The world will lose its stability and man his reason ... A day will come, and it makes me tremble. Do you hear me?"

"Yes, Rebbe. I hear you."

"I ask of you to tell it to our people. Tell them that on that day none will be spared, not even men like me or you. We shall have to delve deep into our consciousness to find the spark. Will you tell them?"

"Yes, Rebbe. But ... when that day comes, what must they do in order not to go under? Do you know the remedy, Rebbe?"

The sick man sighed: "When that day comes, tell our people that I have foreseen it."

He turned against the wall, and was gone.

LEVI-YITZHAK
OF BERDITCHEV

A STORY: The Rebbe notices a coachman, who to save time runs through his morning prayers while greasing his carriage. He does not scold him. Instead, he lifts his eyes to heaven and asks it to be his witness:

"Look at Your people, God of Israel, and be proud. What does this man do while working on his cart? He prays. Tell me, do You know of any other nation that has You so completely in its thoughts?"

Another: On his way to the synagogue to celebrate Shabbat services, he meets an "enlightened" young man who pulls out his pipe in overt defiance and lights it. The Rebbe stops to remind him: "Surely you're forgetting that today is Shabbat?"

"No, I haven't forgotten."

"Then surely you are ignorant of the law that forbids us to smoke on Shabbat?"

"Not at all, I know all your laws," the smoker impudently replies.

The Rebbe looks the young man over. He refuses to be provoked; instead he turns to Him for whom every being also signifies provocation: "Did you hear? True, he violates certain of

Your commandments. But You must admit one thing: nobody will coerce him into telling a lie."

The Rebbe of these anecdotes is of course none other than Levi-Yitzhak Derbaremdiger (the Merciful), better known by the name of his town: Levi-Yitzhak of Berditchev. His stories, dialogues and litanies can be attributed to no one else. His monologues are poems, his poems are legends, and all bear witness for man. Always he appears as our spokesman.

A contemporary of the Great Maggid of Mezeritch, he occupies a very specific place in the Hasidic movement as well as in the life of every Hasid. His popularity equals the Baal Shem's. Even today, today more than ever, he commands our respect and affection. No European Diaspora Master since the Baal Shem has left so profound a mark on the Jewish imagination.

As a child, I visualized him as a powerful, invincible defender of the weak, a dispenser of mercy ready to risk all and lose all in the pursuit of truth and justice. He was my hero then, he still is. Often, when I try to go back in time to my own sources, what I remember are his songs and his pleas. And when what is required is a buffer between victim and persecutor, between moribund and death, it is he who comes to mind. To invoke his name, says Hasidic tradition, is to formulate a wish and have it granted. "The greatness of Levi-Yitzhak of Berditchev?" my grandfather asked. And answered: "He was a fighter."

• • •

Yet he was not a Rebbe in the accepted sense of the word. He sought neither to spread his own doctrine nor to surround himself with disciples, followers and admirers. Berditchever Hasidism originated and disappeared with him. He founded neither school nor dynasty. The house he built, he carried inside him.

That is perhaps the most important reason for the unanimous esteem the other great leaders of the movement manifested for him. He was no one's rival. Shmelke of Nikolsburg called him: "My disciple in *Nigla*—oral tradition—and my Master in *Nistar*—esoteric tradition." Shneur-Zalmen of Ladi put it this way: "God is a Tzaddik up there and Levi-Yitzhak is one down here." Reb Barukh of Medzebozh claimed that angels and seraphim envied him his fervor. Nahman of Bratzlav, himself an ardent rebel, covered him with praise and saw the light of Israel in his light. Another non-conformist, Menahem-Mendl of Kotzk, stated categorically that the gates to the sanctuary of love had been opened by Levi-Yitzhak. After his death, they had fallen shut again.

Though a friend to all Rebbes and Rebbe of all their disciples, he belonged to no clan. He was above rivalries and refused to become embroiled in the many quarrels that divided the movement. Protector of Israel, he pleaded for any and all Jews unjustly accused and unjustly punished. His most beautiful adventures, the most beautiful accounts and stories of his adventures, are those that show him in his role of attorney for the defense, challenging and remonstrating the Judge. As a child, I loved them and saw in them nothing but love and friendship. Today I feel their weight of despair and revolt—and love them even more. I often look at them; I owe them much. Sometimes I dip my pen into their wealth before I write.

· · ·

Who was he? Only the broad outlines of his life are traced. Little, almost nothing, is known of his childhood. We know that he was born in Galicia in 1740. That his was a sharp inquisitive mind. That he became a Talmudic scholar at a very early age and that he married very young. He was twenty when the Baal Shem died. He could have met him, but didn't. He probably wasn't interested; the recently founded movement held no attraction for him. He went to Shmelke of Nikolsburg to study Talmud and its commentaries, not Hasidism. Impressed by his learning and thirst for knowledge, Rebbe Shmelke paid him very special attention. Here was a student to his liking; not a wasted move, not a wasted word. "He has never uttered a single word in vain," Rebbe Shmelke said later. And so he took him along to Mezeritch, where, at the Maggid's side, Levi-Yitzhak was to discover that the Jewish condition must be lived rather than studied.

Newly married, Levi-Yitzhak came to spend the High Holy Days with his father-in-law, an influential personality in the community. One Simhat Torah eve he was invited to recite the prayer opening the procession and dance. Flattered, Levi-Yitzhak went to the pulpit, draped his ritual shawl around his shoulders—and took it off. A moment later he put the shawl back on, only to remove it again. This went on for a long time, under the watchful eyes of an amazed congregation. Suddenly Levi-Yitzhak pulled off the tallith again and shouted angrily: "Since you claim to be both Hasid and Talmudist, you can say the prayer yourself!" And he went back to his seat.

That evening, at the dinner table, his father-in-law protested: "You embarrassed me in public, I would like to understand."

"I'll tell you what happened," Levi-Yitzhak said calmly. "I was wrapping myself in my tallith, when the *yetzer-hara*, the evil one, the temptor, offered to say the prayer with me. 'You?' I asked. 'Are you worthy of it?' — 'Are you?' he countered. — 'Yes,' I said. 'After all I study Talmud.' — 'So do I.' — 'You study? Where?' — 'With you.' — 'But with me it's different. I am a Hasid.' — 'So am I.' — 'Who is your Rebbe?' — 'The same as yours.' — 'The Great Maggid of Mezeritch?' — 'Himself. Every time you go to him, I accompany you.' At that point," said Levi-Yitzhak, "I was overcome by anger. — 'Since you possess so many qualities, so many virtues, you don't need me; take the tallith and say the prayer without me!' "

An anecdote which lets us glimpse his temperament, his total indifference to public opinion. However, if by acting and speaking in this manner he had hoped to convert his father-in-law to Hasidism, it must be said that he failed miserably. His father-in-law forbade him to return to his Masters. To regain his freedom, Levi-Yitzhak began to fast, and this hunger strike, the first in the annals of Hasidism, was crowned with success.

Levi-Yitzhak returned to the Maggid and acquired a reputation as a Talmudist. Several communities offered him rabbinical posts. But luck was against him: wherever he went, he ran into the opposition of Mitnagdim, who provoked and bullied him, not because they bore him a personal grudge but because it was the custom.

This was the time of the first violent clashes between the

Hasidim and their opponents, who adhered to a stricter, more conservative interpretation of Judaism. The Gaon of Vilna had only recently published his first edict of excommunication; it was being read in all the congregations. The Maggid's disciples responded in kind. Fanaticism reigned on both sides. No Jew was permitted to remain aloof. For a teacher to be accepted by one side was sufficient cause to be repudiated by the other. The synagogue became a battleground, the street resounded with insults because of an omitted or added verse. Especially in the Ukraine, people went so far as to call in the authorities to force cantors to officiate in the manner of the conservatives. Worse yet, Rebbe Shneur-Zalmen of Ladi was arrested and indicted for treason. "They denounced him, they did it!" inveighed the Hasidim. The climate of irrational hostility in both camps took on intolerable proportions approaching mass hysteria.

Levi-Yitzhak tried hard to stay out of the scuffle. His faith in God, in man, in what binds one to the other, was too great, too genuine, for him to sanction differences between men. His temperament and convictions being what they were, he could only deplore sectarianism in any form. Yet it was no use: wherever he went, he found himself thrust into the eye of the storm.

Named to succeed Rabbi Shmelke in Ritchvol, he was severely put to the test. Cabals, calumniations, mockery; and no one to come to his aid. Exhausted, spent, he ran away. It was the eve of Simhat Torah.

His tenure in Zolohov, where he assumed a post at the age of twenty-five, left him with equally unhappy memories. Six years later he was unemployed once more. Invited to establish himself in Minsk, he accepted. Only to encounter similar attacks, similar virulent and malicious campaigns of slander. One day, while he was visiting his Master in Mezeritch, people broke into his house, smashed everything in sight and left his home a shambles. Moreover, when Levi-Yitzhak returned, he found another rabbi had taken his place.

More peregrinations followed. In the end he was stranded in Berditchev. He was forty-five and free at last to start his work in a fairly stable if not peaceful atmosphere. Here too, there were Mitnagdim, fewer but as vocal and active as elsewhere and who made life anything but easy for the new rabbi. Yet with the years the hostility waned. Thanks to the Rebbe, Berditchev became a sanctuary of Hasidism. And when he passed away, twenty-five years after his arrival, the community council refused to engage a successor; one does not replace a Levi-Yitzhak. The chronicles confirm the fact that after him there was no *Rav*—appointed rabbi—in Berditchev. There were rabbinical judges—*Dayanim*—yes. But there never was another *Rav*.

Gentle and considerate in his dealings with people, he seemed naïve, almost childish. Yet he did not lack humor. When challenged, his rejoinders were fast and witty, rarely offensive. The following incident was exceptional.

He was invited by a rabbi to address a gathering of tailors and bakers, all hostile to Hasidism.

"It is written," said Rebbe Levi-Yitzhak, "that when the Messiah will come, nature will provide man with ready-made bread and clothing. I could never understand why. But now I do. So as not to need either tailors or bakers, nor even their rabbi."

On another occasion, during a public debate in Warsaw with Avraham Katznelenbogen of Brisk, a Mitnagged and formidable opponent, he became involved in a discussion of certain customs newly introduced into Hasidic services.

"Why do you shout so loud in synagogue?" Rabbi Avraham asked. "Do you think He is so far away? Too far away to hear you?"

"Not at all," answered Levi-Yitzhak. "We know that God is near and that He is listening. If we shout, it is because we want *you* to hear us."

Still, he stayed away from a similar debate in Vilna. The Maggid of Kozhenitz had advised him to abstain: "If they should ask you why, contrary to custom, your eyes remain open while you recite the *Amida,* how will you reply?"

"What?" said Levi-Yitzhak, surprised. "My eyes stay open? But I see nothing when I pray!"

"That," said the Maggid of Kozhenitz, "I know. But they, our adversaries, do they know it?"

Levi-Yitzhak gave in.

Which did not happen often. Usually he could not be stopped in the middle of a project. Too impulsive to consider consequences or worry about ridicule, he charged headfirst, sure of himself, confident that he would find the words that would be needed.

Walking down the street one day, he received the well-aimed contents of a garbage can on his head. Inquiries revealed the culprit to be the wife of a fierce, malicious Mitnagged. Unruffled, the Rebbe continued to the House of Study, where he pronounced the incident closed:

"Don't be angry with her, Lord, it's not her fault. Poor woman, she wishes only to please her husband. Can you blame her for that?"

An episode which gives a measure of the man: His imagination, his ingenuity were never at a loss; somehow he always managed to invoke extenuating circumstances for others. He himself did not get off so easily; he was his own most severe judge. "Why do all Talmudic tractates begin with page two? To remind us that even if we know them from one end to the other, we have not even begun." Every night before falling asleep he reviewed his day: "Levi-Yitzhak sinned to-day," he would cry, "but Levi-Yitzhak promises not to do it again. He made the same resolution yesterday? Yes, but to-night he really means it."

One is tempted to believe that his humor was unconscious, almost involuntary. To get the laughers on his side was not a maneuver or a strategy; he had too much respect for things human—and what is more human than man's weaknesses—to make them an object of laughter. If he amused people, it was done unwittingly.

Infinitely serious, he would transpose trivial offenses and quarrels into theological disputations by introducing a third—omnipresent—character: God, thus conferring a timeless dimension to otherwise childish and futile subjects. By siding with his aggressor, he naturally provoked laughter. Only it was a special laughter, the kind that is aimed not at the adversary but at the entire situation which distributed the roles so badly or so well.

One day he heard a preacher delivering a violent sermon, calling down fire and brimstone upon the community and its sins, real and imagined. Levi-Yitzhak reacted only after the peroration: "Do not listen to him, Lord! What he said, he had to say. Don't You see? This is his trade. Preaching is how he earns his living. Surely he has a family to feed, three daughters to marry. Give him the money he needs and let him cease slandering Your children."

As for Levi-Yitzhak, he never said a bad word about His

children. On the contrary, he extolled their virtues in his own heart and to God. His motto: man must criticize himself and praise his fellow man. He pushed this line of thought to the point of holding himself responsible if mankind was in bad straits.

He told this story: "One morning I noticed that the people of my town did not respect me any more. Troubled, I sought to understand why. At last I found that it had nothing to do with them and everything to do with me. I simply had lost all respect for myself. And why should others be more charitable than I? So I decided to work on myself. As a result, people around me began to treat me with increased consideration. First my family, then my neighbors. From family to family, from street to street, the change made itself felt, until it spread to the whole town. I was esteemed again."

By improving himself, the Rebbe affects others; that is a major principle of mystical thought. Let one human being attain perfection and the entire species shall be saved from falsehood. Levi-Yitzhak subscribed only partially to this form of egocentricity; he preferred to help man in more direct ways. He talked to them, guided them; he offered himself to them, if only as a sounding board.

Meeting a notorious non-believer in the street, he asked him: "Do you know that I envy you?"

"Whatever for?"

"Because, according to our sages, if you ever repent, all your sins will be counted as good deeds."

There are two endings to this story. One is that the non-believer let himself be persuaded. The second, that he cried out: "If you envy me now, Rebbe, wait until tonight, you'll have so much more to envy by then!"

During another encounter, he is said to have succeeded in convincing his opponent, a noted philosopher who enjoyed provoking rabbis and theologians by using dialectical evidence to demonstrate the non-existence of God. This man arrived in Berditchev to find Rebbe Levi-Yitzhak in deepest meditation. Suddenly, without preamble, the Rebbe looked up straight into his eyes and said gently: "And what if it were true after all? Tell me, and what if it were true?" The philosopher later confessed that this question had moved and troubled him more than all the affirmations and arguments he had ever heard before or since.

Levi-Yitzhak knew when and with whom to share his certainties and his quests. He knew when to become embroiled in a heated exchange and when to fall back into the passivity of the collective Wait. Though he had mastered the art of striking rejoinders, he knew when to remain silent.

He had no illusions about men, yet he loved even the most sinful and ignorant among them. When the notables of Berditchev reproached him for associating with people of inferior rank, he replied: "When the Messiah will come, God will arrange a feast in his honor, and all our patriarchs and kings, our prophets and sages will of course be invited. As for myself, I shall quietly make my way into one of the last rows and hope not to be noticed. If I am discovered anyway and asked what right I have to attend, I shall say: 'Please be merciful with me, for I have been merciful too.' "

The destitute, the ignorant, the misfits sought him out. His presence made them feel important; he gave them what they needed most: dignity.

ELIE WIESEL

Was it within his powers to change their lives? Though one ought not to generalize, it would appear from his legends that his impact on people transcended language. His arguments were less important, for instance, than the way he celebrated services. His smiles were fraught with greater meaning than his sermons.

At the time when he was still residing in Minsk, he sent for an obscure teacher named Aharon, who lived in a faraway hamlet. This teacher, young and shy, was reluctant to follow the messenger. Finally he was convinced and was brought before Levi-Yitzhak, who received him warmly: *"Barukh haba,* Rebbe Aharon, welcome. Be seated, Rebbe Aharon of Karlin."* The visitor, surprised by such honors, shook his head. That was all. The two men sat down, one facing the other, without saying a word. Two hours went by; not a sound. Then, obeying the same impulse, they exchanged a smile—in silence. And that is how they parted—in silence. Neither one ever disclosed the meaning of that smile, the content of that silence. All we know is the result. The obscure visitor became a famous Tzaddik.

Like the Baal Shem, Levi-Yitzhak changed those who approached him. And like the Baal Shem, Levi-Yitzhak felt most at ease among ordinary people. He maintained contact with other Rebbes—Elimelekh of Lizensk, Shmelke of Nikolsburg, the Maggid of Kozhenitz and, naturally, the great Maggid of Mezeritch—but he came to them almost as would any Hasid. He preferred following to being followed. Genuinely humble, his love went out to the humiliated and the hungry. Drawn to and touched by their misery, he saw it as a grace. Penniless himself, he pitied the rich "who lose more than they gain."

100

His salary he divided among the beggars. His despairing wife complained to the rabbinical court that her husband—who, incidentally, presided over that court—failed to comply with the terms of their marriage contract. Too busy running from village to fair, from street to synagogue, from shelter to orphanage, he neglected to meet his family's needs. Levi-Yitzhak pleaded not guilty. This contract, he explained, committed him to clothing and feeding his family with money honestly earned. Well, for a rabbi, that is not always easy.

There is a strange story told in this connection. It is rumored that his wife signed certain promissory notes to a local squire, vowing to convert to Christianity if, within the appointed time, she did not redeem her pledges.

In truth, her husband had no notion of money nor did he understand why people seemed so eager to acquire it. Observing a man hurrying down the street, he called to him: "Where are you running?"—"I am looking for work."—"And that is why you run? And what if the work were looking for you? If God were looking for you?" For him, money existed only for man to give or to beg. When the community council considered the creation of a unified appeal for the needy so as to discourage itinerant beggars, he declared that the idea reminded him of Sodom—where beggars were unwanted—and threatened to resign: the poor must not be tampered with. The council was forced to yield.

His was an impulsive, unpredictable nature. One never knew what to expect from him.

Once he climbed to the roof of a building facing the marketplace. He watched the merchants buying and selling, he listened to the screeching horse dealers, and suddenly he began to shout at the top of his lungs: "Good people, do not forget, do not forget that God too is to be feared!"

Every once in a while he dispatched his servant to one or the other of the neighboring synagogues: "Look neither to your right nor to your left, walk straight to the bimah, pound your fist on the pulpit and make the following announcement: "Know ye, men and women, know that God exists and that He is of this world, of this world too!"

People resisted him but—in Berditchev—no one mocked him. People listened to him and respected him, though he was odd and clumsy and everything happened to him. He could not light the Hanukkah candles without burning his fingers, nor could he take the ethrog out of the cupboard without breaking the glass door. Attending the Seder of the pedantic Rebbe Barukh of Medzebozh, he tipped over the table. He went to the well and barely missed falling in. Whether absent-minded or in a trance, he seemed to have little sense of reality. Nor was he aware of the disorder he left in his wake. His inner life detached him from real life. When a gang of hoodlums beat him mercilessly, he did not interrupt his prayers for a moment; as though he never felt his wounds. Impervious to the outside world, he was not afraid of suffering; he ignored it. He fought pain in his own way. Accompanying his dead son to the cemetery, he began to dance, crying: "Lord, you entrusted me my son with a pure soul and that is how I give him back to You."

No wonder that Mitnagdim, opposed to anything that smacked of sensationalism, fought him so bitterly and with such determination, especially in the early days. They complained about his manners, his manias—what they called his taste for dramatics—in short, his way of life. In his capacity as official rabbi, he should have, in their opinion, devoted more time to study and less time to services. He did the exact opposite. Like Rabbi Akiba long ago, he worshipped with such abandon that the frightened faithful instinctively moved away. He gesticulated, howled and danced, jumping from one corner to the other, pushing and overturning whatever was in his way. People ceased to exist for him. When he prayed, he himself ceased to exist. Sometimes the faithful became tired of waiting and went home, leaving him alone in the House of Study. This even happened on a Passover eve.

He prayed with fervor because he believed in prayer. A story he liked to tell: "I was there when a thief was being caught. I heard him whisper: 'Too bad, I'll try again, and next time I'll do better.' From this thief I learned that one must always be prepared to try again."

But he believed just as much, if not more, in fervor. His own was boundless. Whatever he did, he did without reservations, with his entire being. He often fainted in the middle of services. The slightest prayer exhausted him; it involved more than his faith, it involved his life.

But above all he believed in the coming of the Messiah. Drawing up his son's engagement contract, the scribe had specified that the marriage was to take place on a certain date in Berditchev. Levi-Yitzhak furiously tore the contract to shreds: "Berditchev? Why Berditchev? This is what you will write: 'The marriage will take place on such a date in Jerusalem, except if the Messiah has not yet come; in which case the ceremony will be performed in Berditchev.' "

He was flamboyant, like so many among his peers. He, in turn, intrigued, disconcerted, fascinated and frightened many of his contemporaries. Some knew him without understanding him; others loved him without knowing him.

That he made a spectacle of himself is true enough. But that was the man's essence. It has been speculated that he considered his exhibitionism to be his best cover. That was the opinion of Elimelekh of Lizensk, who asked Aharon of Zhitomir: "Why would you wish to stay with me? Follow your Master, Levi-Yitzhak." — "Him I already know, now it is you I want to know." — "You don't realize what your mouth is saying," Elimelekh scolded him. "You think you know Levi-Yitzhak. You don't even know the coat that covers him."

Still, other Masters considered him dangerous for the non-initiated and warned against too close association with him.

A disciple of Moshe-Leib of Sassov, a certain Avraham-David, future Rebbe of Bucsacs, planned to spend Shabbat in Berditchev. The Tzaddik of Sassov asked him: "Will you be able to resist laughter?" — "Yes, Rebbe." But Avraham-David had overestimated his strength. Delirium struck during the first Shabbat meal. Without apparent reason, he burst into laughter and could not stop for thirty days and thirty nights. Rebbe Moshe-Leib then wrote to his Berditchever friend: "I sent you a whole vase and you gave it back to me shattered into a thousand pieces."

An episode which has never been fully explored. Hasidic chronicle limits itself to providing it with a happy ending. Levi-Yitzhak, moved by compassion, rescinded the punishment. The disciple recovered. But why had he laughed in the presence of the Master and the entire audience? How could he have been guilty of such utter lack of respect toward his hosts? After all, he was not just anybody; what did he see, discover or understand in Berditchev to make him laugh at the holiest moment of the week, in front of one of the most exalted and exalting figures of Hasidism? We shall never know.

Levi-Yitzhak admired King Solomon, the wisest of our sovereigns. Why? Because, according to the Midrash, he mastered all languages? Because he knew how to speak to birds? No. Because he understood the language of madmen.

We shall never learn the truth. The entire period is taboo; one particular period of the Rebbe's life. Hasidic texts barely allude to it. It would seem that he succumbed to a severe nervous depression, deeper than any he had experienced before. We know, for example, that one night, having strayed into what was known as Tanners' Street, he was seized by infinite almost inhuman sadness—and fainted. We also know that he was obsessed by the suicide of a poor little beadle who had hanged himself from the synagogue's main chandelier, thinking thus to "honor" God. If he went to see other Masters with such regularity, it was probably to escape his own phantoms, which after being repressed for many years, overwhelmed him in the end.

He withdrew into himself, became a recluse. Suddenly he was incapable of carrying out his official duties, and instead spent his time "reading, very fast, from a small book that never left him." Prostrate, he let his absent gaze wander over beings and places. He whose passion had kindled sparks in every heart was now burned out; a frightened, hunted man. A spring had broken. What exactly was he suffering from? Overwork? Were all the trials and humiliations taking their toll?

Were the accumulated frustrations driving him into despair? A number of Tzaddikim met to help him. They attributed his ailment to deeper causes. Yitzhak-Eizik of Komarno stated: "This is the angels' revenge; he forced their hand." Another thought it a punishment; it seems that Levi-Yitzhak had once doubted both his own powers and his followers' sincerity. A third claimed that he had fallen victim to a quest pursued too far; the secret science may not be practiced with impunity. Whoever defies celestial order leaves himself open and vulnerable. Had Levi-Yitzhak discovered that the soul can become the enemy of reason? Or that fervor, pushed to its limits, opens onto the abyss? That abrupt transitions may beget insanity? Could he have understood that his pleas were not bringing forth the expected results? That God could easily decide not to receive them, not to hear them? No one knows. And more surprisingly: no one even tried to find out.

True, his was not a unique case. Many other Hasidic Masters were similarly afflicted: Barukh of Medzebozh, Nahman of Bratzlav, Elimelekh of Lizensk, the Holy Seer of Lublin and, according to some sources, the Baal Shem himself. All, to varying degrees, struggled against melancholy. Perhaps because they looked so hard and so much at suffering, they could see nothing but sorrow in the end; because they listened so hard and so often to a thousand voices of sadness, they came to wish that they were deaf and dumb. Yet Levi-Yitzhak was a case apart: his breakdown was ignored; it went unmentioned. As though the chroniclers of Hasidism were reluctant to let him be seen as a tortured and broken man. Anyone else—but not him. He had no right to be defeated, even temporarily. Anyone else could be subject to lapses; not he. Legend required him to remain equal to himself, brimming over with faith, vigor and creative rapture.

. . .

Fortunately, his crisis lasted but one year. He recovered almost overnight, and without outside help, closed the parenthesis and was himself again. During the next fifteen years he again plunged into the battle to protect his people against scores of dangers and slanders, a battle that was then reaching its climax. In a way, his fall became a point of departure. After silence and solitude, after the sting of disappointment, Levi-Yitzhak attained new heights and a power whose roots were in his quarrels with God. These quarrels one may safely situate in time between his crisis and his death. His daring, his frankness were drawn from his very despair. So was his revolt.

For the first time a Rebbe took man's defense against his Judge, and that from a position of strength, during the High Holy Days, in the presence of the entire community. And lest someone fail to understand, he expressed himself not in the sacred tongue, but in Yiddish and sometimes in Polish. He did not consider the sacred tongue suitable for battle. Not even for the battle with God.

Others before him had carried on dialogues with God. But none had ever dared take a stand against God. None had gone so far as to judge Him and threaten Him. *"Zol Ivan blozen shofar!"* Levi-Yitzhak cried out during Rosh Hashana services: "If You prefer the enemy who suffers less than we do, then let the enemy praise Your glory!" Nor did the Rebbe hesitate to remind God that He too had to ask forgiveness for the hardships He inflicted on His people. Thence the plural of Yom Kippurim: the request for pardon is reciprocal.

One day he noticed a man in the synagogue whose eyes were filled with tears. It was before *Kol Nidre*.

107

"Why are you crying?" he asked.

"I can't help it. The tears keep coming. I was a pious man and well-to-do. My wife was hospitable' and devout. And suddenly He intervened and turned me into a heap of rubble. I lost my wife, my home. And here I am, desperate and destitute, with six children on my arms. That isn't all. I had a prayer book that meant much to me. He burnt that too. I don't know how to pray any more; all I can do is weep."

The Rebbe ordered that the man be given a prayer book just like the one he once had, and then he asked: "Will you pray?"

"Yes."

"Do you forgive Him now?"

"Yes," said the Jew through his tears. "Today is Yom Kippur; I must forgive."

"Well then, it is up to You to do same," roared Levi-Yitzhak. "You, too, must forgive!" And he intoned the somber, solemn melody of *Kol Nidre*.

Another time he offered God a bargain: "We shall give You our sins and, in return, You will grant us Your pardon. By the way, You come out ahead. Without our sins, what would You do with Your pardon?"

One Rosh Hashana he told this story: A woman arrives at the synagogue out of breath; she is late. She notices that services have not yet started. And so she addresses God: "I wish to thank You for telling Your children to wait awhile. What could I possibly wish You? I wish You to be proud of them, as I am proud of them."

Once he remained standing at his pulpit from morning till night without moving his lips. Earlier he had issued a warning to God: "If You refuse to answer our prayers, I shall refuse to go on saying them."

Another story: It was Yom Kippur. The faithful, weak from fasting, were waiting for the Rebbe to begin the *Mussaf* prayer, but he too was waiting. An hour went by, and another. Impatience turned into anguish. This time the Rebbe was really going too far. It was late. Why was he waiting? When he finally emerged from his meditation, he explained: "There is in our midst someone who cannot read. It is not his fault; he has been too busy providing for his family to go to school or study with a teacher. But he wishes to sing. And so he allows his heart to speak: 'You are God; I am but a man. You are Almighty and know everything; I am weak and ignorant. All I can do is decipher the twenty-two letters of the sacred tongue; let me give them to You to make into prayers for me and they will be more beautiful than mine.' " The Rebbe raised his voice: "And that, brethren, is why we had to wait. God was busy writing."

If other mystics maintained I-and-Thou relations with God, he, Levi-Yitzhak, threatened Him with breaking off these same relations. In this way, he wished to demonstrate that one may be Jewish with God, in God and even against God; but not without God.

He was not content merely to ask God questions, like Abraham and Job before him. He demanded answers, and in their absence, drew his conclusions. To accede to holiness against God, that was what he was seeking. "If we were to accept the Rebbe of Berditchev's reasoning," said Barukh of Medzebozh, "there would not be a single Jew toward whom God is not guilty."

Levi-Yitzhak's arguments were considerable: "From the moment You concluded a covenant with Your people, You have consistently tried to break it by testing it; why? Remember: at Sinai You walked back and forth with Your Torah like a peddler unable to dispose of his rotten apples. Your Law, You offered it to every nation and each turned away contemptuously. Israel alone declared itself ready to accept it, to accept You. Where is its reward?"

Another time he made a terrifying statement: "Know that if Your reign does not bring grace and mercy, *lo teshev al kissakha beemet,* Your throne will not be a throne of truth."

He also said: "When a Jew sees tephillin on the ground, he runs to pick them up and kisses them. Isn't it written that we are Your tephillin? Are You never going to lift us toward You?"

Before *Mussaf* service on Yom Kippur, he cried out: "Today is Judgment Day. David proclaims it in his Psalms. Today all Your creatures stand before You so that You may pass sentence. But I, Levi-Yitzhak, son of Sarah of Berditchev, I say and I proclaim that it is You who shall be judged today! By Your children who suffer for You, who die for You and the sanctification of Your name and Your law and Your promise."

And also: "You order man to the aid of orphans. We too are orphans. Why do You refuse to help us?"

His depressions can probably be linked to the misfortunes he watched rain on his people. One Passover eve, tortured by the mystery of collective suffering and evil, he burst out, pleading: "Tonight we celebrate our Exodus from Egypt. According to tradition, four sons question the father on the meaning of the event. No, not four, only three. The fourth does not even know the question. I am this fourth. Not that I lack questions, Lord. But I don't know how to put them. Anyhow, even if I knew, I wouldn't dare. And so I don't ask You why we are persecuted and massacred in every place and under every pretext; but I would at least like to know whether all our suffering is for You."

Despite his public outbursts, it never occurred to anyone to accuse him of blasphemy. For two reasons. First: Levi-Yitzhak never sulked indefinitely. Once he had spoken his mind, he came back to God. His reproaches vented, his threats uttered, he resumed—freely and as a free man—the ancient, majestic litany of *Kaddish*. The questions remained questions, but he could go on. He could begin and build on the ruins. Second: Jewish tradition allows man to say anything to God, provided it be on behalf of man. Man's inner liberation is God's justification. It all depends on where the rebel chooses to stand. From inside his community, he may say everything. Let him step outside it, and he will be denied this right. The revolt of the believer is not that of the renegade; the two do not speak in the name of the same anguish.

Thus the revolt of Levi-Yitzhak of Berditchev enhanced his legend. He emerges from it more than a guide, more than a Master. One sees him as the strong and daring brother on whom one may rely.

Let us conclude this sketch with a story an anonymous Hasid told me in the kingdom of night and mist:

Before he died, Levi-Yitzhak swore in the presence of his closest followers that once up there, he would refuse all rest until he would be allowed to put an end to man's distress. To prevent him from keeping his promise, the celestial creatures turned him into an angel of fire. And that is why the Messiah is so late in coming. And that is also why, added the Hasid, we are here, forgotten, forsaken, expelled from divine and human memory. None of these atrocities would be possible if Levi-Yitzhak, our defender, could intervene.

But the questions of the Berditchever Rebbe, and his challenges too, flung at the face of a sky in flames, have survived him. They follow us and give us the strength and courage to claim them and retell them as if they were our own.

ELIMELEKH
OF LIZENSK

Once upon a time, somewhere in a Lithuanian village, a certain Eliezer Lipman, known for his wealth and generosity, meets a beggar on the way to the village. He stops his carriage and invites him to get in.

The beggar refuses: "I still haven't earned anything all day."

"How much could you possibly earn?"

"A lot. Twenty-five ducats. Maybe."

"I'll give them to you, come along."

"No," says the stubborn beggar. "I can't."

"Why not? Since you won't lose anything!"

"True—but money isn't everything. I must think of the people who regularly, once a week, open their doors and hearts to me. If they don't see me today, they'll worry."

"Don't let that bother you, I'll go myself—I'll go from door to door—to reassure them on your behalf. But do come along—I can't bear to see you walk so far."

Dropping his mask, the beggar—a messenger in disguise—congratulates Eliezer on passing the test: "As a reward, you may look into your future. The fact is, you have only one year to live. I tell this to you so that you may use the time to good advantage and put some order into your life."

Eliezer gave up his business, and devoted himself so completely and exclusively to serving God, that he was granted a twenty-year reprieve.

And five children, including Zusia and Elimelekh.

One night while the brothers were still leading a deliberately anonymous and restless existence, they were stranded at a village inn where a wedding was being celebrated.

Excited by the wine and noise, a band of ruffians, eager for new distractions, decided to have some fun with the two uninvited guests huddled in a dark corner behind the hearth. For no particular reason, Zusia was the one they grabbed. They made him twirl and stumble and let the blows rain on him before letting him go. An hour later they started all over. And so it went until late into the night.

"Why does it have to be you, always you?" whispered Elimelekh.

"Such is the will of God," Zusia groaned weakly.

"I have an idea. Let us change places. They are too drunk to notice. You'll see, next time they'll take me—you'll be able to rest."

He was wrong. For at this very moment one of the drunkards cried out: "But there are two of them! And it's always the same one we honor with our company! That's not good, that's not right! Let's take a look at his friend . . ."

Later Zusia told his brother: "You see? It's not up to us; we are powerless. Everything is written."

This anecdote beautifully illustrates the lives of Zusia and Elimelekh—the great figures of Galician Hasidism toward the end of the eighteenth century.

Elimelekh of Lizensk

All his life Elimelekh aspired to fulfill himself through suffering, which taunted him by eluding him. Whereas Zusia, constantly beaten by life and tormented by Him who gives life, considered himself to be the happiest of men.

Zusia: a picturesque character, rich in color, worshipped as a saint, praised as a Tzaddik and affectionately remembered as the "Fool of God." His younger brother: a natural leader, founder of a major new school. Without either, Hasidism would have been different. Together they gave its future a countenance. In years to come, for a Rebbe to be whole, he had to be both Rebbe Zusia—innocence and humility personified—and Rebbe Elimelekh, supreme incarnation of authority and power. Their two portraits—so distinct and yet intertwined—have remained singularly alive in Hasidic memory.

Zusia was the first to be attracted to Hasidism—by its way of life more than by its doctrine—and had to use great persuasiveness, for a long time, to draw Elimelekh along. But once he succeeded, they became inseparable.

Together they experienced the awe and rapture that characterized Mezeritch; together they were received by the Great Maggid, who accepted them as disciples; together they chose to live three years of exile and abstinence to purify their souls and thoughts; and still together, they traveled through the Polish countryside, "raising sparks" and kindling flames everywhere they went.

One tradition has it that every place they stayed—even for just a night—became annexed to the Hasidic kingdom. And that the places they could not reach remained outside Hasidism. There is a curious legend that tells of the two brothers arriving in a small village near Cracow with the intention of staying overnight. But they were restless and felt compelled to leave. As dusk fell, they left. The name of the village: Auschwitz.

Disciples of the Maggid, they could have known his Master. Elimelekh was forty-three when the Baal Shem died. Both he and his brother had many opportunities to leave their native Lithuania and seek him out. Yet they did not. Perhaps because Lithuania, stronghold of the Mitnagdim, was closed to Hasidism more completely and for a longer time than Poland and the Ukraine.

Little is known about the years that preceded their adherence to the movement. Only that their mother, a devout though utterly uneducated widow—she couldn't read the prayer book but knew all the prayers by heart—had not only the earliest but a major influence on their development. Also that Elimelekh's passion was the Talmud, whereas Zusia was a dreamer and leaned toward pure contemplation. Perhaps he had heard a wandering preacher, a storyteller, evoke the wonders to be seen and experienced in Mezeritch, for he decided to go there. Not in search of scholarship or wisdom, but of fervor and salvation.

While Elimelekh was studying and working his way through the tangled texture of Talmudic concepts and arguments, Zusia spent his days and nights roaming the woods, singing and dancing for God. To his brother he explained: "I am like the servant who loves his king but may see him only through a hole in the wall. You are like the prince who may stay in the presence of the king provided you have learned the art of using words."

Of all the disciples of the Great Maggid, said Israel of Rizhin, Rebbe Zusia was the only one not to pass on what he had learned. And this is why: because as soon as the Maggid began talking, Zusia would fall into ecstasy and make so much noise that he would be sent out. How could he have repeated what he hadn't heard?

Not Rebbe Elimelekh. He listened so well that he eventually became almost a copy of the Maggid. Like the Maggid, he was somber and moody, while Zusia was the extrovert constantly astonished to discover himself alive in God's world. People remembered Elimelekh as "a tall man, with a short overcoat and a straw belt around his waist." Zusia wasn't even noticed. Elimelekh liked to carry a watch and concentrate his attention on it so as "to link himself to time and the world." Zusia was far too absent-minded to attach himself to any object. One brother was as demanding and merciless as the other was tolerant and gentle. Zusia, like Levi-Yitzhak of Berditchev, was incapable of finding fault with others; his brother wanted all men to be perfect. Elimelekh preached severity. Zusia advocated compassion. Totally dissimilar, they were united by legend. One cannot mention the one without remembering the other. Elimelekh was feared, Zusia was loved. Fear and love: the two feelings a Tzaddik must inspire.

Zusia, of course, refused to be looked upon as a Tzaddik. He was content to remain the failure, the victim of victims, the eternal child. Though a member of the Maggid's intimate circle, he was the only one not to wear a crown, not to hold court, not to have his own Hasidim. But if there were blows falling somewhere—chances were they would fall on him. Honors he despised, preferring to admire rather than be admired, preferring the poverty of the poor to the poverty of the rich.

To a wealthy villager who offered the two—now famous—brothers his big comfortable house, one of them—probably Zusia—gave this reply: "This is not the first time we visit here; on previous occasions we stayed with a poor farmer who received us as if we were his brothers. Why do you invite us now? Are you impressed by our carriage and horses? Then invite the horses; we shall stay with the farmer. As we did before."

Another pair of famous brothers, Shmelke of Nikolsburg and Pinhas of Frankfort, put the following question to the Maggid of Mezeritch: "It is written in the Talmud that man must thank God for the good things as well as for the bad; is that not asking too much of man? Who would have the strength to praise the Lord for being punished?"

"Go and have a little chat with Zusia," said the Maggid.

Zusia was well known in Mezeritch. And everyone there knew that he was sick and burdened with countless miseries and ailments; that he was spared nothing.

"Zusia, how can you thank the Lord? What about your suffering?"

"My suffering?" asked Zusia, amazed. "Who is suffering? Not I. I am happy. Zusia is happy to live in the world that God, blessed be He, created. Zusia lacks nothing, needs nothing. Everything he wants, Zusia has, and his heart is filled with gratitude."

He had not even understood the question.

On another occasion he nevertheless felt it necessary to explain the problem of good and evil, and he did it in his own inimitable way: "True, suffering exists. Like everything else, it too comes from God. Why does it exist? I'll tell you: man is too weak to accept or absorb divine charity, which is absolute. For that reason, and that reason alone, does God cover it with the veil that is pain."

•   •   •

In his extreme naïveté, he simply could not conceive of anything in creation not testifying to God's mercy. Unhappiness he dismissed as a figment of the mind. Wounds were opened only to be healed. When his own wife made his life miserable, he showed her his pillow, drenched with tears, and she repented and became good. No tear is in vain, no prayer goes unheard. If woman can be moved, would God remain inflexible? Man has no reason to complain.

He came to an inn and noticed birds in a cage. Naturally he freed them. Birds are meant to fly. And naturally the innkeeper thought otherwise—and gave him a lesson without words. No matter, here was Zusia, back on the road, his body aching but his spirits high, carefree and deliriously happy. Man is made to be happy, even when his tormented flesh cries out in pain.

His capacity for happiness was equaled only by his humility. Once he was heard groaning: "I am unworthy of addressing my prayers to You; I am not even worthy of giving You my tears. Instead—listen—I shall whistle. That's all."

In his own eyes, he was the worst of sinners. He was convinced that if he was alive so long, it was to suffer—and expiate —as long as possible. It is said that every day he recorded all his deeds and thoughts in a little notebook; in the evening he would reread what he had written and cry until his tears had erased all traces of his writing.

Menahem-Mendl of Kotzk said of him: "Just as there are scientific geniuses, there is one in matters of humility, and I mean Rebbe Zusia."

He had a secret admirer and benefactor, a merchant who occasionally dropped a few silver coins into his bag. Ever since he had begun this practice, this man's business flourished. So he thought to himself: If this poor devil can do so much for me, why not go to his Master, who can do more! And so he went to see the Maggid of Mezeritch and gave him a donation. Next day his affairs took a turn for the worse. Perplexed, he sought out Zusia. Who explained to him that when man makes no distinction in giving, God makes no distinction either; but when man shows himself particular, God does the same.

Before Rebbe Zusia died, he said: "When I shall face the celestial tribunal, I shall not be asked why I was not Abraham, Jacob or Moses. I shall be asked why I was not Zusia."

His brother, imagining the same scene, lent it a more optimistic ending: "They will ask me if I was just; I shall say no. Then they will ask me if I was charitable; I shall say no. Did I devote my life to study? No. To prayer perhaps? No again. And then the Supreme Judge will smile and say: 'Elimelekh, Elimelekh, you speak the truth—and for this alone you may enter paradise.'"

With the advent of Rebbe Elimelekh, Hasidism enters a new phase. The era of Tzaddikism opens.

Not that he was the first Tzaddik—or the only one. The Maggid of Mezeritch had more than one disciple, and each in his own way, in his own area, became his successor. But it was Rebbe Elimelekh who developed the concept and role of the Tzaddik and built a movement if not a doctrine around him.

The time: the last decades of the eighteenth century. On the surface, all signs are encouraging. The movement has withstood the death of its founder—in 1760—and of its organizational architect, the Maggid of Mezeritch, twelve years later.

If in the beginning there was a danger that Hasidism would become too centered on one person, one leader, that danger has now vanished. The movement proved itself strong enough to withstand the first internal dissensions and power struggles among the pretenders to the throne left vacant first by the Baal Shem, then by the Maggid. The Maggid had had to overcome considerable resistance before asserting his authority; his successors did not, for they were many. Hasidism now had several centers—and all were flourishing.

The Maggid had wanted this decentralization for his own reasons—which had to do with Jewish politics, not with international relations. Events confirmed his vision. With one center built around one figure, Hasidism might not have survived the series of severe crises which began erupting throughout Eastern Europe in 1772—the year of the Maggid's death.

Poland was divided among her three neighbors: Russia, Prussia and Austria. And once more the Jewish community broke up into newly created geopolitical entities, each facing a new set of problems from within and without. The fact that each region, and in many cases, each city and town, had its own guide to rely upon, surely helped Hasidism maintain its initial momentum, while continuing to spread in various directions at once. One Master could not have coped with all the different needs.

Elimelekh settled in Lizensk in 1777, and that is where he died eleven years later. During that period Lizensk became one of the capitals of Hasidism. Among Elimelekh's disciples one could find such distinguished figures as the Holy Seer of Lublin, Menahem-Mendl of Riminov, the Maggid of Kozhenitz, the Apter Rebbe . . .

After the founder—the Baal Shem—and the architect—the Great Maggid—came Elimelekh—the teacher, the practical man who translated abstract concepts into simple language for simple people.

What and who is a Tzaddik according to Lizensk? Rebbe, rabbi, guide, conscience, tutor; he is the sublimation of man's self. He is what man can be, wants to be. He is the chosen one who is refused nothing, in heaven or on earth. God is angry? He can make him smile. God is severe? He can induce him to leniency. His followers owe him blind and unconditional allegiance. *Emunat Tzaddikim*, faith in the Rebbe, is one of the basic tenets of Lizensker Hasidism. He who hesitates, who waivers, cannot be helped. To question the Rebbe is worse than sin; it is absurd, for it destroys the very relationship that binds you to him.

If his behavior appears bizarre, it means the Hasid does not possess the required powers of understanding. So complex is Elimelekh's dialectical approach that the Tzaddik's relationship with the "higher spheres" is never clearly defined—yet the common mortal may not question its existence or its efficiency. Whether he chooses to sing or laugh, to smile or be unpleasant, to open up or withdraw into meditation—*he* knows what he is doing; that should be enough. One must not try to understand. One must admire, that's all. Let him choose poverty while accepting donations; let him simulate joy but spend nights in lamentation; let him *boast* of his humility—nobody has the right to take exception. What he does, he does well, and for you. A superior, almost perfect being—meaning that his thirst for perfection is almost perfection—he uses his mysterious powers to redeem the sins of his generation. No matter what the Tzaddik does, he transcends his own person. His suffering confers a meaning upon all suffering; and when he eats, he cleanses the very act of nourishing the body.

"If they had left me alone, if they had left me in peace for two years," said Rebbe Elimelekh, "I would have made the Messiah come."

Like the Baal Shem and the Great Maggid of Mezeritch, Elimelekh linked individual salvation to universal redemption. A Tzaddik is called upon to play the most vital role in human drama, just as the Messiah would in cosmic drama. Though the two roles are not identical, they are related. Which explains why, at one point, a Tzaddik *must* assume responsibility for the Messiah's *not* coming. Like his two immediate predecessors, Elimelekh is said to have planned a momentous journey to the Holy Land—and like them, had to abandon the project: times were not propitious as yet.

His asceticism, his self-flagellation are legendary. "Whoever shows self-indulgence will die without repentance," he stated flatly. Sometimes he would tell his servant to follow him into the forest: "Let us go and punish a rebel." Out of sight in the woods he would ask the servant to whip him, "for I am the rebel."

Once he remarked: "So many people come to me with their pleas. One cries for health, another for bread, a third for a better life. Why do they come to *me?* Because in truth I am responsible for their sickness, their hunger and their misery."

Does that mean the Hasid's own responsibilities are diminished? Surely not. Only shifted. He is responsible for what happens to the Tzaddik—for *his* crises, for *his* spiritual anguish. One needs the other. For the Tzaddik represents man's potential; he is all that every Hasid wishes to become, could become. Granted, it is given to every man to attain perfection. Granted, too, that the Tzaddik owes his position of Tzaddik only to himself. Whoever works on himself long enough, obstinately enough, will in the end break his chains. Ancestry means nothing. A descendant of the Baal Shem is no worthier than any other man. Like the Baal Shem, Elimelekh left his throne not to his sons but to his disciples, none of whom had titles other than those they had acquired themselves. Titles every Hasid can acquire, if only he tries. Failing that, he can set his sights on a secondary project: to labor for salvation by attaching himself to a Tzaddik who thus becomes his other self. If he cannot be Tzaddik, he will be Hasid. And the Tzaddik will be Tzaddik to the extent that the Hasid will be Hasid. Except that a perfect Hasid is worthier than a Tzaddik who no longer is Tzaddik.

The Hasid-Tzaddik relationship, therefore, must exist under the sign of faith, and contrary to what one may think, it reinforces the faith in God.

Faith in God was so absolute in Lizensk that Rebbe Mendl of Riminov—so the story goes—once refused to pick up a gold coin he saw lying on the ground. If God wishes me to have it, he thought, I will get it without having to bend down.

It is because the Hasid believes in God that he believes in the Tzaddik, who, according to the terms of their tacit agreement, must bring him closer to God. The school of Lizensk illustrates this relationship with the Biblical verse: *Vayaaminu baadoshem uv-Moshe avdo,* and they had faith in God and in his servant Moses. Because they believed in the one, they could believe in the other, thus becoming worthy of the miracle of the Red Sea crossing. And enabling Moses to speak on their behalf —and sing. *Az Yashir Moshe,* and that's when Moses began singing. Singing? He? Wasn't Moses a stutterer? He could sing, Hasidim say, because his people now had faith in him. Thus, faith in one's Tzaddik makes one an active participant in the Tzaddik's work and partly responsible for his being the omnipotent, omniscient figure he is. When Rebbe Elimelekh says: "I remember perfectly the scene of revelation at Sinai; not only do I remember myself standing there, but also the souls on my left and on my right," the miracle is not only his memory, but also the fact that he raised other souls by linking them to his own. Because the Tzaddik does not speak for himself alone, he has great authority in heaven. The Talmudic saying *Hatzaddik gozer vehakadosh barukh hu mekayem*—the Just Man commands and the Lord obeys—is taken literally in Lizensk. Elimelekh, inadvertently or unconsciously, compares the Tzaddik to the Just Man who is obeyed by the Lord, his servant; a comparison that drew sharp criticism even from his peers. Can it be interpreted in a context other than blasphemous? Yes, since God is everywhere, they claimed in Lizensk, and every act derives from His will, it follows that this applies also to the Tzaddik's "orders"; even when he addresses God, he is but carrying out His will.

One understands why in Lizensk, even more than in Mezeritch, the struggle against vanity played a major role: because of one spark of silly pride, the entire structure could collapse, no matter what its initial purpose.

Nothing is worse than pride; it lures man into usurping the place of the Creator, Rebbe Elimelekh taught his followers.

Rebbe Zusia asked his brother: "It is written that Adam's soul contained all others. Which means ours too. How then do you explain that you did nothing to prevent him from committing his sin?" Rebbe Elimelekh's reply: "If Adam hadn't sinned, he would have become vain."

At the ritual baths, Elimelekh met a Jew who had come from Hungary to spend Shabbat at his court. "You took the trouble to come from so far away for this idle faker, this liar, this make-believe Rebbe?" asked the Tzaddik, whom the visitor had not recognized.

"How dare you?" the Hungarian Jew replied angrily. "How dare you slander a saint and sage of Israel?"

In the evening they met again, but this time in the Master's house, in the presence of his disciples. The visitor, petrified at first, began to sob, asking to be forgiven: "I didn't know, holy Master . . ."

"Dry your tears," the Rebbe reassured him. "You told me your truth, and I told you mine."

A somewhat similar anecdote has Zusia as its hero.

In an inn somewhere, a wealthy guest mistakes him for a beggar and treats him accordingly. Later he learns his identity and comes to cry his remorse: "Forgive me, Rebbe, you must —for I didn't know!"

"Why do you ask Zusia to forgive you?" Rebbe Zusia said, shaking his head and smiling. "You haven't done anything bad to him; it is not Zusia you insulted but a poor beggar, so go and ask the beggars, everywhere, to forgive you!"

Both replies sound authentic, though one seems more humble than the other. Elimelekh was complicated; his brother was all of one piece. Zusia was Zusia all the time—and wanted to be nobody else. Elimelekh wanted to be both Elimelekh and Zusia; hence he could simultaneously preach joy and practice asceticism, cling to the external marks of power and denounce power, put his hands into the fire and oppose mortification. Like many Tzaddikim after him, he led a double life. Publicly, he followed the path traced by the Baal Shem, while privately exploring labyrinths of pain and suffering.

Yet at no time did he go so far as to suggest that the average Hasid try to follow in his footsteps. At his school, the Tzaddikim of Apt, Sassov, Lublin, Ropshitz, Riminov and Kozhenitz learned that they must be available to their followers at all times and in all matters. They learned to take a part in the lives of their Hasidim, to be interested in their business affairs, to help arrange their marriages, settle their differences and organize collections to pay their debts. Elimelekh taught them the art of counseling in times of distress, of jolting the complacent and appeasing the tormented. Lizensk meant total involvement on the part of the Master and the disciple alike. "Solitude is no solution," Elimelekh said. "Rather than isolating your lives, isolate your thoughts." Lizensk meant total concern on the part of every Hasid for his fellow man. A disciple—Rebbe Zekharia-Mendl—wrote: ". . . At Lizensk, Hasidim love each other more than husbands love their wives and fathers their children. They live in harmony. They help each other in every way. All he possesses, the Hasid shares with the others. Including his fears and hopes . . ."

Rather than teach Kabbala or theology to his Hasidim, Elimelekh gave them a *zetl koten:* a short list of little things to do every day, when rising in the morning, when praying, when engaging in business, when being alone or with others. It is a seventeen-point program on how to be a good Jew . . . with a minimum of effort. Theology was left to the Tzaddikim; Hasidim needed simple answers to not so simple questions.

It is said that the Rebbe's involvement with his followers was such that they could be identified instantly. Anyone who saw him or was seen by him, carried him away in his eyes. Nobody passed through Lizensk unchanged.

•   •   •

But Rebbe Elimelekh was not to enjoy a peaceful old age. He had succeeded too well. His teaching had borne fruit sooner and in greater abundance than he had expected. He who had wanted, like his Master the Maggid of Mezeritch, to provide the greatest number of leaders to the greatest number of communities, suddenly felt left behind, superfluous. Unlike the Maggid, he seems to have succumbed to jealousy. He who had helped his disciples to become Tzaddikim, now found their success intolerable. He who had urged his favorite disciple Yaakov-Yitzhak—the future Seer of Lublin—to free himself of his hold and start on his own course, regretted it now. Yaakov-Yitzhak, established in a small locality named Lanzhut, attracted the best elements away from Lizensk. Legend has recorded a heart-rending cry of the great old man: "I still want to live!" He sent emissaries to Lanzhut, alternately demanding, urging, pleading for a reprieve. Let Yaakov-Yitzhak wait—a few months, a few years at most—and I'll lift him up even higher, even higher than myself. Too late. Yaakov-Yitzhak had already entered Hasidic history. Elimelekh then asked that he at least move farther away; Lanzhut was too close to Lizensk. Yaakov-Yitzhak could not bring himself to refuse. He moved to Lublin, where he became known as the Holy Seer. The break between Lizensk and Lublin was sad but absolute.

Hasidic scholars try very hard to explain and even justify this break by comparing it to the "breaks" that long ago had occurred between the Prophet Elijah and his successor Elisha, and between Moses and Joshua. They say that the Seer understood that old Rebbe Elimelekh was too saintly for the new generation. And that for a disciple to show his measure, he must cut the ties with his Master. Moses and Joshua, Elijah and Elisha could not reign together; neither could Elimelekh of Lizensk and the Holy Seer of Lublin.

Too facile—and superfluous—an explanation. Judaism never claimed to be monolithic. Its teachings are a sum, a synthesis; they represent all currents, those of the Masters *and* those of the disciples. Though given once, Torah is received a thousand times in a thousand ways; each man contributes to its enrichment.

The reasons for Rebbe Elimelekh's resentment toward the Seer of Lublin must be sought not in theories but in human nature. For jealousy—any jealousy, even that of a Master toward his disciple—is human.

And agonizing. Hasidic tradition refers to it with embarrassment and sadness. Elimelekh appears as a changed person, unrecognizable. Bitter, ill-tempered, physically ill, he refuses all food, all contact with the outside world. He hardly speaks; after *Maariv*, the evening service, he retreats into total silence. Suspicious, he sees treason everywhere. He thinks himself surrounded by spies; he doubts even the most loyal of his admirers and calls them flatterers and hypocrites.

One Saturday night, as soon as Shabbat was over, he hurried to a certain Reb David to check whether he was at home; no, he wasn't. Later Reb David, who had spent Shabbat with the Seer, tried to justify himself: "I thought I would climb onto his shoulders so I could reach you, Rebbe." But Elimelekh wasn't fooled. And legend, with more than a touch of cruelty, adds that Reb David was punished for his betrayal; he died the following year.

Rebbe Elimelekh seems also to have harbored resentment toward his own children, though they cherished him and defended his throne and name to the very end. He left them nothing: "Let them be poor, let them live off charity, and if they themselves are not deserving, they should be given nothing."

When he died—in 1786—he took even Lizensk with him; it left geography to enter legend.

Yet he had unquestionable greatness. Few schools can be compared to his. His disciples, founders of dynasties all, worshipped him. Even the Seer never disavowed his Master, just as his own disciple, the Jew of Pshiskhe, did not disavow him when he left Lublin to establish his own school and lead his own rebellion.

But that belongs to another story.

DISCIPLES III

A GREAT MIRACLE-MAKER himself, it is by miracle that Rebbe Israel, Maggid of Kozhenitz, stayed alive. Emaciated, so weak he had to be carried to services for more than fifteen years, he regained his strength only when he prayed. Then he became a changed man. He would sing and dance feverishly, his body rejuvenated and well again. The rest of the time he spent in bed muffled up in heavy blankets, receiving admirers and disciples, and if need be, interceding on their behalf, frequently with success. As a wonder rabbi, he had no equal.

A healer of bodies and souls, he "gave" children to childless couples, redistributed the wealth of the rich among the poor, appeased the dead and their mourners. For Jews and Gentiles alike, he was a last chance, an ultimate hope.

It is said that princes and generals came knocking at his door, requesting his advice before they made a decision, before they went to war.

Those who believed in him, and they were many, did nothing without his approval. They came from far away to see him, if only for one fleeting moment. Some considered him a second Israel Baal Shem Tov.

A story: When Elimelekh of Lizensk felt his hour approach, he made his last will known. To Mendl of Riminov he bequeathed his brain, to Yehoshua Heschel of Apt, his tongue; to Yaakov-Yitzhak of Lublin he left his sight, and to Israel of Kozhenitz, his heart.

That is what the Maggid of Kozhenitz became: his generation's heart.

He said: "What is man? A speck of dust, flawed and doomed to nothingness. And yet, here he is addressing God, familiarly at that, is that not a reason to be grateful?"

And also: "Man aspiring to heights must reach for them through others, with their help and helping them. If all of Israel's children joined hands, they would form a chain and touch the celestial throne."

Another time: "Every man must free himself of Egypt every day."

A woman begged him to pray for her; she wanted a child.

"My mother was as unhappy as you are, and for the same reason," he told her. "Until the day she met the Baal Shem Tov. She presented him with a cape. I was born the following year."

"Thank you," the woman said, beaming. "I'll do as your mother did. I'll bring you the most beautiful cape I can find."

The Maggid of Kozhenitz smiled: "No, that won't help you. You see, my mother didn't know this story."

Adam, ancestor of all mankind, visited him in a dream: "You have prayed for yourself—for your purity—and your prayer was heard. Now I would like you to pray for me."

He said: "The greatness of Torah lies in the way it changes

every day, thus providing man with a primary satisfaction every day."

As a young man he would stay up late into the night studying. His father suspected him of wasting his time playing and wandering through the streets. He would punish him for being idle. Israel suffered the blows in silence.

Later, when he was famous, he was asked why he had not protested his innocence to his father.

"It is not given to everyone to suffer for the Torah," he explained.

In his relationship to God, he saw himself as a messenger: "Send me anywhere to do anything, I am ready."

This he was still repeating after years of confinement to bed.

His favorite prayer is mine too: "Master of the Universe, know that the children of Israel are suffering too much; they deserve redemption, they need it. But if, for reasons unknown to me, You are not willing, not yet, then redeem all the other nations, but do it soon!"

They were called the "Holy Brothers": Samuel, nicknamed Shmelke, the older of the two, was a rabbi in Nikolsburg, while Pinhas served in the same capacity in Frankfort.

During Reb Pinhas's formal investiture, while notables and dignitaries were extolling his virtues, a strange expression came over his face.

"What are you thinking of?" he was asked.

"I have the odd feeling I am attending my own funeral," he replied.

During the corresponding ceremony in Nikolsburg, Shmelke

attracted people's attention by talking to himself in a low voice: "I tell my mouth to repeat what my ears are hearing; and it all sounds absurd."

The two brothers enjoyed extraordinary prestige even in non-Hasidic circles. The anathema cast upon the disciples of the Maggid of Mezeritch hardly affected them. Their scholarship was too well known for them to be excluded from the community; their Halakhic works set new standards.

Still, legend recalls them not as scholars but as Hasidic Masters.

A story: Once upon a time there was a beadle who would awaken the faithful and call them to prayer. Frail, sickly, he would scratch at the door or window, nothing more. Terrified, people would jump from their beds and hurry to services.

"This power," said the beadle, "I have from Rebbe Shmelke. Years ago I was in his service and he taught me the art of jolting people without making a sound."

Whoever came to see Rebbe Shmelke with outstretched palms left bearing a gift. One day, when he had not a single piece of change, he gave a beggar a ring he saw lying on the table. It belonged to his wife, who, when she heard the story, complained loudly: "How could you, didn't you know this was a valuable ring, a diamond ring?"

Whereupon Shmelke ran out of the house in pursuit of the beggar, shouting: "Friend, listen, that ring is valuable! Don't let the jeweler cheat you! You mustn't sell it too cheap!"

He said: "The rich need the poor more than the poor need the rich. Unfortunately, neither is conscious of it."

Rebbe Shmelke told the following: "Basing myself on the Talmudic saying that if all men repented, the Messiah would come, I decided to do something about it. I was convinced I would be successful. But where was I to start? The world is so vast. I shall start with the country I know best, my own. But my country is so very large. I had better start with my town. But my town, too, is large. I had best start with my street. No: my home. No: my family. Never mind, I shall start with myself."

Accompanied by his faithful disciple Moshe-Leib of Sassov, he went to Vienna, where he was received in audience by Queen Maria-Theresa.

"Why don't you look me straight in the eyes?" Her Royal Highness inquired.

"I cannot detach my eyes from the ground, Your Majesty, I owe it more than I owe you; earth gives us man and also takes him back."

Before he died, he told his followers not to cry. He said: "Death is not a stranger to me. For my soul is that of the Prophet Samuel. Like him I am a Levi, like him I shall die— today—at the age of fifty-two. Only they called him Samuel, whereas I shall remain Shmelke. Is that a reason for you to cry?"

And he drew his last breath.

Rebbe Yaakov-Yitzhak was almost blind, but in Lublin he was called the Seer; between fits of depression, he preached joy. He presided over a royal court, but he personally served its paupers. His disciples—according to tradition they numbered four hundred—were held to a rigorous discipline permitting no deviation, though he himself had dared to be a rebel during his years of apprenticeship.

He was a disquieting, awesome figure. From all accounts, he

frightened people. His strange eyes, one different from the other—the right very large, the left almost invisible—reputedly could see "from one end of the world to the other," and had the power to scan the stifling depths of the soul. One glance at a person would tell him whether he was a descendant of Cain or Abel. This gift of vision he considered a burden; that is what he stated in public. He did not wish to see what the world had to show him; he did not like his eyes.

It is said that in his youth he deliberately chose to live seven years with his eyes closed.

And also that he took walks through the forests and sat on anthills.

And also that having climbed to the peak of a very high mountain one day, he attempted to throw himself into the abyss.

"But why, Grandfather?"

"Don't try to understand. One either likes or dislikes the Seer. But one mustn't try to understand why."

"Who saved him?"

"A friend. He grabbed him by his belt."

After a pause, my grandfather added: "The Seer never forgave him."

Desperately, he fought the anxiety that undermined him. He even tried to "outlaw" it by proclaiming it the worst of sins. But it came back, day after day, choking him and squeezing him as in a vise. He startled his followers by forming a friendship with a non-believer, a well-known rake. "I like him," he said, "because he's cheerful."

His first Master, Rebbe Shmelke, had understood and sent him to Rebbe Zusia. With a note of recommendation: "Try to teach him joy."

"Not easy," my grandfather said to me, his eyes shining with mischief. *"Joy can be learned only from Hasidim, not from Masters."*

Yet, despite his depressions, the Seer was constantly growing in stature in the eyes of his followers; his sphere of influence widened from one Shabbat to the next. People came to Lublin to study, to meditate, to do penance and rearrange their inner life. Some came to stay, others came and went.

He said: "How strange, all these people who come from far away, they are sad when they arrive, but by the time they leave, they are gay and confident, whereas I . . ."

A long pause: "I am somber, and so I remain; mine is a black fire, one that gives no light."

But that, his followers did not see or refused to see.

Perhaps they found it easier that way. They were content simply to watch his fire burn.

The disciples he guided on the path to perfection were bound to him by an intense admiration that bordered on worship. One of them was asked: "Since you were so many and so powerful, and had a Master of such outstanding talent, why could you not make the Messiah come?" And the disciple replied, unsmiling: "The question is a valid one. But you see, in Lublin we lived in such ecstasy, we hardly felt the hardship of exile."

The Seer's powers of suggestion were exceptional; they transcended the individual. His battles he fought alone; his victories he shared with all his disciples and followers.

Thence the prestige and esteem he enjoyed with the other Masters. The Maggid of Kozhenitz and Menahem-Mendl of

Riminov were his allies; Ber of Radoshitz and Naftali of Ropshitz, his devoted admirers. Even Barukh of Medzebozh showed him affection. Welcoming him to his home one Shabbat, he questioned him: "They say you are a Seer; where are we?"

And the Tzaddik of Lublin's answer: "I see us in the Holy Land; we are entering Jerusalem, soon we shall cross the sanctuary's threshold."

And the same landscape appeared before the two men's eyes.

In his moments of despair, he was known to say: "Woe to the generation whose leader I am."

Also: "People come to me because I do not understand why they come."

And also: "The wicked man who knows he is wicked, well, I prefer him to the Just Man who knows he is just."

Demanding of man that he assume his condition and not till his neighbor's field, he said: "There are many paths leading to perfection; it is given to each of us to choose our own, and by following it with great dedication, we can make it become truth, our only truth."

The Seer's best disciple, the Jew of Pshiskhe, took him at his word. And left him to teach new, revolutionary ways. And so the circle closed; like his Master, Elimelekh of Lizensk, the Seer in his turn thought himself betrayed, abandoned, robbed.

But unlike Elimelekh, he continued the struggle. Instead of foundering in his personal tragedy, he went back to work with renewed vigor. Better still, there was a new dimension to his purpose, a universal dimension. He wanted nothing less than to put an end to all conflicts, to all wars; he wanted to end exile.

With his two friends and allies, Mendl of Riminov and the Maggid of Kozhenitz, he devised a detailed strategy, combining their powers to bring about final redemption. The tasks were divided—the roles distributed—the secret well kept. Unfortunately, the mystical plot failed. Punished by God, all three conspirators died during that same year (1814–1815).

Six months before his death, the Seer, who had been meditating in the privacy of his room, fell out the window; a mysterious fall, referred to as a divine malediction.

"It was Satan's doing," my grandfather assured me, *"it was Satan's vengeance."*

As far as my grandfather was concerned, the Seer, whose personality he loved, had come too close to his goal. Satan could not help but wish his downfall.

A valid hypothesis. Except that it fails to take into account the future Seer's earlier suicide attempt. And his illness. And also the timing: his fall occurred on the eve of Simhat Torah.

"The Seer's life belonged to the crowds who worshipped him," said my grandfather. *"His death belonged to him alone. One must respect it and approach it with great care."*

So be it. May legend have the upper hand. Once more. Satan: the obvious culprit, he explains everything but settles nothing. And so, after all, he was the one who pushed the Seer and provoked his fail. No wonder: solitary men attract him.

... Outside, in Lublin, there was dancing and singing. The throngs were rejoicing in the Law, becoming drunk on memories and hope. Defeated, the Seer lay on the ground, his body writhing in pain. The celebration was at its height.

ISRAEL
OF RIZHIN

WHEN ISRAEL BAAL SHEM TOV felt his hour approaching, he promised the disciples gathered at his bedside that as soon as he would arrive in heaven, he would use all his influence to hasten the coming of the Messiah.

When his soul reached heaven, he expressed the wish to meet the Redeemer. His wish was granted; one refuses nothing to a Baal Shem. But the encounter provoked in him such exultation, such ecstasy, and lifted his soul to such heights, that he forgot his promise.

His successor, the Great Maggid of Mezeritch, knew of this mishap and was determined not to fall into the same trap. "I shall know how to immunize myself against ecstasy," he vowed before he left this world. "I shall not ask to see the Messiah. I shall see everyone but him; and so he will go down to earth."

But to disarm him, he was made into an angel, and he too forgot what he owed the people below.

"I shall not let it happen to me," promised Levi-Yitzhak of Berditchev. "I shall not succumb to temptation or submit to any order. I shall refuse to enter paradise, I shall refuse to leave human history. I shall annoy and go on annoying the Judge of all judges, the Father of all living things. I shall tell Him what

His duties are toward His children, who are less stubborn than He. I shall speak, I shall shout . . ."

He did stir up much noise, and did oppose resistance. To their astonishment, the angels had to use force to push him into paradise.

"Do not worry," said Israel of Rizhin, who told this tale, "do not be afraid, I tell you. I shall resist better and longer. I shall not forget."

I confess my prejudice in favor of this last Rebbe. As a Wizsnitzer Hasid, my grandfather felt close to Rizhin. And so do I. Wizsnitz is but a branch of Rizhin, and Rizhin is . . .

"What is Rizhin, Grandfather?"

"Rizhin is the House of Rizhin, full of daily wonders and splendor. Rizhin is the Hasidic kingdom in constant state of celebration, it is Jerusalem away from Jerusalem."

And after a while: "And the Rizhiner . . ."

He smiled nostalgically. My grandfather always smiled when talking about the first Rebbe of Rizhin, usually referred to as "the Rizhiner." And my childish heart was pounding while listening to him.

"The poorest land has its king; and this king has the Rizhiner's face. I am sorry I didn't know him. I was born too late. Ten years or so after his death . . . It seems that our Rebbe looks like him . . . so they say . . . Well, the same sap nourishes the tree and the branch; still, the branch is not the tree."

Grandfather stopped talking but went on dreaming. He smiled at someone and I tried vainly to guess at whom. But in my memory his smile remains associated with the Rizhiner.

●　　　●　　　●

To evoke his image is to tell his story, a disturbing story, both beautiful and deceptively simple. A story which marks the beginning of an era and the end of another. After him the Hasidic movement was no longer the same. After him came the inevitable process of decline. The source recedes into the distance and we find that we are no longer thirsty.

It happens whenever and wherever man, moved by compassion, attempts to change the existing order and accepts responsibility for a world he has not created. He takes a step forward, he stretches out his hand to a friend, a companion, a stranger perhaps. Refusing merely to speak of love, friendship and truth, he decides to live them. He rejects mediocrity and evil, vulgarity, falsehood and easy solutions. He considers himself a revolutionary, determined to discover new paths, willing to fight the universe and its ruler. If he fails, no great harm is done; he'll start again tomorrow.

But woe unto him who succeeds. Nothing corrupts revolutionary movements more—and more radically—than success. For the first generation, the pioneering one, is followed by that of opportunists. The third continues the fight out of habit; the fourth, out of inertia. Eventually the movement turns its battle inward, splitting into factions, groups, sects, one against the other, one against all. Substance gives way to superficiality. Personalities replace ideas; slogans replace ideals. The lofty goals are lost; the message is forgotten. Now the struggle revolves around titles and positions. The process is predictable, ineluctable. No surprise is eternal, no passion immortal. At dawn, night will have lost its prophets and their promises. No school ever succeeded in keeping alive the vision and aspirations of its founders. Nothing is harder than to maintain the dream after it has molded reality. Nothing is as dangerous for victory, be it spiritual, than victory itself. If Moses led the Hebrews through the desert for forty years, it was perhaps to preserve the authenticity of their first victory over the Pharaoh and themselves. One does not win battles without paying a price, and it is usually one's innocence. Whatever the triumph, sooner or later it begets conditions which call it into question.

All this has been illustrated by most movements. And in a way, on a reduced and infinitely less harmful scale, it has also been illustrated by the non-violent though revolutionary movement of Hasidism. The story of Israel of Rizhin could therefore serve as both example and warning.

Born in 1797, Israel of Rizhin was Hasidism's favorite child and last undisputed leader. Was it because he was the great-grandson of the Maggid of Mezeritch that he enjoyed a special privileged status? Be that as it may, he had no known enemies or even opponents. People loved him, asked nothing more than to love him. They forgave him everything: his predilection for solitude, his lack of erudition, his pride, and in a more general way, the new path he was taking, so different from the one the Baal Shem had opened a century earlier in the Carpathian Mountains.

From the very beginning, he behaved like a spoiled child, a prince entitled to all honors. "I was seven," he said, "when I visited Vienna. There I was received with such pomp that nothing impresses me any more." Nothing but the best was good enough for him. Whatever he wanted, he was given. His every whim was satisfied. His elegant suits were made to measure. He was both handsome and rich, and from the beginning he craved wealth and loved beauty. During the latter part of his reign he owned a palace with servants, musicians and stables. His synagogue in Sadigor accommodated three thousand worshippers. He never went anywhere without a suite of a hundred or so aides, cooks, coachmen, musicians and intimates. On Passover his guests were served on golden dishes. Rizhin was a temple and the Rebbe its royal presence. Every Shabbat brought another attempt to re-create the lost splendors of Jerusalem. The singing was reminiscent of the Levites; the repasts evoked memories of sacrificial ceremonies.

Hasidim, by the thousands, converged upon Rizhin and, later, Sadigor, simply to be in Rizhin and Sadigor, simply to see the prince in his palace, the prince on his throne, the prince and his wealth—and strange as it may sound, nobody was shocked, nobody called it scandalous; the Rebbe was above reproach, beyond judgment.

There were great Masters among those who came to see him: Hersh Riminover, Yitzhak-Meir of Ger, Yitzhak of Worke, Haim of Tzanz—and even a rabbi as far removed from Hasidism as Shamshon-Raphael Hirsch of Frankfort. None lifted an eyebrow. All returned to their homes impressed if perhaps not conquered by the Rizhiner's personality.

True, they realized how different his concept of Hasidism was from theirs, from the one they had received from their Masters. Once upon a time, in Medzebozh and Mezeritch, in Tchernobil and Berditchev, the Hasid had tried to overcome poverty by means other than money, to defeat sadness by means other than ostentation. Hasidism in those days mocked appearances and denigrated comfort. The Baal Shem had lived in misery and so had his disciples. They had advocated joy within misery, hope despite misfortune, despite injustice. They had believed in generosity toward others and severity toward themselves. They had lived for each other, for their fellow man; they had helped one another attain knowledge, and above all,

144

self-knowledge. They had lived and survived, fully realizing their needs and desires.

Once upon a time Hasidism had meant emphasis on inner truth and fervor; a return to nature, to genuine beauty, to identification. A Hasid would see a tree and become that tree; he would hear the song of a shepherd and become that song and that shepherd—that was his way of coming closer to the essence of man. He had no need for castles and servants in order to feel at home in God's creation. To possess meant nothing, to be meant everything. Thus, it is no coincidence that the heroes of the Baal Shem's legends were mostly beggars. His way of telling us that it is more important to possess oneself than to possess; more important to be than to appear.

But in Rizhin it was the aristocracy that set the law. In Rizhin, greatness had to be displayed to be recognized. What counted was the mask, not the face; the reflection, not the source.

The question naturally arises; why? What did Israel of Rizhin want to prove, discover or refute? Whom was he challenging? What game was he playing and—most importantly— why was he permitted to play?

The fact is he could have been criticized, castigated for his style of living, for the economic and social gap he was creating between himself and his followers; but he wasn't. He could have been opposed and challenged on the grounds that within Hasidic terms of reference, his extravagance was bordering on heresy. But he wasn't. He was free to do and say whatever he wanted, in any way he chose. As a founder of a dynasty, he was protected, untouchable.

It is said that when Avraham Yehoshua Heschel of Apt proclaimed a day of fasting and prayer out of solidarity with a

certain Jewish community in distress, on that same day the
Rizhiner Rebbe summoned his musicians to play for him. Yet
the Apter Rebbe did not take it as an affront. His only comment: "No one can understand the ways of the Rizhiner."
Other Rebbes adopted the same attitude. Out of respect rather
than complacency. He was a Rebbe unlike others, a special
case, a destiny apart.

But why such favoritism? Why such privileges? What made
him so special? The fact that he was the direct descendant of
the Mezeritcher Maggid? Or because he represented, almost
from the beginning, a real force within the movement, a force
with which other leaders had to reckon? Was there something
else, and if so, what was it?

Whatever the reason, the fact remains that his popularity
kept growing; his fanatic followers saw to it. His legend exerted
a magic appeal on the masses, it captivated their imagination,
starved for things sublime. His biography—embellished by
popular storytellers—became that of a saint, prophet and
prince in Israel. It was said that his soul was among the four
Moses brought back with him when he returned to earth at
Sinai. The other three being those of Shimon Bar-Yohai,
Yitzhak Lurie and Israel Baal Shem Tov.

The Rizhiner himself claimed that he had been on earth
three times. First as a young prince in the Kingdom of Judea,
then as a young priest in the Temple; this was the third time.

Once, when he was five—or ten, opinions vary—his ritual
belt slipped and fell to the ground in the presence of his powerful protector, the old Rebbe of Apt. The old Tzaddik bent
down, picked it up and girded the youngster's waist, explain-
ing: "This is how one performs the commandment of *Glila,* of
girding the scrolls of the Torah." On another occasion he said:

"The Rizhiner has forgotten nothing of what the angels taught him before he was born."

Perhaps that explains why, as a child, he refused to study. His tutor reportedly complained that his illustrious pupil was not the most promising of students. Could young Israel's refusal to read the required books, to prepare his homework be ascribed to lack of interest or ambition? That seems unlikely. More probably, it was excessive ambition and a desire to do everything better and faster by taking shortcuts. And also to show he had received the Torah "directly from God." Soon he became so sure of himself that he professed having no need to study. Whatever he said became interesting and important because he said it. To Moshe of Savran, who came to visit, he showed his stable and spoke with pride of his magnificent stallions. All the pious and saintly visitor found to say afterward, in the way of commentary, was: "All this talk of horses was allegorical. Actually, the Rizhiner was referring to the celestial chariots, symbols of the mystical relationship the Creator maintains with creation."

His more formal discourses, though rare, were not particularly scholarly. A few commentaries on Torah, several ingenious findings on Midrash and Zohar. What people remembered mainly were his sayings. For instance: "How is one to distinguish the silent sage from the silent fool? The sage doesn't mind being silent." Also: "Look around you. Works of art everywhere are cherished, honored and protected, while man —God's masterpiece—lies in the dust." But even his most ardent admirers admit that his personality was his strength; his impact was due to the quality of his presence, not to his scholarship.

A certain Yaakov-Yosseph of Koretz told him of his plans to

move to a remote village to be a schoolteacher. "What?" exclaimed the Rizhiner. "Another schoolteacher? No! I want you to become rich!" And so great was the Hasid's faith in his Rebbe that he went into business and in a few short years amassed an immense fortune.

Was that the Rizhiner's secret? His ability to push his followers to the limits of their potential? And beyond? Perhaps. But then why did he need such pageantry? The Baal Shem in his wooden hut had caused incomparably deeper changes in his faithful. In fact, the Rizhiner's ostentatious wealth should have repelled and offended many a visitor. It didn't. On the contrary. As his fortunes multiplied, more and more poor people flocked to his court. What attracted them? Curiosity? A possibility of sublimation? Escapism? The fact that they liked him, worshipped him, proves that they needed someone like him to admire and idolize. Perhaps they needed to see that it was possible for a Jew to live like a prince; for them he was a reflection of past grandeur, a continuation of ancient and glorious times. He reminded them of what they had once been. There was so much poverty lurking behind every door, so much fear to be contained in every heart, that the sight of a Jew crowned and gratified was enough for them. He was their illusion, their holiday.

Still, it became necessary to invent a plausible explanation that would justify his eccentricities. So they said: "Poor Rebbe. Beneath his princely robes he is dressed in straw. We honor him, but his heart is in mourning." And they would shake their heads: "Poor, poor Rebbe. His shiny leather shoes are without soles; he walks on snow, his body is bruised. He suffers even while he appears happy." The proof? He never ate in public, slept three hours a night, spoke little, sought solitude and eschewed noise. In constant meditation, he moved in other worlds. But what about his properties? His valuables? His riches? He had to accept them. In order to fool Satan. For where would Satan set his traps for the Just? In synagogues, in Houses of Study, in the poorhouse, but surely not in a princely palace, under the golden robes of someone whose demeanor was that of a nobleman, not that of a Tzaddik. Satan covets only the humble; the conceited, the already corrupted leave him indifferent. That is why, they maintained in Rizhin, the Rebbe had to cover himself with gold and show himself proud.

And proud he was. Just like his father, Rebbe Shalom-Shakhne, the Maggid of Mezeritch's grandson.

The Kotzker Rebbe had said: "God is where He is allowed to enter." For Shalom-Shakhne, it was: "God is where I am." To Barukh of Medzebozh, who offered to join forces with him and rule the world, Shalom-Shakhne is said to have replied: "Thank you, but I can manage perfectly well alone."

Thus the Rizhiner followed a pattern. Authoritarian, arrogant, he brooked contradiction from nobody. To annoy him was a risky affair. He warned people that "he who speaks evil of me is guilty of blasphemy and will be blackened in this world and the other." By offending him, one exposed oneself to losing one's sanity, one's livelihood, one's life.

Once he urged a merchant to increase his donation to a certain charity.

"Rebbe," the man objected, "I don't mix in your business, please don't mix in mine."

"*Nu-nu*," answered the Rizhiner. "We shall see."

The man went bankrupt.

Another version of the same story:

149

"If you don't mend your ways," the Rizhiner warned, "you won't stay rich."

"Then you won't stay Rebbe," came the reply.

"*Nu-nu*," said the Rizhiner. "We shall see."

And the poor rich man discovered the price of disrespect and the meaning of poverty.

To his admirers who were indulging in Hasidic "elbow-pushing" around him, he said: "Why must all of you be near me? Isn't it enough to be in one room with me, under one roof, sharing one sky?"

When the Seraph Uri of Strelisk died, his followers came to the Rizhiner and asked him to be their Rebbe.

"If you want to stay," he told them, "stay. But on one condition: learn to say your prayers silently, respectfully."

To a child crying with disappointment because the Rebbe did not have six wings—like the angels in Talmudic descriptions—he murmured softly: "But yes, I do have them; I have six sons."

Yet despite his fame and munificence, his life unfolded under the sign of tragedy. The son who went astray. The twenty-two months spent in prison. The escapes, the tribulations, the years of uncertainty and waiting, the burden of responsibilities. Like his father and grandfather before him, he died young. Of his grandfather he said: "He came down, did what he had to do and went back. What's the use of lingering down here?" He, too, owed it to himself to live as fast and as intensely as possible—and not linger.

He was engaged at seven, married at thirteen, and at sixteen he ascended the rabbinic throne. At forty he was arrested and jailed in the fortress at Kiev, summarily charged with treason and complicity in murder. He was linked with a vaguely formulated plot aiming to crown him "King of the Jews," and the assassination of two informers. Eighty other Jewish dignitaries were taken into custody at the same time.

The Rizhiner's imprisonment sent shudders through the Jewish community. His faithful moved heaven and earth to free him. Clergymen were asked to intercede. Ministers were petitioned, governors bribed. The Czar himself was approached. Intrigued by the story of a "Jewish king," the ruler of all Russians ordered him brought before him. The story goes that just as the Czar was about to set him free, their eyes met, and the Czar decided he had "the eyes of a revolutionary" and sent him back to solitary confinement. Chronicles relate that the august prisoner cried often, "but never in the presence of strangers."

After his release on bail he fled to Austria, where he changed his name and nationality. Austria and Turkey offered him citizenship, but to the astonishment of officialdom, he requested to have his documents show him to be a citizen of . . . Jerusalem.

Nor were his troubles over. He continued to be a hunted man. The Russian authorities wanted him back. His case became a complicated international affair involving governments on the highest level. Metternich studied his case, the British ambassador was instructed by his government to follow developments closely and report back. St. Petersburg requested, demanded, threatened and spared no effort to secure his extradition—and failed. The Rizhiner, settled in his new estate at Patik near Sadigor, now had influential Austrian protectors. Thanks to his presence and his activities, the area prospered and bloomed. The economic situation of the people in and around Sadigor had never been so good. The region had become a new center of attraction. Thus, even the Gentiles had good reason to pray for the Rizhiner's safety and freedom.

Among Jews, his fame reached unprecedented heights. With the added aura of martyrdom his position now was even more secure and unchallenged. The most puritan Hasid could no longer object to his royal privileges: he had paid for them. Even the Rebbe of Kotzk, the fierce and savage seeker of truth, the uncompromising enemy of vanity, paid him homage. Only a man chosen by God becomes target and victim of the Czar. Any man who suffers unjustly becomes God's instrument. If punishments bear the divine seal, the same is true for rewards. After spending almost two years in prison—for nothing—a man acquires certain rights, including the right to assert that life in a palace is but a new, unexplored dimension of his trials. To deny him this right is to repudiate the cause of the one who suffers and of suffering as well.

Thus, people flocked to him in ever larger numbers. To see, to touch the one who had come from far away bearing such memories. Add to that the striking beauty of his person. Whoever saw him could not forget him. He inspired such awe as one might expect to feel in the presence of a king risen from the depths. Everything about him was regal, even his melancholy air, his reassuring gestures, his reserve. His painful past became a bond. It is easier to confide in someone who has suffered greatly. And then, he knew what words were needed to inspire confidence, to reassure. His good sense and logic were proverbial; many famous Gentiles came to seek his advice. A frequent visitor was Marshal Wittgenstein (in 1828), who liked to discuss world events with him. Rich and poor, pious and enlightened, peasants and intellectuals, to all of them Sadigor meant warmth and reassurance, if only for one encounter, one Shabbat.

Was the Rizhiner considered a miracle-maker? Not really. Rather a sage. He was known for his wisdom, not for his mystical powers. He was too modern, too liberal a man to indulge in meddling with the supernatural. When told that gangs of hoodlums were attacking defenseless Jews in his own town, he was not content just to pray for their safety: he ordered the younger men to organize groups of self-defense. He wanted his Hasidim to be healthy and normal, free of complexes. To set an example, he himself rode horses, exercised, and cut his own wood every morning.

He possessed yet another quality that made him even more appealing to his people: a sense of humor.

A man once said to him: "Rebbe, I so wish to repent, but I don't know what to do."

"And to sin, you knew what to do?"

"Yes, but that was easy. First I sinned, then I knew."

"Exactly. Now do the same the other way around. Start by repenting; you'll know later."

Rebbe Meir of Premishlan once sent him a letter with an urgent question: "Custom requires one to eat kreplach on Shavuot. How many should one eat? There is no book to tell us. Yet one would be too little, three too many, and two is an even number, and we know that even numbers come from unholy spheres. What is one to do?" The Rizhiner—unruffled—provided this solution: "Eat one—but make sure it is as large as two."

A pragmatist, he urged his Hasidim not to waste the possible for the impossible, immediate gains for remote or abstract rewards. He advised them to help one another instead of aspiring to redeem generations yet unborn, to raise themselves one step above the ground instead of walking on clouds.

He urged them to keep their means as pure as their purpose, if not more. Often he illustrated his ideas with tales and parables. One theme came back again and again: A traveler loses his way in the forest; it is dark and he is afraid. Danger lurks behind every tree. A storm shatters the silence. The fool looks at the lightning, the wise man at the road that lies—illuminated—before him. The first task of the traveler is to find his way back to man's world; then he may think of ways to change its face.

"Rebbe," a Hasid asked, "how is one to worship God without lying to oneself?"

"I'll tell you how. Make believe that you're an acrobat walking a tightrope high above a precipice. What can you do to keep your balance? Whenever your body pulls you to one side, you must pull to the other."

And also: "In your daily occupations, remember this: don't do anything that is forbidden, and even that which is permitted, do without undue haste."

Eloquent and pithy, he knew how to laugh at himself.

"The Talmud," he said, "compares Satan to an old, foolish king. I understand why he may be a king; he rules over man's passions. Why old? Because he is older than man himself. But why a fool? This I finally understood when I was in jail. He was with me, even there. I said to him: 'Fool that you are! Why are you here? I have no choice—but you?' "

He disliked Maimonides. First, because Maimonides was a philosopher, and philosophy was not the Rizhiner's strongest subject, and second . . .

"I'll tell you why. Theoretically I should like him, for he refutes Aristotle's theories, so dangerous for the faith. But imagine Jews like you and me reading Aristotle's theories in Maimonides' work and falling asleep *before* he refutes them?"

Like all Hasidic Masters, he saw God's presence in every man, in every thing: "Man," he said, "cannot *not* do God's will. Even the wicked obey Him. If their negation has any strength, it is His. Fortunately for them, they are not aware of it. If they were, they would die of spite."

Yet despite his agile mind and sharp tongue, he lost three verbal duels.

The first to a ferryman, the man who helped him flee Czarist Russia by carrying him on his shoulders. They were wading through the river at night when the man suddenly stopped and said: "Rebbe, if you want me to continue to the other side, you had better promise me a place in paradise right now."

The Rizhiner conceded: this was not the place or the time to argue.

His second defeat came on the occasion of the engagement ceremony of his son to Hersh Riminover's daughter. In the presence of dozens of noted guests and hundreds of their admirers, the Rizhiner addressed them as follows:

"It is the custom on such occasions, before the signing of the contracts, for the parents of the future couple to recall who they are and who their ancestors were. Well, know that my grandfather was Rebbe Avraham Malakh, a saint, an angel among men. His father was the celebrated Maggid of Mezeritch, who was himself a direct descendant of Yehuda Hanassi, Yohanan the Shoemaker and King David. And you, Riminover Rebbe, what is your lineage?"

"Oh, I am neither son nor grandson of rabbis," Hersh of Riminov answered. "My father was a simple tailor, poor but honest. He taught me neither the timeless truths of Torah nor the splendors of the Zohar. Still, he did teach me something about his trade. Yes, he taught me never to spoil what is new, and always to mend what is old."

The Rizhiner smiled and kept silent.

The third episode opposed him to his friend Meir of Premishlan. They met on the road. Rebbe Meir traveled in a modest cart drawn by a pitifully skinny horse, while Israel of Rizhin was seated in a sumptuous carriage with four exuberant horses in harness. The Rizhiner, ill-at-ease, felt the need to explain, apologize: "The roads are bad, there has been so much rain. One horse alone would not be enough to pull me out of the mud ... just in case."

"I understand," said the Rebbe of Premishlan, who liked to speak of himself in the third person. "Yes, Meir understands. Mud is a danger and horses can be of help. But, you see, Meir has only one horse and so he must be careful, very careful indeed, not to sink into the mud."

Again the Rizhiner smiled and said nothing.

But usually the last word was his. And not only when talking with friends or admirers. There are those who insinuate that what he really wanted was to be the last man to pronounce the last word in history and the first thereafter; in other words, that he dreamed of incarnating the Messiah.

Did he actually believe himself qualified for the role? Some of his remarks indicate that he did. For instance, he said: "All the Tzaddikim speak of the day of redemption, but I remain silent. It reminds me of a wedding. The parents and relatives are agitated. And noisy. Only the bridegroom stands aside, somber and impassive. And remains silent!"

This theory would in a way explain his affinity for silence, his whims, his taste for pomp, by linking them to the expectation that the Messiah will be more than Savior; he will be King, the king of times to come.

And here I must confess that I, grandson of Dodye Feig, Hasid of Wizsnitz, am unable to accept this theory. The Rizhiner was too clever, too lucid a man to play a game whose perils he well knew. He knew the end that lies in store for false Messiahs. The true Messiah does not behave like a Messiah. He does not covet honors or gold. Nor does he reveal what must remain hidden. The Rizhiner knew all this, he had to know.

How then is one to interpret his parable about the wedding? Could he have seen himself not as the bridegroom, but as a guest, a special guest close to the bridegroom, and closer than anyone to the Messiah? Was that why he spoke of him so often? More than any of the other Hasidic Masters? Hasidism, as conceived and elaborated in Rizhin, was more Messiah-oriented than any other.

He may have sensed that only the Messiah could save future generations of Jews from the fate that was awaiting them. The last of the great early Masters, he saw himself as heir to the Maggid of Mezeritch and the Baal Shem. Like them, he strove to mark the future. His failings and failures do him honor; they are those of a man determined to force God's hand. Such a man must lose.

Obsessed, literally, by the messianic promise, the Rizhiner understood that man will never be strong enough to bring about universal change. Like the Grandfather of Shpole and Levi-Yitzhak of Berditchev, he turned to God and took part in His quarrels with man, and like his predecessors, pleaded the cause of man.

He said: "It is written that *it is because of our sins that we were chased from our land;* and I say that is false. Exile preceded our sins. Just bring us back and You shall see that not one Jew will feel like sinning."

Another time: "You must put an end to exile because exile itself is a sin; the most dangerous of all."

And also: "Be our Father and we shall be Your servants; we shall be Your servants only if You are our Father."

He addressed God in terms reminiscent of Levi-Yitzhak of Berditchev, but with less humility: "I am not a slave come to ask favors of the king. I come as a counselor to discuss matters of state."

One day he cried out: "Master of the Universe, how many years do we know each other? How many decades? So please permit me to wonder: is this any way to rule Your world? The time has come for You to have mercy on Your people! And if You refuse to listen to me, then tell me: what am *I* doing here on this earth of Yours?"

Another time he shouted angrily: "Why is the Messiah so late in coming? Does he think the next generation will be better? More deserving? I tell him here and now that he is wrong! They will be worse, much worse!"

His exceptional intuition helped him decipher the future. He foresaw what was to come. The world was doomed, mankind rushing to its fall. In a dehumanized, arid universe, robbed of desire and salvation, disorder would be on a cosmic scale and so would guilt. With the dawning of the end of time, good and evil would go hand in hand, would become one. Light would become indistinguishable from darkness, daybreak from dusk, silence from words, words from truth, truth from fear and fear from death.

Yes, he was a tragic figure, for he sensed the futility of his endeavors. "A day will come," he said, "when ignorance will reign. Mediocre men will feel at ease on earth and above, while men of spirit and conscience will be alienated. The most pious Jew will be incapable of reciting a verse from the Psalms. I tell you this so you will know: that is how it will have to be, that is how it will be."

Another prediction: "A day will come when all nations will begin hating Jews; they will hate them so much, with such passion and violence, that the Jews will have no choice but to go to the land of their ancestors, to the Holy Land. And then, woe unto us and woe unto them, for it will be the beginning of redemption."

Once he explained why he liked to marry people but refused to intercede in heaven for them to have children: "I foresee that from the next century on, people will have souls so ugly, so repulsive, that one will not be able to stand their sight. Well, we must accept what we are given—but pray to obtain it? No."

The most striking of his visions: "A day will come when man will stop hating others and hate himself; a day will come when all things will lose their coherence, when there will be no relation between man and his face, desire and its object, question and its answer."

And then, this story he loved to tell:

A young Hasid of the great Maggid of Mezeritch married the daughter of a fierce Mitnagged, who forced him to choose between his family and his Rebbe. The son-in-law swore that he would not return to Mezeritch. But after a few months, or perhaps years, he could not resist the impulse to join his companions and their Master. When he returned home his angry father-in-law marched him to the local rabbi for a judgment. The rabbi consulted the *Shulkhan Arukh* and issued this verdict: since he had broken his promise, the young man was to give his wife a divorce at once. Overnight the young man found himself on the street. He had no means of his own, no relations. Inconsolable, refusing all nourishment, the young Hasid fell sick. With no one to care for him, he died shortly after.

"Well," continued the Rizhiner, "when the Messiah will come, the young Hasid will file a complaint against his father-in-law and the local rabbi, both guilty of his premature death. The first will say: 'I obeyed the rabbi.' The rabbi will say: 'I obeyed the *Shulkhan Arukh*.' And the Messiah will say: 'The father-in-law is right, the rabbi is right and the Law is right.' Then he will kiss the young plaintiff and say: 'But I, what do I have to do with them? I have come for those who are not right.'"

The messianic idea and dream were so deeply rooted in the Rizhiner that he—or his son David-Moshe of Chortkov, opinions vary on this—prepared a special room in his apartments called the "Messiah's chamber." All his most valuable and valued belongings were stored there and no one was allowed inside.

Still, as time went on, the Rizhiner must have felt that he would die without having welcomed the "Bridegroom." He had long struggled with sadness. Toward the end of his life, he yielded to sorrow.

The prison experience had marked him, and made him withdraw further into solitude. He now received his disciples only on Fridays. Like his great-grandfather, the Maggid of Mezeritch, he would retire to his room for prayers, while in an adjoining room, the faithful prayed, relying on a disciple posted at the door to signal the beginning or end of various passages in the service.

Little is known about his last moments. Not as much as about his son Nahum's, who, several hours before he died, washed from head to toes, put on his Shabbat clothes, lay down on his bed and bade his friends sing; and sang with them until they sang no more.

The Rizhiner was given more time to prepare. On the eve of his last Yom Kippur, he paused on the synagogue's threshold, put his hand on the mezuzah and murmured: "May I become sacrifice and expiate for the entire household of Israel."

He died one month later. He was fifty-four.

One hundred and twenty years later, the Rizhiner is more enigmatic than ever.

His habits, his talents, his tastes and his charisma; his tendency toward exhibitionism and theatrics remain a mystery for the student or Hasid who, like myself, believes in his greatness.

It is difficult to accept the idea that he loved riches for the sake of riches. True, he was neither philosopher nor teacher, but he was a remarkable figure, an influential leader; all testimonies agree on that point. Such a Rebbe is not drawn to wealth for the usual reasons. I choose to think that his ambitions were not materialistic. I would like to believe that he was trying to prove something, defy someone; we shall never know what or whom. And perhaps that is the way he wanted it. It may be part of the mystery he wished to create around himself. Just as we do not understand the extreme asceticism of the solitary Rebbe of Kotzk, we find it difficult to understand the extreme taste for luxury of the Rizhiner. Who knows, perhaps the two attitudes were meant to conceal one and the same secret.

That he did not amass the gold and silver for himself is certain. An austere Master such as Haim of Tzanz said: "The Rebbe of Rizhin is ready at every moment to sacrifice himself for the people of Israel."

For the student assessing the totality of his deeds and words, there can be no doubt: the Rizhiner, his gaze reaching far into the distance, thought and acted always in collective terms; his plans transcended the limits of possession. He was concerned with what was in store for man and his soul; nothing else.

The pomp and pageantry of his court? Perhaps this was his way of consoling and comforting his poor Hasidim by showing them that the dream was there; that they could see it if they tried, and that the reality of exile does not preclude the royal vision of redemption. Perhaps this was his way of reminding them that *malkhut*—royalty—is also an attribute of God, and that the God of Israel is also King of Israel, a king whose often destroyed and dispersed kingdom nevertheless remains indestructible. Perhaps he wanted to add emphasis to Reb Aharon Karliner's warning: "We are all princes; to forget that, is the gravest sin of all."

Could he have had still greater ambitions and justifications? Perhaps. Renunciation contains a certain joy, a certain kind of ecstasy no possession can provide. Could the Rizhiner Rebbe have chosen flagrant dramatics and wealth out of despair, or rather: to attain despair? Could he have tried to go to the end of his satiated desires in order to reach his own naked being? Is it conceivable that having come to the realization that he would never resemble his ancestors, the Maggid and the Baal Shem, he wished to show them that despite his wealth and marks of distinction, despite appearances, he was following in their footsteps? And that appearances have their own secrets? Is that why he so frequently referred to the Messiah? To bring an end, once and for all, to appearances?

Of course, these are so many hypotheses. For me, Israel of Rizhin remains a mystery; he resists analysis. As much as I like the character, something about him troubles me. I feel it is too pat an explanation to point out the ease of attaining purity inside misery, and that true merit consists in living alone in a crowd; in remaining humble at the peak of fame and poor in the midst of wealth. Instinctively, I am suspicious of material gains accompanied by spiritual justifications. The scenery may well influence both the action and the cast on stage. The means *can* influence the end. And every game runs the risk of ultimately defining itself by its own rules.

We are back to the question: who is Israel of Rizhin? I see him as a poet, a tragic visionary condemned to agonizing lucidity. He may have known he was the last of his dynasty. He may have known that after him Hasidism would not be the same. That future disciples would have the Masters they would deserve and that all would live and perish in a world that did not deserve them.

One thing he must have known: that it is not enough to call the Messiah to make him come.

DISCIPLES IV

Before Hersh Ziditchoiv's soul was sent down to earth, Satan appeared before the celestial court to lodge a complaint: "This soul must not be given to men; it will make saints of them. And signify my end. With Hersh of Ziditchoiv as my adversary, I am beaten in advance. I protest, I demand justice . . ."

The court deliberated and decided: "Your argument is valid, but we cannot turn back. Our decisions are irrevocable. This soul that frightens you will inhabit Rebbe Hersh. But, to reassure you, another soul will be sent down for another man who will have all the signs, qualities and virtues of a Rebbe; the crowds will admire and praise him. And with the exception of this court and yourself, nobody will know that this man owes allegiance not to our sacred and divine authority but to you alone."

How is one to know? How does one recognize purity in a man? And how can one be sure? I remember putting this question to my grandfather. He chuckled and his eyes twinkled when he answered: "But one is never sure; nor should one be. Actually, it all depends on the Hasid; it is he who, in the final analysis, must justify the Rebbe."

• • •

David Zlates, disciple of the Seer of Lublin, refused to
become a rabbi. He persisted in wanting to remain disciple.
After the Seer's death, he joined Hersh of Ziditchoiv's followers, then Meir of Premishlan's and, finally, Israel of
Rizhin's.

It is said that one Shabbat, the Seer invited him to recite the
blessing customary at the end of a meal. Rebbe David de-
murred. "I order you to obey," shouted the Seer. "Whoever
accedes to the higher spheres may not retreat from them!"
David did as he was told. But thereafter, whenever his followers
came to seek his advice or help, they found his room empty.
David the Hasid was with another Master. As a simple Hasid.

*"You'll grow up, you'll see," my grandfather had said.
"You'll see that it is more difficult, more rare to find a Hasid
than a Rebbe. To induce others to believe is easier than to
believe. To give, easier than receive. And," added grandfather,
"a Hasid is more to be envied than his Master."*

Menahem-Mendl of Riminov said: "To pronounce
useless words is to commit murder."

Moshe of Ujhely waited his whole life for the Messiah;
he never went to bed at night without reminding his sons: "If
he comes, wake me right away!"

Near the end of his life, this is how he spoke to God: "Master of the Universe, my strength is gone; I am exhausted. You
must send us the Messiah. You have no choice. Don't think

I'm asking this for my own salvation. If you wish, I am ready to deny myself even a single ray of light and joy. Believe me, I am ready to sacrifice my life and my soul and undergo the terrors of eternal night if that be the price of Israel's redemption. I know, Master of the Universe, that I am the last of the last, but I love truth and I say: if I had known that my hair would turn white without my eyes ever beholding the Savior, I could not have gone on living. You held me, you kept me going with hope, with faith. You procrastinated, day after day, hour after hour. You fooled me. Is it really so clever, so charitable, to mock an old man like me? I ask You!"

I remember. Grandfather blessing me: "May you see the Messiah put an end to exile and the reign of evil." A blessing that almost came true. It was night. I found myself transported into a strange and distant kingdom. In the shadow of the flames, the exiled were gathered. They came from everywhere, they spoke every language and all told the same story. Seeing them together under the fiery sky, the child in me had thought: This is it; this is the end of time, the end of everything. Any moment the Messiah will appear out of the night, the Messiah of fear, the Messiah of death. I thought of my grandfather and I trembled for him, for myself. And for his blessing.

Said Hune of Kolochitz: "Nothing and nobody down here frightens me; not even an angel, not even the angel of fear. But the moaning of a beggar makes me shudder."

And Moshe-Leib of Sassov to his friend Uri of Strelisk: "You cross the country from one end to the other, collecting money to free this man from prison, marry this orphan girl, help that widow. I know, I know all that. But I have no money; never had any. I would like to help you and I don't know how. I would like to do something for you, but I don't know what— Wait! I've got it! I know what to do; I know how to help you: Uri, my friend, Rebbe of Strelisk, I shall dance for you!"

And I try to imagine my grandfather in the train that carried him away. They tell that some danced, others sang and still others prayed—fervently, joyously, as though they anticipated a celebration, a reunion. And he? I try to see him, but I cannot. And so I shall never know whether my grandfather, Dodye Feig, the Wizsnitzer Hasid, went to his death singing or dancing for a man, for a child, or for a tale he will never tell.

When the great Israel Baal Shem Tov saw misfortune threatening the Jews, it was his custom to go into a certain part of the forest to meditate. There he would light a fire, say a special prayer, and the miracle would be accomplished and the misfortune averted.

Later, when his disciple, the celebrated Maggid of Mezeritch, had occasion, for the same reason, to intercede with heaven, he would go to the same place in the forest and say: "Master of the Universe, listen! I do not know how to light the fire, but I am still able to say the prayer." And again the miracle would be accomplished.

Still later, Moshe-Leib of Sassov, in order to save his people once more, would go into the forest and say: "I do not know the prayer, but I know the place and this must be sufficient." It was sufficient and the miracle was accomplished.

Then it fell to Israel of Rizhin to overcome misfortune. Sitting in his armchair, his head in his hands, he spoke to God: "I am unable to light the fire and I do not know the prayer; I cannot even find the place in the forest. All I can do is tell the story, and this must be sufficient." And it was sufficient.

It no longer is. The proof is that the threat has not been averted. Perhaps we are no longer able to tell the story. Could all of us be guilty? Even the survivors? Especially the survivors?

NAHMAN
OF BRATZLAV

ONE DAY THE KING summoned his counselor and told him of his anguish: "I have read in the stars that all those who will eat of the next harvest will be struck with madness. What shall we do, my friend?"

"Nothing could be more simple, Sire," replied the counselor, "we shall not touch it. Last year's harvest is not yet exhausted. You have but to requisition it; it will be ample for you. And me."

"And the others?" scolded the king. "All the subjects of my kingdom? The faithful servants of the crown? The men, the women, the madmen and the beggars, are you forgetting them? Are you forgetting the children, the children too?"

"I am forgetting nobody, Sire. But as your adviser, I must be realistic and take all possibilities into account. We don't have enough reserves, not enough to protect and satisfy everyone. There will be just enough for you. And me."

Thereupon the king's brow darkened, and he said: "Your solution does not please me. Is there no other? Never mind. But I refuse to separate myself from my people and I don't care to remain lucid in the midst of a people gone mad. Therefore we shall all enter madness together. You and I like the others, with the others. When the world is gripped by delirium, it is senseless to watch from the outside: the mad will think that we are mad too. And yet, I should like to safeguard some reflection of our present glory and of our anguish too; I should like to keep alive the memory of this determination, this decision. I should like that when the time comes, you and I shall remain aware of our predicament."

"Whatever for, Sire?"

"It will help us, you'll see. And thus we shall be able to help our friends. Who knows, perhaps thanks to us, men will find the strength to resist later, even if it is too late."

And putting his arm around his friend's shoulders, the king went on: "You and I shall therefore mark each other's foreheads with the seal of madness. And every time we shall look at one another, we shall know, you and I, that we are mad."

In a distant land, a prince lost his mind and imagined himself a rooster. He sought refuge under the table and lived there, naked, refusing to partake of the royal delicacies served in golden dishes—all he wanted and accepted was the grain reserved for the roosters. The king was desperate. He sent for the best physicians, the most famous specialists; all admitted their incompetence. So did the magicians. And the monks, the ascetics, the miracle-makers; all their interventions proved fruitless.

One day an unknown sage presented himself at court. "I think that I could heal the prince," he said shyly. "Will you allow me to try?"

The king consented, and to the surprise of all present, the sage removed his clothes, and joining the prince under the table, began to crow like a rooster.

Suspicious, the prince interrogated him: "Who are you and

what are you doing here?" — "And you," replied the sage, "who are you and what are you doing here?" — "Can't you see? I am a rooster!" — "Hmm," said the Sage, "how very strange to meet you here!" — "Why strange?" — "You mean, you don't see? Really not? You don't see that I'm a rooster just like you?"

The two men became friends and swore never to leave each other.

And then the sage undertook to cure the prince by using himself as example. He started by putting on a shirt. The prince couldn't believe his eyes. — "Are you crazy? Are you forgetting who you are? You really want to be a man?" — "You know," said the Sage in a gentle voice, "you mustn't ever believe that a rooster who dresses like a man ceases to be a rooster." The prince had to agree. The next day both dressed in a normal way. The sage sent for some dishes from the palace kitchen. "Wretch! What are you doing?" protested the prince, frightened in the extreme. "Are you going to *eat* like them now?" His friend allayed his fears: "Don't ever think that by eating like man, with man, at his table, a rooster ceases to be what he is; you mustn't ever believe that it is enough for a rooster to behave like a man to become human; you can do anything with man, in his world and even for him, and yet remain the rooster you are."

And the prince was convinced; he resumed his life as a prince.

The author of these tales is Nahman of Bratzlav, whose stories are among the most spellbinding in Hasidic literature. They constitute a universe of their own in which dreamers go beyond their dreams, beyond their desires, swept away by their quest for imagination and salvation and an infinite craving for innocence and wonder.

(He reminds one of Franz Kafka, whom he preceded and—according to some—inspired. A tempting and even plausible hypothesis. Separated by more than a century— Rebbe Nahman was born in 1772—the two men seem to have shared the themes and obsessions that lend their work its realistic yet dreamlike quality. Their heroes live their lives by imagining them, and their deaths by telling them.

There are more striking similarities: the Tzaddik from the Ukraine and the novelist from Prague both died young; the Rebbe at thirty-eight, the writer at forty-one. Cut down by the same ailment: tuberculosis. Both demanded that their writings be burned. And each had a faithful friend, a devoted interpreter, an apostle to whom we owe their work's survival. What Max Brod was for Kafka, Reb Nathan had been for Rebbe Nahman.

But while Rebbe Nahman wished his writings destroyed, he wanted to preserve their essence: "Make my tales into prayers," he told his followers. Prayers and not relics.

Before he died, he gave orders to throw his notes into the fire: "To send them back up there." Nathan believed it to be his duty to obey—and did. He lacked the combination of vision and audacity of a Max Brod. The tellers of tales resembled each other more than their two fervent apostles.)

Another story: that of the royal messenger unable to accomplish his mission.

The king had sent a letter to a wise but skeptical man, who, in his faraway province, refused to accept it. He was one of those men who think too much, who complicate their lives by complicating small things. He couldn't understand, not in the slightest, what the king might want of him: "Why would the sovereign, so powerful and so rich, address himself to me, who am less than nothing? Because he takes me for a philosopher? There are more important ones. Could there be another reason? If so, what reason?"

Unable to answer these questions, he preferred to believe the letter a misunderstanding. Worse: a fraud. Worse yet: a practical joke. "Your king," he said to the messenger, "does not exist." But the messenger insisted: "I am here, and here is the letter; isn't that proof enough?" — "The letter proves nothing at all; besides, I haven't read it. And by the way, who gave it to you? The king in person?" — "No," confessed the messenger. "It was given to me by a royal page. In his name." — "Are you sure of that? And how can you be sure that it comes from the reigning sovereign? Have you ever seen him?" — "Never. My rank does not permit or warrant it." "Then how do you know that the king is king? You see? You don't know any more than I."

And without unsealing the letter, the sage and the messenger decided to learn the truth once and for all. They would go to the end of the world, they would question the very last of mortals, but they would know.

At the marketplace, they accosted a soldier: "Who are you and what do you do?" — "I am a soldier by trade and I am in the king's service." — "What king?" — "The one to whom we swore allegiance; this land is his. We are all here to serve him." — "Do you know what he looks like?" — "No." — "Then you have never seen him?" — "Never."

The two companions burst into laughter: "Look at him! This man in uniform insists upon serving someone he has never seen and will never see!"

Further on, they met an officer: yes, he would willingly die for the king; no, he had never had the honor of seeing him, neither from close by nor from afar.

A general: same questions, same answers, clear and precise. He, too, thinks of nothing but to serve the king, he lives only for him and by him; and yet, even though he is a general, he cannot boast of ever having set his eyes upon the king.

"You see?" says the sceptical sage to the messenger. "People are naïve and credulous, and rather foolish; they live a lie and are afraid of the truth."

And they laugh. They laugh with such despair that in the end, they will understand that there must be a link between the voice and the call, between man and his road; in the end they will understand that their feeling of despair is not absurd, for it may well be the link that binds them to the king.

The king, in Rebbe Nahman's terms, is not the enemy of the sage, nor is the sage the enemy of the prince. All aspire to a particular metamorphosis in order to escape their condition. But whereas the hero of the Jewish novelist from Prague moves in a sordid universe, a universe dominated by dark violence and implacable ugliness, the Rebbe's hero wins the favor of the king.

All of Nahman's characters find themselves before obstacles to be overcome, walls to be climbed, strangers to be conciliated; only they succeed, their adventures end happily, in harmony rather than in renunciation. Once arrived at the end of their tribulations, they understand their meaning. Cast into the secret that awaits them and no other, they know that it is not evil; on the contrary, it spells liberation and salvation. Nothing in the romantic universe of Rebbe Nahman is truly evil; in the end, all things become man's allies.

Rebbe Nahman—or Hasidic imagination, the celebration of the word, the glorification of legend, inspired and bewitching. Rebbe Nahman—or flight directed inward.

A figure so complex as to either make you dream or make you lose the very desire to dream. His life, rich in exploits, seems to lie under the sign of paradox and fever, on mountain peaks and precipices, in outright hallucination and never, never in security.

A great-grandson of the Besht, he quarrels with almost every great personality that claims his heritage. As a Master, founder of a school, he transmits his vision of the world by telling tales, masterworks of their kind, rather than by enunciating theories. As a Kabbalist he is accessible, as a Rebbe he is not. Ascetic, an enemy of doubt, he frequents the so-called emancipated intellectual circles whose vocation and pastime it is to doubt and oppose asceticism. An intolerant believer, he plays chess with free-thinkers; their faith in nothingness intrigues him. Sick, he hates doctors; poor, he despises the rich. He forbids his disciples to read philosophical works, Maimonides included; yet he has read them all. Arrogant with some, humble with others, and always with the wrong person, he is never the same though he never changes, as though there were two of him. And sometimes the saint behaves like a comedian.

All this we know, thanks to Reb Nathan, his biographer turned hagiographer. His confidant too. The Master told, and went on telling, him his intimate thoughts fired up by delirium. His tormented childhood, his adolescence and his crises, his paroxysms of anxiety followed by surges of ecstasy. Detailed episodes, startling images often clumsily sketched: the facts and how they are told bear the mark of authenticity.

Thus we know that Nahman was a turbulent child, secretive

and stubborn. A poor pupil, he cried easily and complained to
God about God. He was a troubled, anxiety-ridden adolescent
who sometimes would run away from home, visit the Baal
Shem's grave and come back exhausted, his eyes aflame.

When he discovered his body, he had to muster all his
strength to fight its desires, an excruciating fight described at
great length in the notes taken down by Reb Nathan. But he
emerged victorious. "For me," he said, "men and women are
all the same; I react to both in the same way." And another
time: "From now on I shall fear woman no more than I fear
the angel."

His was an intense life, filled with "falls and staggering
ascensions," punctuated with fasting and sleeplessness. He suffered silently, "his teeth clenched until they could have cracked
a piece of wood"—and sometimes he would "scream and howl
quietly." It was a life of disorder, streaked with lightning
and painful, exalting sensations. "He had ups and downs by the
thousands, by the tens of thousands," Reb Nathan said later.
"After much work, he would succeed in rising high—only to
fall, over and over again, innumerable times in the course of a
single day."

Before Reb Nathan's advent, he had acquired a close friend
in the person of a certain Reb Shimon; they studied together.
One day Rebbe Nahman abruptly invited him to leave with him
for Hungary and live there in anonymity and poverty. "Here,
too many people know me," he said. "They respect me for my
lineage. In Hungary they won't think twice about making me
suffer." The journey never took place. "No need to leave,"
he announced to his companion. "I shall be persecuted here,
too."

He was right. When he was married at thirteen, he was already more famous than many spiritual leaders of his time.

He couldn't help but arouse their hostility sooner or later. "Only a bundle of straw does not provoke opposition," he remarked later. His temperament was so unstable, his sensitivity so acute, his intelligence so lively and precocious, that he experienced and received life like a wound. That, too, we know, thanks to Reb Nathan.

A strange fellow, this Nathan, referred to as "from Nemerov." To view him as a simple witness, or as a scribe by appointment to the court of Bratzlav, would be to underestimate his worth. He was no less original a disciple than his Master was a Rebbe. Each in his way attained fulfillment. If the interpreter lived solely for the Rebbe, the Master in turn expressed himself solely through his biographer. Who said of the Rebbe's work: "In it you will find the mind of the Master, only the voice is mine."

That Reb Nathan was more than an instrument became evident at the death of Rebbe Nahman. His favorite collaborator, first among his peers, was accepted almost as an independent Rebbe. People sought his advice, solicited his blessing and attended his services. They described his prayer as a commentary on the Prayer. But he himself, faithful and unassuming to the end, refused all roles other than that of disciple; it was the only one to his liking. He said: "The whole world is mad and so am I; except that I had the good fortune of seeing one lucid being." He also said: "Blessed is he whose eyes have met the eyes of Rebbe Nahman; blessed is he whose eyes have met mine that have looked into the eyes of Rebbe Nahman."

What had driven him to the Tzaddik of Bratzlav? A dream, he said. "In my dream, I went to the bakery to buy rolls. On the way, I halted, deeply troubled: could this be my life's purpose? To take little rolls from one man in order to give them to another? Nothing else, nothing more? At that moment, a man appeared before me and said: 'If you would like me to help you, hold on to me.' It was Rebbe Nahman."

Rebbe Nahman gave him a warm welcome: "We know each other a long time, but this is the first time we see each other." The visitor was moved and won over. From that moment on he was another man.

For him, it was love at first sight. He gave up his travels, neglected his affairs and even his home. He changed his own life to better integrate himself into his Master's. "If the earth were covered with daggers," he said, "I would willingly walk it from one end to the other for one glimpse of the Rebbe's holy face."

His task: to collect the Rebbe's teachings, his table conversations, scraps of thoughts and sentences uttered here and there; his dreams, his moods, his anecdotes; absorb them all, then write them down, giving them continuity and form. A grateful Nahman praised him. "Every one of you has his share in my tales," he told his intimate disciples, "but you, Nathan, have the biggest share of all."

A compliment? No. A statement of fact. Thanks to Nathan's talent, his foresight and vigilance, the thoughts and legends of the Master have been preserved for us. Scrupulous, exacting to the point of fanaticism, he submitted his notes to the author for corrections and comments. Thus we sometimes may read a certain story on two levels, from two points of view: as told and as listened to by the teller himself. Nathan went even further; with future readers in mind, he did not content himself with transcribing a particular piece, but added his own explanatory observations, sometimes even describing the circumstances surrounding its creation. Thanks to him, Rebbe

Nahman's readers are privileged to be present at the birth of several of his fables.

It is Nathan who tells us exactly when and why Nahman decided to become a storyteller. In 1806 when he declared: "I can see that my ideas have no effect on you, therefore I shall tell you stories; and I shall tell them in Yiddish so as not to give you the excuse of having misunderstood." He also said: "If one is to believe what people say, stories are written to put them to sleep; I tell mine to wake them up." Another time: "I tell you my dreams also because a dream is but the story of a dream; yet the story of a dream is more than a dream."

Five years after the Master's death, Reb Nathan turned editor and printer to further his cause. Prohibited in Russia—where they were considered too sad and depressing—Rebbe Nahman's tales were published in Poland. In his foreword, Reb Nathan wrote:

"Pause and marvel at these wonders. If you are a man, if you have a soul, you cannot help but bite your lips and take your life into your hands; your hair will stand up on your head, for stunned, you will read words that will entrance the most hardened of hearts. Every word here conceals a deep intention, every character is linked to an ancient and timeless truth."

Rebbe Nahman himself considered his tales sacred; he thought of them as being inspired, perhaps even revealed. And to this day, his followers repeat them—after saying a special prayer—to probe them for secrets accessible only to the initiated. They repeat them to one another like incantations, to purify themselves by purifying the word that names beings and voices in time and space.

•   •   •

I remember reading these stories as a child and, spell-bound, thinking that I had understood them. Now I reread them, and though I am still under their spell, I no longer understand them. Some seem too simple, others too complicated; sometimes both at the same time. Frequently their form is what misleads me; sometimes it is their inner structure. The more I read, the more I get the feeling of being left behind, of being incapable of continuing to the end. And then I fear that there will always remain a zone of silence, a zone of darkness which I shall never pierce. Never will I retrace the steps leading back to the teller; I shall see neither what he saw nor what he refused to see. I shall not live his adventures, though I may sometimes claim those of his heroes and their victims as my own.

His tales? Each contains many others. Imagine a series of concentric circles whose fixed centers are buried in man's innermost being: the I inside the I, conscience become silence and peace, memory inside memory. And all are inhabited by princes and sages. By haunted creatures seeking one another, one in another. By survivors of calamities, refugees, fugitives, messengers and innocent children, orphans and beggars endlessly roaming the world only to meet again in a cave or in a palace, reunited and fulfilled in ways that go beyond the experience they have gone through or been subjected to, perhaps unwittingly. Following them, we plunge into the supernatural, and yet the word miracle is never pronounced. For in the Bratzlaver's universe everything is miraculous, even the most common event. On his lips, the most deprived, most primitive of men are endowed with powers; his objects have the gift of song, just as his forest, his trees, his animals and his morning breezes all have the gift of laughter.

More daring than the most daring of the surrealists, trusting only his intuition, Nahman creates freely, impulsively; he rejects all logic, inductive or deductive; he obeys no law, acknowledges no influence. "Time does not exist," he asserts, meaning his tales as well as the world; he goes so far as to exclude it from primary creation. According to him, God gave man everything—except time.

Thus, the notion of time never enters Rebbe Nahman's work. Neither does the notion of place. Continuity? He prefers unbridled, irresistible and sovereign fantasy disdainful of frontiers, all frontiers; those of the mind as well as those of lands inhabited though cursed. His characters are forever leaving one another: sometimes to hide behind others for no reason. Impossible to know who is playing what role and for how long. The episodes arbitrarily fit into one another, follow one another, becoming inextricably tangled. And then, just as arbitrarily, they reach an abrupt ending, as though the teller had exhausted his patience and wanted to finish quickly in order to start anew. The tone is epic, the pace fast and erratic. Every fable contains ten fables, every scene is a mosaic whose every fragment is a tale, a scene in itself. One easily loses the thread. There are too many *maassioth betokh maassioth,* too many tales inside the tales Rebbe Nahman tells us. One ends up forgetting the main, subterranean plot. Like Nahman's heroes, the reader-listener no longer has any notion where he is or what might be awaiting him at the next step; he is helpless, lost in a strange land.

At first glance, this may seem surprising, for Rebbe Nahman could impose a discipline on himself when he wanted to or deemed it necessary. He was too skilled a craftsman to botch a tale. If he sustains our attention to the end in spite of the dispersion of his characters, it is only because he is a master of his craft. But then, how could he who in the secondary, not to say minor, episodes attached such importance to the smallest intricate pattern, to every detail—the color of a cloud, of twilight; an old man's expression of wonder, a passer-by's sneer—how could he neglect the framework and underestimate the importance of the work's very structure? Why did he leave so many gaps? Threads leading in too many directions at once; action ten times suspended—and seven times resumed? Have they a purpose? The answer is contained in the question. The same failings—or apparent failings—may be found in all his tales, in everything he created; therefore they must be deliberate, translating his concept of creation, of the art of transmitting legends and also of their author.

It is as though he wanted people to understand that it is more important for man to halt and consider the mystery of his own life than that of the world's origins. Danger and evil are not in the walk toward death, but in the digression. Man advances toward more than one goal, lives on more than one level, loves and despairs in more than one way for more than one reason. Yet he does not even know whether his deeds fall into a main or secondary pattern or if his awareness is blessing or curse. The human condition gains in impact at the very moment it breaks apart. Every fragment contains the whole, every fissure bears witness that man is at once the most fragile and the most tenacious of creatures.

Rebbe Nahman is more concerned with man than with mankind. Because he reacts more directly to the individual. His relationship to earth and heaven is filled with as many secrets as are contained by heaven and earth. Rebbe Nahman tightens the episodic events and lets the canvas flutter because he prefers the moment to years, the infinitely small to the infinitely large, the jolts of a life to a lifetime without surprises.

• • •

Here is the most beautiful of his tales, the most obscure too, entitled: "The Story of the Seven Beggars." It was his favorite. We know this because, once before telling it in public, he confided to Reb Nathan: "I am now going to tell a story which, since the creation of the world, has been heard only one time: before the destruction of the Temple. Even the Prophets don't know it. Only one man knew it—the one who put it into words." And he added: "We should go into town, as far as Brodi, enter the main synagogue, ascend the bimah and invite the public to come in throngs and listen . . ."

Once upon a time there was a king who abdicated in favor of his son. The coronation took place amid merriment and exuberance. There was singing in the streets and drinking in the squares. Comedians and musicians, troubadours and jugglers amused the people of the court; others entertained the crowds from morning till night and into the early hours. At the height of the festivities, the king turned to his son and said: "I see in the stars that one day you shall lose your throne. Promise me you will not let it sadden you; promise me that you will continue to be of good cheer. Then I will be too, though my gaiety will be of a special kind."

The new king was kind and charitable. He was a patron of the arts and encouraged the free exchange of ideas. He wanted his subjects to be happy. If someone wanted money, he made him rich. If someone aspired to honors, he helped him attain them. Thus the kingdom gained in wisdom and love what it lost in military power; the warriors forgot their trade and their desire to reap glory by killing or defying death. And then the king was overcome with sadness and began endlessly questioning himself: what am I doing in this world and what is my place in it? He had changed.

Well, in another country a great panic broke out and its inhabitants fled. While crossing a forest, two very small children —a boy and a girl—became lost. They cried and cried, for they were hungry. Along came a beggar, a bundle on his back, his eyes empty, expressionless. The children appealed to him and he gave them some bread. "Where do you come from," he asked.—"We don't know," answered the children. When he wanted to leave they begged him to take them along. He refused. Only then did they realize that he was blind. He left them with a wish: "Be like me."

The next morning, famished, they began to cry again. And a second beggar came to their aid; he was deaf. Like the first, he refused to take them along, but also formulated the wish that they be like him. The third day it was a stutterer's turn to offer them some bread and his blessing: "Be like me." The fourth beggar had a twisted neck, the fifth was a hunchback, the sixth had no arms and the seventh, no legs. And each wished them to be like him.

Then the children left the night and the forest, and becoming full-time beggars, they visited towns and fairs. Wherever they went they aroused compassion. And so, they made a career. And became famous. Whereupon it was decided that they should marry. The engagement was celebrated on a market day. As for the wedding, it was to take place on the king's birthday, in a huge cave decorated with leaves and large stones in place of tables. They would be given what was left from the royal banquet, and all would eat to their hearts' content. And all would sing with joy.

But the newlyweds remembered their early years in the forest and regretted the absence of their first benefactors, the seven beggars with big hearts and curious benedictions. More than anything, they wanted to see them again, just once. And lo and behold there appeared at the entrance of the cave, their very first friend, the blind beggar. "I have come to take part in your celebration and bring you my present . . ." And he began to tell them a fable: "It is not I who am blind; it is the world. Moreover, I am neither old nor young; I have not started to be. The great eagle has confirmed it to me . . ."

The next day, the second day of festivities, the second beggar made his appearance before the newlyweds, who silently had evoked his memory. This is what he told them: "I am not deaf, but my ears perceive only the absence in the world. Some mourn the absence of happiness, others rejoice in the absence of misfortune. It is to this absence I am deaf. Therein lies my strength. The population of the great city of abundance has confirmed it to me . . ."

The third day saw the arrival of the third beggar, the stutterer, who said: "I do not stutter at all. On the contrary, I am an orator by profession and avocation. But I like to express nothing but perfection. Furthermore, I am a singer, and my song contains the wisdom of wisdom. The man of true grace has confirmed it to me . . ." And he, too, began to tell them a story:

In the center of the world there is a mountain and on this mountain there is a rock and out of this rock there spouts a spring. Well, every thing has a heart. Even the world has a heart, a heart that is a complete being with a face, hands, legs, eyes and ears. And this heart is full of fire and anxious to go back to the spring, at the other end of the world, at the other side of the abyss. This heart is doubly unfortunate; the sun pursues and dries it. To survive, it contemplates the spring. But the longer it contemplates the spring, the greater its desire. Yet, as soon as it comes closer to the mountain, the peak disappears, and with it, the spring. And then its soul leaves, for it lives only in the love it feels for the spring. And if it were to stop, the whole world would be reduced to nothingness. Thus it must remain far away, on the other side, protected by a bird, its wings spread wide, condemned to look at the spring, knowing that they can never meet.

And so it went. The young couple had the joy of a reunion with the fourth beggar and the fifth and the sixth. And every day they listened to another tale. But when Rebbe Nahman reached the sixth day of the wedding week, he stopped. Later he confided to Reb Nathan that the story of the seventh beggar would be told only after the coming of the Messiah.

As for the beginning of the tale, it had been forgotten long before. As a matter of fact, what happened to the king who was crowned in his father's lifetime? Did he lose his throne? Did he succumb to sorrow, or did he succeed in safeguarding the "special gaiety" of his father?

No matter. What is important for Rebbe Nahman is the fable inside the story, the legend begotten by the fable, the dream buried inside the dream. The king matters less than the beggars, less than the possessed creatures with extraordinary gifts who reign over horses, sounds and eyes. Creatures that are kind, disinterested, understanding, ready to fly to the aid of princes lost in the forest, of princesses abducted from their castles or of old men deprived of their childhood. They all know where to look, where to go. And they tell us. As soon as they come onstage, they make us the richer for having heard their tale, for having felt their talent. There is one who knows how to listen to noise. Another who knows where day and night meet. And a third who hears the moon complaining to the sun.

A bewitched magic world, dominated and magnified by the

word. "Words can silence rifles," says Rebbe Nahman. And also: "One may give life to words with words." Words can tear down the most solid of walls. The word is the most exciting of all discoveries, the most terrifying too.

"It is written," Rebbe Nahman says, "that the Just Men obey the word of God. This should be read differently: Just Men make the word of God." A literal translation, which on the Master's lips means: Just Men compose the language with which God creates His universes. Prophets transmit the word of God, Just Men conceived it. Often in the form of tales.

Every word is a tale, they said in Bratzlav. Example: Torah. Or Talmud. Or Zohar. The tale of the Law is as important as the Law. And it is more profound than its commentaries.

Should one attribute an intention, a mystical content, to Rebbe Nahman's legends? The school of Bratzlav says yes. The king is said to be God; the unhappy prince, the people of Israel; the princess, the Shekhinah, the Torah or the Messiah. The fable is said to be nothing but a showcase. The characters and their obsessions are said to come from an ancient source, sacred and perennial. Their ephemeral and invented relationships are said to conceal a superior and timeless meaning.

Example: Once upon a time there was a prince who was forced to leave his father's palace. Months went by. Even years. He became homesick and restless. Exile was weighing heavily on him, he was losing ground, changing, closing himself to hope. Then one day a messenger brought him a letter from his father. Which only made his pain more acute, for it reminded him of his home and of what he had lost. He would have given anything to see his father again, to embrace him or touch a fringe of his royal robes. He was crying soundlessly when suddenly he pulled himself together; the thought had come to him that he need not be sad and sorry for himself—didn't he have a precious, unique letter in his hand? For the handwriting of the king reflects the will of the king and therefore *is* the king . . . Smiling, he began to kiss the letter. It was a link to his royal past and proof that his father was alive. That this letter was written and sent, meant that the king was king and that the prince, though in exile, still was prince.

The parable is clear enough: to bear exile, Israel must console itself by and in the Torah. It must retain a strong hold on the letter and the will of God.

For, said Rebbe Nahman on another occasion, every man is called upon in his own way and at his own level. God summons one man with a shout, another with a song, and a third with a whisper. As with the shepherd and the sheep: so long as the sheep do not stray too far, they can hear the shepherd's flute, who in turn can hear their bells. But as soon as they stray too far, they will no longer hear—or be heard.

Who is the shepherd if not God? Who are the sheep if not Israel? And the bell is the Torah which reminds both of the dangers of distance and separation.

Several of the Hasidic Masters of the period evidently did not greatly appreciate the symbolism of these tales. That a Rebbe should waste his time and that of his faithful inventing fables, well, one could accept that. But that his tales should speak not of saints or miracle Rebbes but of princes and shepherds, of anonymous beggars and horsemen, of sages and messengers—and not even Jewish ones at that—could only dismay them. If only he had spared their feelings by inserting a few more conventional Hasidic legends here and there, praising the powers of the Tzaddik and the faith of the followers, the rest would have aroused less resentment. But Rebbe Nahman was stubborn: he cared about his beggars and his princes.

Nor was criticism restricted to his literature. His general conduct also gave cause for disapproval. The "bad company" he was keeping, his fierce individualism, irked many. So did his pronounced taste for mystery and ambiguity, his disdain of public opinion. He was castigated for his contacts with the clandestine Frankists, who, perpetuating the thoughts and practices of their late leader, believed in redemption through evil.

Of course, in Bratzlav people knew how to explain and justify the Master's behavior. To pull a man out of the mud, the Just Man must set foot into that mud. To bring back lost souls, he must leave the comfort of his home and seek them wherever they might be. "In every man, there is something of the Messiah." In every man, in every place. The Kabbala says it, the mystics repeat it. To free mankind one must gather the sparks, all the sparks, and integrate them into the sacred flame. A Messiah who would seek to save only the Just, would not be the Messiah. The others must be considered too—they must be prepared. Miscreants need redemption more than saints. And that is the reason—we are told—why Rebbe Nahman braved so many dangers in so many inhospitable territories—alone.

An explanation that failed to placate his opponents. They had other reasons to be vexed with him. The Grandfather of Shpole, who liked him in the beginning, turned against him the day Rebbe Nahman came to settle in his town; he felt that Nahman was taunting him. Others were appalled and angered by the way he lived, which was different from their way. Though as famous as they, he refused to resemble them. He rejected what they paraded; he disparaged what they praised.

Stability and honors meant nothing to him. He surrounded himself with young people and brushed aside the old and the rich, for the same reasons. The first he dismissed as "loaded with sadness" and the second as "loaded with debts." Yet everywhere else, old men were respected for their wisdom and rich men for their generosity.

Furthermore, he prescribed solitary and silent meditation to his followers; he even advocated retreats far from the community, which seemed contrary to Hasidic tradition in which collective living and praying are indispensable to salvation. Traditional Hasidism had enounced: the self finds fulfillment by losing itself in the collective self. Rebbe Nahman said that it is better to first concentrate on the individual self by isolating it from the rest. Thus, every Bratzlaver Hasid devoted an hour a day to solitary meditation. Removed from the world and even from the Rebbe. Here it must be remembered that since the Baal Shem's time, the links between Rebbe and Hasid were presumed to be indestructible and necessary, necessary for the Rebbe to be Rebbe and the Hasid, Hasid. What right had Rebbe Nahman, great-grandson of the Baal Shem, to extol the virtues of isolation and silent song? Was he denying the importance of these links?

Sometimes he would go away for weeks, leaving his disciples confused and his family penniless. He abhorred customs and possessions, considering that they impede freedom. He moved from place to place, from discovery to discovery; he loved to travel and to live anonymously. One knows that he played with the idea of breaking away: "I shall take my wife and go far away, and from the sidelines I shall observe people and laugh about the things they do." He feared boredom more than illness, repetition more than sin. "The angels never repeat their litanies," he said, quoting the Talmud. And he went on to explain: "The angels praising the Lord are never the same; the Lord changes them every day." Rebbe Nahman's conclusion: "Whoever repeats himself displeases God and moves away from him."

Precepts and demands of such severity inevitably provoked crisis upon crisis. Living in a constant state of anxiety, Rebbe Nahman frightened those around him with his sudden, unpredictable changes of mood. Perfectly illustrating his own comparison of human thought and self-awareness with the perpetual movement of a pendulum, he alternated between highly communicative ecstasy and the blackest of depressions, toppling from *gadlut hamokhin*—exuberant frenzy—into stifling depths, *katnut hamokhin*. Gay, his gaiety knew no bounds; the story of the seven beggars is a story he told to "show you how one rejoices." Sad, he dragged the whole world into his despair.

From his window facing the marketplace, he saw one of his followers, a certain Haikel, hurrying down the street. He called to him and invited him up. "Haikel," he said, "have you seen the sky this morning?" — "No, Rebbe." — "And the street, Haikel, have you seen the street this morning?" — "Yes, Rebbe." — "And now, do you see it still?" — "Yes, Rebbe, I see it." — "Tell me what you see." — "People. Horses. Carts. Gesticulating merchants, excited peasants, men and women coming and going, that is what I see." — "Haikel, Haikel," said Rebbe Nahman, shaking his head. "In fifty years, in two times fifty years, there will be—on this very spot—a street like this one and another market similar to this one. Other carriages will bring other merchants to buy and sell other horses. But I shall no longer be here and neither shall you. So I ask you, Haikel, what's the good of running if you don't even have time to look at the sky?".

One of his disciples left us this prayer: "Master of the Universe, You know the extent of my ignorance since I don't even know if I shall die one day. Help me. Make me know, make me aware. Make me conscious of death awaiting me without any chance of escape. And that I shall be alone to confront it. Alone. Without friends, without anyone. Alone and abandoned by memories, desires and passions. Make this image penetrate me. The yellowed image of a sullen corpse."

And of man's destiny, Rebbe Nahman leaves us this description: "A man condemned to death, seated in a cart drawn by two horses who know the way, the way to the gallows. The two horses are called Day and Night, and how they run, how they gallop!"

No Rebbe before him had ever spoken of life and death in these terms. None had ever imposed such a nightmarish vision upon his disciples.

A Rebbe owed it to himself to appear strong and stable, sure of himself and his powers. A Master owed it to himself to be a solid support, readily accessible to any follower in distress.

And so, Rebbe Nahman's peers had little use for him. Some set upon him with a savagery without precedent in Jewish tradition. The Grandfather of Shpole said: "To anyone tormenting Rebbe Nahman, I promise a place in paradise." There were those who went so far as to ban him and his faithful. The text of the excommunication edict includes a series of astonishing prohibitions: "It is forbidden to marry their offspring, to share their meals, to negotiate with them. Also forbidden: to attend their services, to speak to them, to answer their questions. Also: to pity them or feel for them even a semblance of compassion..."

It must be noted that this kind of proclamation must not be taken too seriously—it wasn't then. Intramural quarrels were relatively frequent in those days, in those circles, and there was an excessive use made of bans and counterbans on all sides; nobody followed them to the letter. Still, there was a difference in this case; most of the in-fighting took place among disciples —with the Rebbes staying outside and above the scuffle. In Nahman's case, even the Rebbes were implicated. At first the conflict was ideological. The Grandfather of Shpole said: "He came three generations too early!" To which Rebbe Nahman is said to have replied proudly: "No. I came three generations too late!" Fueled by rumors and gossip peddled from court to court, the philosophical disputation degenerated into personal feud. Being in the minority, Nahman and his disciples were subjected to many humiliations, which sometimes took on the proportions of a veritable campaign of persecution.

Rebbe Nahman expressed satisfaction. The more he was attacked, the more content he claimed to be. He said: "My opponents think they do me harm; in fact, they help me enormously. My every success I owe to them."

He also said: "I need people to take issue with me. It allows me to raise myself moment by moment—at every moment I change being. If I thought that I am now where I was before, I wouldn't want to live in this world."

Nor did he remain passive. He returned every blow. And elegantly at that, never debasing himself to designating his persecutors by name. Rather than answering anyone in particular, he settled his accounts with all of them at once. For him, all his adversaries were alike—he called them "the stars" or "the celebrities." He put them in their place with a few well-chosen sentences that cracked like a whip. "These people who don't know how to behave, here they are calling themselves leaders of men!" Also: "Since Satan is overworked and cannot take care of the whole world by himself, he relies on the services of the celebrities." And again: "Incapable of fulfilling his mission, which is to kill mankind, the Angel of Death has enlisted the aid of the physicians—who demolish the body—and of the 'celebrities'—who destroy the mind." In the presence of his daughter, he ridiculed a famous Tzaddik who for nine years had prayed with fervor thinking that his Hasidim were listening in the anteroom; he thought he could hear their whispers. At the end of nine years he opened the door. A cat was scratching the floor.

He recognized but one authentic Rebbe: himself.

Pride? Yes. Egocentricity? Yes. Disconcerting traits in a Rebbe? Yes again. Ordinarily the Hasidim are the ones to sing their Master's praise. In Bratzlav, the Rebbe outdid, in this respect as in many others, his own admirers. To the latter he said: "Every one of you is a non-inhabited, non-inhabitable desert, that is why the Shekhina avoids you . . . and that is why I walk day and night. I cross the desert to make it habitable."

Another time: "If I were to reveal my wisdom, mankind could subsist without food or drink." And also: "The roads languish with desire to feel themselves trodden by men who go to see the Tzaddik. Whenever a man interrupts his journey, the roads go into mourning."

And to his faithful he said: "There are three things I have already done for you. One: I broke your vanity, even in your prayers. Two: thanks to my influence on you, your sins will be lame sins. Three: from now on, you will be able to unmask impostors, for you have tasted wine of quality."

And still another time: "The Messiah will be the one to comment on my work."

His peers were enraged by such arrogance. Nobody else mattered, nobody else deserved to be heard and admired. Once he started, nobody was spared, not even the Baal Shem: "I have no use for his secret writings; and if my grandfather wishes to see me, he knows where to find me." He considered himself an equal of the Ari Hakodesh and Rabbi Shimon Bar-Yohai. "In the world of eternal truth," he said, "they will all need me and all will want to hear what I have to say on the fleeting moment."

How is one to reconcile such pride with one's image of a Rebbe whose virtues, by definition, should include humility?

Rebbe Nahman would answer that a Tzaddik is comparable to the Creator and not to His creature. He is beyond our comprehension; we are incapable of understanding and incompetent to judge him. His standards, his criteria are not ours. He is above pride and humility. "He alone is humble who says he is and remains so," he said.

And also: "Those who admire and praise me don't know me any more than those who hate and denigrate me."

Also: "There are two erroneous concepts going around the world. The first: that a Just Man cannot make a mistake; and the second: that he cannot remain great even if he has made a mistake." The Tzaddik has the right not only to err, but even to boast of it. He has the right not only to appear vain, but even to be vain. "Actually," he remarked one day, not altogether seriously, "I possess all the attributes, all the qualities of the Messiah. Except that he will come—I won't."

Let us stop here. Rebbe Nahman had a sense of humor. The key to his enigma? His ability to laugh. To better understand its full import, we must study attentively an event that marked his life: his journey to the Holy Land.

The journey of a visionary, a pilgrimage worthy of the teller and of his tales. Abounding in unpredictable, incredible adven-

tures that succeed one another at dazzling speed, it is a race toward the unknown, toward nothingness.

The Egypt campaign is at its height; Napoleon wants Jerusalem. Once again war is pounding at the gates of the Holy Land. That is the time Rebbe Nahman, accompanied by an anonymous disciple, chooses for his visit. In vain do people try to reason with him, to dissuade him; he seems drawn by an irresistible force. Communications with Palestine are infrequent, dangerous? Never mind. He cannot stay still, his impatience turns into suffering. And yet, a while later, hardly has his foot touched holy ground than he has had enough; he wants to retrace his steps and return home without losing another minute . . .

As reconstituted by Reb Nathan, this true epic is among the strangest and most beautiful the Bratzlaver Rebbe ever told.

Both journeys, going and coming, are strewn with mishaps lying in wait for him. All the obstacles in the world seem to accumulate in his path. He attracts danger, he flirts with disaster. No trial is spared him. No sooner does he take to the sea, than a storm breaks out; no sooner does he decide to rest in a certain town, than the plague makes its entrance. Everything frightens him, everything happens to him. In the Holy Land a young Turk spends hours staring at him silently before challenging him to a duel. Elsewhere he is suspected of being a spy in Napoleon's service. He escapes the epidemic that ravages Tiberias only to find himself in beleaguered Akko. He climbs the walls of a fortress only to awake on board a warship where sailors try to teach him the use of guns. The sea is his enemy, but so is land. Hunted, persecuted, he moves from town to town, from prison to prison. Trial follows trial as he appears everywhere at the most inopportune moment and attracts the attention of the most merciless men. He even succeeds in falling into the hands of pirates. In the words of Reb Nathan: ". . . our Master and his companion fell prey to many mishaps in every town and every village, but the Holy One, may He be blessed, came to their aid and protected them from plague and sword, from hunger and thirst and captivity, and they returned home in peace."

But let us go back for a moment. During his first passage through Istanbul, Nahman—if one is to believe his biographer —behaved in a more than strange manner: "Like a good-for-nothing, he wandered around barefoot, without belt or hat, his clothes turned inside out showing their lining, and indulging in all kinds of childish pranks. He went through the marketplace like those urchins who run and gesticulate and snicker among the merchants; he threw himself into make-believe fights, just like a boy playing war against the Frenchman, using real war tactics."

Moreover: Rebbe Zeev, a venerated Tzaddik then living in Istanbul, had welcomed him with respect and honors. In return, Rebbe Nahman mocked him openly: "On Shabbat, while Rebbe Zeev was praying on the bimah as behooves a saintly man, Rebbe Nahman was serenely partaking of his meal. Just as he pretended to be asleep when Rebbe Zeev, surrounded by his followers, sat down at the table singing."

And also: to the many people who assailed him with questions, Nahman refused to disclose who he was and where he came from. One day he claimed to be Cohen; the next, he chose to be Levi or Israel. As though he deliberately wished to cover his tracks and arouse anger. He flew into a rage over nothing and humiliated all who approached him, provoking people into beating and insulting him. In the end they doubted his reason and thus fulfilled his profound wish.

Yes, he did want people to look at him askance. That is why

he changed his identity every day, and his disguise as well. He wanted to be *another*. Comedian, impostor, clown. Anything but Rebbe. Anything but Tzaddik. Hence his disconcerting behavior of simpleton, of escaped lunatic. He wanted people to see him as a poor vagrant forsaken by God and forgotten by man, adrift, coming from nowhere and going nowhere.

Why this game? To what end? To acquire what knowledge of what subject? These grotesque movements, these borrowed masks, what could they mean? Why was the Rebbe posing as a madman in Istanbul's public square?

From Bratzlav comes the following explanation: it was only a ruse. To deceive Rebbe Zeev? Not at all. To fool Satan, who was endeavoring to thwart Nahman's project, the way he had done with the Baal Shem. By disguising himself, by playing the carefree, careless madman, Nahman succeeded in outwitting the enemy and pursuing his journey.

As for me, I would rather not apply to Rebbe Nahman the Hasidic standards implied by this hypothesis. I lean toward an explanation that places the accent on his laughter.

Laughter occupies an astonishingly important place in his work. Here and there, one meets a man who laughs and does nothing else. Also a landscape that laughs. And a man who hears time, and everything he touches, roar with laughter—and hears nothing else.

Laughter that springs from lucid and desperate awareness, a mirthless laughter, laughter of protest against the absurdities of existence, a laughter of revolt against a universe where man, whatever he may do, is condemned in advance. A laughter of compassion for man who cannot escape the ambiguity of his condition and of his faith. To blindly submit to God, without questioning the meaning of this submission, would be to diminish Him. To want to understand Him would be to reduce His intentions, His vision to the level of ours. How then can man take himself seriously? Revolt is not a solution, neither is submission. Remains laughter, metaphysical laughter. "Hell exists," said Rebbe Nahman, "not in the other world, but here. Only no one dares to admit it." Also: "God, I pity You, yes, I pity You! You should not have invented the world, created man. They cause You nothing but trouble." And also: "When the Messiah will come, nothing will change, except that people will be ashamed of their foolishness."

Rebbe Nahman knew how to laugh, wanted to laugh. Mostly about himself. He played with the urchins to mock the Rebbe inside him. He played war to show the absurdity of wars. He posed as a madman to deride reason and appearances, and as a penniless nomad to underline the grotesque aspect of possessions. He played the clown to rid himself of the last vestiges of pride that persisted inside him. All this he could not do where he was known. That is why, at home, he went to the other extreme: he disarmed his pride by pushing it to its limits, by exaggerating his own importance in all areas, in all spheres. By conferring upon himself unlikely dimensions, he deliberately made himself into a caricature. To provoke laughter. And certainly also to exasperate his adversaries. These adversaries he used as a pretext, as a front. He aimed higher. Pride, his falsest and most successful mask, allowed him to laugh louder yet.

In one of his tales we read: "Once upon a time there was a country that encompassed all the countries of the world. And in that country, there was a town that incorporated all the towns of the country; and in that town there was a street in which were gathered all the streets of the town; and on that street there was a house that sheltered all the houses of the street; and in that house there was a room, and in that room there was a man, and that man personified all men of all countries, and that man laughed and laughed—no one had ever laughed like that before."

Who is that man? The Creator laughing at His creation? Man sending Him back His laughter as an echo, or perhaps as a challenge? Will we ever know?

Describing Rebbe Nahman on his deathbed, Reb Nathan speaks of "a kind of smile on his face" while he whispered: "And here there approaches an immense and terrible mountain. And I am not sure whether we are walking toward it or whether it is coming toward us." Taking notice of his sobbing faithful, he threw them this sentence: "My flame will glow till the end of time. Don't cry, I shall not forsake you." His Hasidim took his words as a promise and gave them a literal interpretation. As a result, they decided that he would have no successor. For them, the Tzaddik of Bratzlav remains alive. When they speak of him, they use the present tense. That is why they are surnamed "the dead Hasidim," or, "the Hasidim of the Dead."

In my town, there were none. I met some of them later in Jerusalem, where their *shtibel* is a center of attraction for those who like stories and songs of a particular quality, marked with nostalgia.

If you should ever go there, you will see Rebbe Nahman's armchair. Dismantled by his Hasidim before they left the Soviet Union, this armchair crossed many borders, piece by piece, before landing in Jerusalem. Not one part is missing. Not one Hasid of this strange brotherhood died on the way. The old watchman of the Rebbe's tomb, a Russian convert to Judaism and Bratzlaver Hasidism, benefited from the same miraculous protection: eluding a thousand dangers, he arrived unscathed in Israel.

Many are the followers of Nahman who to this day travel as far as Oman to commemorate the date of his death by meditating at his grave and reciting psalms.

But my first Hasid of Bratzlav, I met *over there*, in the kingdom of night. He repeated to anyone willing to listen the words of his Rebbe, the only Rebbe to survive himself: "For the love of heaven, Jews, do not despair!" He prayed and told stories. I have forgotten his name. But not his voice. I can hear it still: "Do you know when Rebbe Nahman was really alone? When he was not alone. That is what he said. He could scream silently in the midst of a crowd and his cry was heard in the far corners of the earth . . . Like us here. We are never alone. And yet, we have never been so alone. Nor so silent. Only our cry has not been heard."

He also liked to quote another of Rebbe Nahman's thoughts: "Two men separated by space and time can nevertheless take part in an exchange. One asks a question and the other, elsewhere and later, asks another, unaware that his question is an answer to the first."

One night someone asked him: "What would your Rebbe Nahman say to the thousands of men, women and children who live and die here in one place, in one night? Who could answer their question?" There was silence, and then a whispered sigh escaped his painfully twisted mouth: "Who says that we are question? And what if our death were answer?"

●   ●   ●

To conclude, let us retell one of Rebbe Nahman's tales, a tale which, like all those he left behind, is both of this moment and timeless:

"Once upon a time there was a king who knew that the next harvest would be cursed. Whosoever would eat from it would go mad. And so he ordered an enormous granary built and stored there all that remained from the last crop. He entrusted the key to his friend and this is what he told him: 'When my subjects and their king will have been struck with madness, you alone will have the right to enter the storehouse and eat uncontaminated food. Thus you will escape the malediction. But in exchange, your mission will be to cover the earth, going from country to country, from town to town, from one street to the other, from one man to the other, telling tales, ours—and you will shout, you will shout with all your might: Good people, do not forget! What is at stake is your life, your survival! Do not forget, do not forget!' "

And the friend in question could not help but obey. He entered the legend with fiery shadows. And this legend encompasses all other legends. It is haunted by a creature that reigns over all others, and this creature is laughing, laughing and crying, laughing and singing, laughing and dreaming, laughing so as not to forget that he is alone and that the king is his friend, his friend gone mad—but the king, is he laughing too? That is the question that contains all the others and gives life to its own tale, always the same tale, the tale of a king and of his friend separated by madness and united by laughter, fire and night.

THE SCHOOL
OF PSHISKHE

O NCE UPON A TIME, a time when there
were still Jews in Cracow, Jews who were not afraid to dream at
night, there lived in that city a man named Eizik, son of Yekel.

Devout, poor and naïve to boot, he found life more than he
could handle; night and day he worried: there was rent to be
paid, and the butcher and the tutor; there were daughters to
clothe and marry. And time was getting shorter and shorter.

Eizik, poor Eizik, what was he to do? What was there to do
except worry? He prayed. Day after day, at every service and
even between services, in the synagogue and in the street and
at home, he begged the Lord to remember His debt-ridden and
tormented servant who could go on no longer. To no avail. God
seemed not to listen. Nevertheless, our Eizik continued to send
Him his requests; it made him neither less pious nor less poor.

And then, one night, he had a strange dream: he saw himself swept away into a distant kingdom, inside its capital, under
a bridge, in the shadow of an immense palace. And a voice told
him: "This is Prague, this is the Vltava and over there, the
palace of the kings. Now look and look well, for under this
bridge, at the spot where you are standing, there is a treasure;
it is waiting for you, it is yours. Your problems are resolved."

In the morning Eizik mocked himself: dreams are very pleasant, they don't cost anything, but they don't serve any purpose either. He dismissed the entire matter from his thoughts. But that night, as soon as he closed his eyes, the same vision took hold of his mind: the capital, the palace, the bridge. And the same voice asking: "Do you want to be rich, or would you rather keep your worries?"

What nonsense, Eizik thought. Go to Prague? What an idea! He had no desire to go there; he didn't know anyone there. And furthermore, it was far. And expensive. And he had no money. If he did, he would know what to do with it. The rent, the butcher, the tutor. Well, between dreams and prayers, Eizik would choose the prayers; in fact, there's even one to exorcise dreams.

Of course, the tale does not end there. Next evening, for the third time, Eizik heard the voice: "What? You haven't left yet?"

Annoyed more than intrigued, he decided to put an end to all this foolishness; he decided to obey. Or at least go through the motions. And so he started the journey, on foot. A few weeks later he arrived in Prague, famished and exhausted. He recognized the river, the bridge, the palace; it was starting all over: he was dreaming again! But no, it was not a dream. This really is strange, he thought. There was a certain spot under the bridge that looked oddly familiar. What if I tried? What do I have to lose? I should dig a hole, take a look. But careful, not so fast. The bridge is guarded, the soldiers must not become suspicious. Eizik prowled the area indecisively, trying to summon his courage, until he was noticed and arrested. The captain of the guards accused him of spying. Too frightened to invent a story, he told the truth. The dreams, the worries, the long walk begun in Cracow, the memory and the voice of that memory. He was convinced, Eizik, that the officer would call him a liar and order him shot. And so, he thought he was dreaming again when the dangerous captain burst out laughing. He laughed so hard that tears ran down his cheeks: "No, is that really why you came from so far away? You Jews are even more stupid than I thought! Now look at me, such as you see me here, if I were as stupid as you, if I too listened to voices, do you know where I would be at this very minute? In Cracow! Yes, you heard me correctly. Imagine that for weeks and weeks, there was that voice at night telling me: 'There is a treasure waiting for you at the house of a Cracow Jew named Eizik, son of Yekel! Yes, under the stove!' Naturally, half the Jews there are called Eizik and the other half Yekel! And they all have stoves! Can you see me going from house to house, tearing down all the stoves, searching for a nonexistent treasure?"

Of course Eizik was not punished. Of course he hurried back home, moved the stove and, of course, he found the promised treasure. He paid his debts, married his daughters, and as a token of his gratitude, built a synagogue that bears his name: Eizik, son of Yekel, a poor and pious Jew who remained pious even when he was no longer poor.

Like most Hasidic tales and parables, this one has more than one author. It has at least two: Nahman of Bratzlav and Simha-Bunam of Pshiskhe. Rebbe Nahman replaced Prague with Vienna, and said: "The treasure is at home but the knowledge of it is in Vienna." Rebbe Bunam liked to repeat it every time he accepted a new disciple: "Remember Eizik, son of

Yekel; the treasure, the one that is yours, is to be found only in yourself and nowhere else, not even in your Tzaddik."

An intelligent and unintimidated student could have asked the Master an embarrassing question: Did the treasure in fact belong to Eizik, to Eizik alone? What about the captain of the Royal Guard? What about his share? But then Rebbe Bunam could have answered—as some of his followers do—that this tale illustrates the importance of dreams and not treasures. And also that two people may have the same dream, and that one man's dream may become another's reality.

However, on Rebbe Bunam's lips—and in the tradition of Pshiskhe—the parable had a more precise meaning, more directly linked to the problems and preoccupations of his times: man may attain perfection without a Tzaddik—and knowledge of the absolute may be acquired only from within, never from the outside. He who thinks he must go somewhere—anywhere —to find someone—anyone—to help him discover truth, had better stay home. Alone. That is the message of Pshiskhe . . .

Pshiskhe: a small *shtetl* in Poland, where the Baal Shem's Hasidism, born of fervor and contemplation, experienced a renaissance under the sign of anger and anxiety.

We are at the beginning of the nineteenth century, right in the middle of the Napoleonic wars. Churning in blood and fury, Europe is turning itself upside down. Frontiers, thrones, loyalties, and systems change overnight. The earth trembles. Nations discover new passions, liberating but deadly. History moves and bursts into flames. And the blood flows. Priests change their styles, kings their thrones. Patriotism, romanticism, nationalism—so many words newly come to life

—prove themselves powerful enough to drive men to breaking their visible and invisible chains.

In the rabbinical courts, these events are endowed with a messianic dimension. One speaks of Gog and Magog, of their gigantic, apocalyptic war. The Hasidim are more and more convinced that the real battles are being waged not by emperors and generals but by Tzaddikim, who, unfortunately, are to be found on both sides. If only they could mobilize their powers in support of the same emperor, the same army, the war would come to an end and redemption would be near.

To hasten that event, three great Masters combined their efforts: the Seer of Lublin, the Maggid of Kozhenitz and Rebbe Mendl of Riminov. They drew up a plan of action. Which failed. And the three conspirators, punished by God, died before the year's end.

An undeserved punishment. The three Masters had meant well. The Jews needed the Messiah, perhaps more than ever. Society as a whole was moving forward in all areas, and as usual, left the Jews excluded from the family of nations.

In Eastern Europe especially the Jewish people needed redemption. Persecuted by the Poles, fanatic anti-Semites, the Jews felt just as threatened by Austrian liberals. A young Talmudist had a choice of military service on the one side and emancipation—that is, secular education, free-thinking morality; in short: atheism—on the other. Add to this the various economic measures that made the Jews' life miserable everywhere and especially in the more isolated townships, where they were forced to live like outlaws, dependent on the good graces of the curate and the whims of the landowner. They were hard hit with taxes, ransoms and laws enacted for the sole purpose of keeping them in a state of perpetual humiliation. Drained by the pogroms and false messianic hopes, they had reached the end of their endurance; they were on the brink of despair. Without Hasidism, they would have resigned themselves to perdition.

Let us recall: What was Hasidism in the beginning? One man—and then many—who knew how to restore to the individual a sense of sacredness and confidence in his ties with the community.

To the isolated Jew, living as an outcast, the Rebbe said: "Your experience is not meaningless, it is part of an entity that takes it into account. Know that eternity is present in every moment; that every table may become altar and every man high priest. Know that there is more than one path leading to God, but that the surest goes through joy and not through tears. Know that God does not like suffering and sadness and least of all those that you deliberately inflict upon yourself. God is not that complicated; He is not jealous of your happiness nor of the kindness you show to others. On the contrary: the road to God goes through man. The sleeping child, the mother caressing him, the old man listening to the rustling of the leaves: God is close to each of them, in each of them God is present."

At that moment in Jewish history, it was a powerful, irresistible message. By putting the accent on friendship and love, on impulse rather than on asceticism, erudition and the strict observance of the Law, Hasidism brought back to the fold large numbers of Jews who, faltering under the weight of their burden, came close to conceding defeat.

That is why, in less than fifty years, the movement swept over these parts of Europe. The Baal Shem's companions and the disciples of the Maggid had succeeded beyond their hopes:

the spark kindled between Kossov and Kitev, here it was, illuminating the sky of the night, the faces of the night, over there, beyond the horizon. Not one community that did not bear its mark. There were three major centers of Hasidism: in Ukraine, in White Russia and in Poland. And the movement was proud of its philosophers such as Shneur-Zalmen of Ladi, of its defenders such as Levi-Yitzhak of Berditchev, of its preachers, storytellers, heroes and saints. Their opponents tried to stem their rapid-fire progress. In vain. Hasidism triumphed because it made itself the advocate of a new Judaism, a smiling Judaism as it were, reconciling man with the idea of happiness. It was, in fact, a resounding call to joy.

Hasidism succeeded also because it created Rebbes who symbolized it. The Rebbe: confessor, master, guide and above all: father. He does not invoke lightning; he is gentle, kind. As the shepherd of an ill-starred flock, he defends it against the iniquities of man and heaven. Thanks to him, those who have been tried may catch their breath and no longer feel forsaken by the God of Israel and the people of Israel.

As a result, it was suddenly easy to be a Hasid, to be a Jew. One knew where to go, what to do and say, what blessing to request and how to obtain it. The Rebbe had all the answers. By taking upon himself the suffering of his followers and of the entire Jewish people, he alleviated that suffering. Did he really accomplish miracles? Yes or no, yes and no; it didn't matter. What was miraculous was that the Jew suddenly discovered within himself the desire and strength to sing and celebrate life at a time when the sky was darkening with crimson clouds and the threat was becoming closer and more defined. Thanks to the Rebbe, the Hasid could persevere and gradually regain self-confidence; he could claim his place in time and in hope. Within the confines of exile, he built his temple and his kingdom and lived in them. Yes, the Baal Shem had won his battle. The Jew, in his oppression, had freed himself from the inside; he was going to remain Jewish. The Maggid of Mezeritch, too, had reached his mark; he had opened the way, the others had but to follow. Every Rebbe now had his disciples; every Tzaddik, his faithful.

The most striking triumph of all was in Poland, where the opposition lacked men of the Gaon of Vilna's stature. They had no one strong enough to challenge the early Masters. They tried here and there, in Cracow, in Brodi, in Lemberg, to organize campaigns; some fanatics even excommunicated "the new sect." To no avail. People shrugged their shoulders and followed the call, the song of Hasidism.

Which was fine, but had its disadvantages. The victories were too swift. Without resistance, a new movement risks weakening from within. Intellectually and socially. And sometimes even morally.

In Lithuania, where recruiters and followers had to fight for every position, every new member, Hasidism benefited. Opposition stimulates and enriches; it adds depth to thought and mind. To challenge an Avraham Katznelenbogen or a Gaon of Vilna was no trifling matter. Forced into a defensive position by the attacks and accusations of the most prestigious rabbis, and into accepting confrontations on a level that precluded subterfuge, the leaders of Hasidism had to remain in a constant state of alert and fight every abatement in intensity, every tendency toward vulgarization.

In White Russia and, to a certain extent, in the Ukraine, the movement also succeeded, often for the same reasons, in forming a considerable intellectual elite.

In Poland it developed the other way; Hasidism was in control and became, very quickly, very popular, in the best and the worst sense of the word. It was an establishment, respected, respectable, with its own set of laws and customs, celebrations and prohibitions. And here the Mitnagdim were the ones to be harassed, for they were in the minority; the privileges went to the Hasidim. Who, on the strictly Jewish level, felt secure.

Thus, it was easy success, rather than adversity, that loomed as the obstacle. Hasidism's objectives changed even though its essence remained the same. The role of the Rebbe evolved. From trusted friend and adviser, the Master turned into miracle-maker and creator of effects, easy effects. Unlike the Baal Shem, who brought man closer to God and His creation, the new Tzaddikim presumed to mediate between individual and destiny. Result: Jews neglected their studies and craved glitter and luxury. After all, the rest was up to the Tzaddik; let him accomplish miracles, since that was his vocation. Result: the movement lost in quality what it gained in numbers; form replaced content, fame replaced purity.

This was particularly true in small communities, centered around Tzaddikim of secondary rank. So much so that, in Riminov, Rebbe Mendl protested against a growing influx of miracle-makers: "Gather a thousand worshippers around a piece of wood, tell them to shout that there is a miracle, and the piece of wood will start to produce them, your miracles!"

Another danger: some of the Masters were beginning to found dynasties, a practice totally alien to early Hasidism. The Baal Shem had said that every man is a potential Baal Shem, spiritual values not being hereditary. Thus he had been succeeded by the Maggid of Mezeritch rather than by his son Rebbe Tzvi-Hersh. And so it had been with the Maggid; he was succeeded by his disciples. The seat of Pinhas of Koretz remained empty. And at the death of Mendl of Riminov, his friend and servant was called to replace him. But traditions had changed: in Lublin the son of the Seer was treated as a crown prince. Elsewhere the Hasidim were deep in quarrels over prerogatives and influence.

What had happened to the adventure started in the Carpathian Mountains one generation earlier, an adventure that had required those who participated to reject ornaments and external symbols of distinction? In the beginning, Hasidism had represented a promise, a commitment, a vow of authenticity that every man renewed every day; it had all been simple then, and filled with grace. And now? On one side there was the Rebbe and on the other his admirers, different and therefore separated from him. The Baal Shem's message, the Baal Shem's song, could this be what they were, all they were? Having swept away rigid institutions with a gust of fresh air, was Hasidism in turn becoming just another institution? With its guides and guided, its princes and servants? With a Rebbe who was important and a Hasid who was not? Was this Hasidism as conceived and lived by the Baal Shem?

It is against this background that one must enter Pshiskhe, if one wishes to understand what took place in Pshiskhe and why and at whose behest.

Three rebels. Yaakov-Yitzhak, called the "Jew," Simha-Bunam, and Menahem-Mendl: the school of Pshiskhe

All three had spent time with the Seer, in Lublin. The youngest, Menahem-Mendl, had been the first to leave; the oldest, Yaakov-Yitzhak, the last and most reluctant.

A rabbi's son, Yaakov-Yitzhak had an ordinary and studious childhood. Even as an adolescent he stood out among his comrades because of his erudition, and also because of his reserve, his shyness, his melancholy ways. He married young. His wife, a baker's daughter, did not bring him happiness; in fact, she made him rather unhappy. (He once told the story of an angel who was punished for being too harsh with man; he was condemned to live on earth and marry.) Was that why he never laughed? He was obsessed by the idea of death, particularly in his youth. Rumor has it that he wanted to die. Fortunately, he met Moshe-Leib of Sassov and Avraham Yehoshua Heschel of Apt, who took a liking to him and won him over to the movement. Shortly afterward he left for Lublin on their advice, and there became the favorite disciple of the Seer, who for many years accorded him special consideration. His knowledge, his memory and analytical gifts were legendary. In Lublin, anyone who was not content with the scraps of wisdom the Seer distributed to the crowd, came to study with Yaakov-Yitzhak. Eventually, the Seer ordered him to preside at his own table, his own court. But the disciple succeeded too well, mostly with the younger intellectuals. Confronted with the intrigues and calumniations resulting from his success in the Seer's circle, he left Lublin and went to settle in Pshiskhe, determined but with a heart heavy with remorse.

Remember: what the Rebbe of Pshiskhe did to the Seer, the Seer had done to his Master, Elimelekh of Lizensk. The two Masters and the two disciples had many traits in common; even their relationships had evolved in the same manner. In Hasidism, history repeats itself. The Seer had never blamed Reb Elimelekh; the Rebbe of Pshiskhe never showed any resentment toward the Seer and considered himself his disciple to the end. Nor did Yaakov-Yitzhak of Pshiskhe ever concede that there had been a break between him and the Seer. And yet, as we shall see, it was indeed a break; the disciple had veered from the Master's course, until in the end they frequently opposed one another.

The names they acquired are revealing. The Seer—the visionary, the prophet—saw himself as an exceptional, superior being, whereas his disciple, choosing anonymity, rejected his very name and identity.

Why was the latter called the "Jew"? The texts of Pshiskhe offer many explanations. Since his name—Yaahov-Yitzhak —was the same as the Seer's, he did not want to use it, out of respect for his Master. Another: he had of the Jew—Jewish man—so noble an image, that all his life he aspired to be worthy of it. Still another: out of modesty, he never gave himself credit for his scholarly innovations, but instead attributed them to an anonymous "Jew," which, after all, he was. Also this one: going from fair to fair, following the Baal Shem's example, he came upon the Prophet Elijah disguised as a peasant. And he stared at Elijah so intently that he moved the prophet to anger. "Jew," he burst out, "since you know, why do you talk?" Actually, the "Jew" hadn't done any talking at all, but he kept the name so as not to refute the prophet.

However, there is another, more plausible hypothesis which sees in the nickname a choice, a conscious or subconscious act of protest; there were already too many Tzaddikim, too many Masters. Therefore, he preferred to define himself simply as Jew, a man like any other. All his sayings and fables reflect his aversion to the excesses of the crowned elite. Just like the Baal Shem Tov, he placed man—and not his title-bedecked leader —at the center of creation; like the Baal Shem Tov, he distrusted the establishment.

The "Jew" saw himself as the Baal Shem's disciple. His taking up residence in Pshiskhe was meant as a return to Medzebozh. Like the movement's founder, he had begun his vocation by tutoring small children; like him, he dressed as did the village men and, like him, roamed from place to place, in search of experiences and encounters. If the Baal Shem was the Master of the Name, he became the Master of the Surname.

His departure from Lublin provoked an outcry. His enemies spread rumors that there had been a personal feud between Master and disciple. It was not true. He regularly went back to Lublin from Pshiskhe; he did everything possible to avoid secession. He remained faithful to the person of his Master—though not to his views—even after the Seer rejected him in the end, asking him never to return.

Ideologically, the break was interpreted as a warning signal. Beware! anyone indulging in excessive comfort runs the risk of succumbing to illusion! His key word was *teshuva*—which means both repentance and return. Return to God and to the sources. It was time to rethink values and concepts, to take stock and start anew.

It was the first conflict, the first revolution, inside Hasidism. Never before had young purists dared question what was established, and put their elders, their parents and the entire movement on trial. These rebels, guided by the Masters who formed the school of Pshiskhe, acted out of idealism; therefore no official sanctions were ever taken against them.

Which is surprising, since the "Jew" and his two successors had rather unkind things to say about the Hasidic establishment. Of the Seer, the "Jew" said that he was a great teacher *in spite of* his miraculous powers. Miracles, he would say, are not difficult to perform; it is more difficult to be a Jew. He also said: "I think that I could make the Messiah come, but these so-called Tzaddikim, with their lack of humility, are hindering me." To his friend Bunam, he complained: "I am sad. When I think of the history of our people, I despair. Though there are many dark spots in our history, God has always given us leaders, guides to help us pull through. We have had Moses. Then Joshua. The judges, the kings, the prophets. Then the Tanaim, the Amoraim, the Gaonim, the Kabbalists. Lately we have had the Baal Shem, the Maggid. And they have helped us. Now I realize that with the passing years, the light is waning; darkness is closing in on us. What will happen to our people?"

His disciple, Menahem-Mendl of Kotzk, echoed his words in a still more alarming way: "We are going farther and farther away from the light at Sinai, yet we do not come any closer to the light of the Messiah!"

"When the Messiah will come," said the Pshiskher Jew, "all the Rebbes and their followers will run to welcome him. But he, the Messiah, will turn them away, saying: 'Take your leaders, take them out of my sight!' Then the Hasidim will come back—alone."

Characteristic, too, his praise of an unknown blacksmith: "Whatever I know, whatever I possess, I owe to him. He was my neighbor when as a newlywed I lived in my father-in-law's house. The blacksmith would rise before me and wake me each day when he started pounding his anvil. One morning I said to myself: 'If he works so hard and gets up so early just for money, can I do less to enrich my soul?' The next day I was up before him. The blacksmith took it badly; he thought: 'If this green-horn who does nothing and needs nothing, sacrifices his sleep for nonsense, how can I, who have a family to feed, stay in bed?' Next day he rose even earlier. This tacit competition was a boon to me; every day I studied a little more, and thanks to it, thanks to the blacksmith, I acquired everything I possess."

Yet, to the question "What did you learn in Lublin?" he replied cryptically: "To fall asleep without difficulty."

Clearly: in Pshiskhe one preferred blacksmiths who plied their trade to Tzaddikim who plied theirs; namely, who exaggerated.

But then, why did the "Jew" accept the title, the crown of Rebbe? Because he was compelled to? Possibly. For it was customary among the Hasidim of the period to elect a leader among themselves. And once elected, whether he liked it or not, he had to accept their decision. This happened in the case of Rebbe Bunam, Rebbe Mendl and, much earlier, the Great Maggid of Mezeritch. The Jew of Pshiskhe was in no position to refuse. In his case, the Seer himself had made the decision. But the real reason was more subtle: the "Jew" accepted because he was convinced that he would not be a Rebbe like the others. And he was right.

He refused honors, privileges, rejected flatterers and overly servile admirers. He did not claim to impose his will upon heaven. In contrast to his peers, he did not discuss their day-to-day problems with his callers; he had no desire to solve them in their stead. His primary goal was to restore a climate of spirituality to the movement. The practical problems and worries of the individual were not his concern; he left those for God to handle. His task was to save the movement, which was losing ground, relying more and more on artifice. Fervor and prayer were given precedence over study and knowledge. The external signs of Hasidism were assuming too much importance; what was needed was a return to inner life. Masters and disciples were too pleased with each other and themselves; what they needed was a jolt.

His faithful disciple and companion, Rebbe Peretz, accompanied him to the forest one day. Listening to the birds' chirping, Peretz said: "I would like to understand what they are saying." — "And what you, yourself, are saying, you already understand?" was the Master's retort.

Another time: "One talks and talks of paradise; one does this and that to earn one's share of it. As for me, I would gladly give up mine to anyone who will offer me a drink!"

One Shabbat, after the third meal, he averted his face, and in a voice echoing his distress, addressed his guests: "Tomorrow you will be going back to work—and you work hard, I know. If I asked you why you work so hard, you would tell me that it is not for your sake, but for the sake of your children; that you wish them to grow up to be good Jews, loving man and fearing God. Yes, that is what you would tell me. That is what, for thousands of years, man has been saying in every language. Man works and works, never for himself but always for his child, who in turn will work for his ... As for me, I am waiting ..." He paused, before continuing even more sadly: "I am waiting for the true child."

Whom did he mean? The Messiah? Perhaps. But it is also possible he simply meant the father who would admit in all honesty that he was working for himself. For the "Jew" despised nothing as much as insincerity, as feigned sincerity.

To tear down his disciples' defenses, to jolt them out of their patterns of behavior, he would resort to shock tactics. The student who had chosen silence to purify language, he ordered to attain his goal by speaking. An emancipated Jew came to discuss theology with him. Without a word the "Jew" took off his hat and placed it on the man's head. The visitor began to stammer and found nothing further to discuss.

To him, what mattered was the effort spent rather than the result obtained. He said: "The Just Man loses at night what he has won during the day; to earn it again the next day, he must work just as hard as the day before." Nothing is given and everything remains to be taken, it was thought in Pshiskhe. Better to raise the profane to the level of the sacred, than to lower, to debase, the sacred to the level of the profane. Better to bring man to the Messiah, than to bring the Messiah to man. Not easy? Never mind. What was important was to know. To know that the goal was not yet reached. To believe that by saying the truth one has told the truth is a delusion. To believe that one can lie to man without lying to God is another. "The seal of God is truth," said the Jew of Pshiskhe, "for it precludes any possibility of forgery; a counterfeited truth is no longer the truth." A truth that is broken or divided is not truth. In Pshiskhe, nothing was lower than hypocrisy. "I think," said Reb Bunam, "that I could reform any sinner—except a liar." And the worst liar, according to Pshiskhe, is the one who lies to himself.

Pshiskhe's militancy understandably antagonized many of the more traditional Hasidic strongholds. There were those Rebbes who felt themselves personally attacked, and therefore started their own offensive. They tried to move the debate from the ideological to the personal level.

Pshiskhe became the subject of gossip and defamation within the Hasidic universe. People said anything they could think of to discredit the "Jew" and those who rallied around him. They went so far as to call a meeting of noted Tzaddikim—including Naftali-Hersh of Ropshitz—to put the new school on trial. The "Jew" was accused of lacking respect for the Seer, of wanting to take over his throne, of introducing dangerous ideas and reforms into the movement, of shifting services (in Pshiskhe, there were no set hours for prayers), of inciting the young against their fathers and against the Masters they followed.

In vain did the "Jew" implore the great figures of Hasidism, the Maggid of Kozhenitz, Mendl of Riminov, to use their authority to make peace between Pshiskhe and Lublin; the conflict continued.

Even more so since Pshiskhe had its own uncompromising fanatics who were opposed to any compromise or reconciliation. They believed in *azut dikdusha,* the virtue of saintly arrogance; and they used it. In-fights are always the most bitter, and this one was no exception. Each side accused the other of deviating; worse: betraying the vision and doctrine of the Baal Shem. Pshiskhe claimed that the others had renounced their Hasidic ties. Lublin returned the compliment.

Still, as long as the "Jew" was alive, the quarrels were somehow kept under control. Faithful to the Seer to the very end, he did not want to cause him pain, he did not want his image to be marred. Though he was slandered and dishonored by the intrigues of the Lublin court, the "Jew" refused to turn against his old Master. Had he lived longer, he might have averted the final break. But he died young, at the height of his powers. What contributed to this premature death? The disappointment of being repudiated by the Master he loved? The death-urge of his youth? He who was so strong physically—he could "crack five nuts with one hand"—suddenly took ill. Nothing is known of the specific nature of his ailment or the circumstances surrounding his death; his final days are shrouded in mystery. All one knows is that he died at forty-eight, in 1818. Precisely one hundred years before the end of the First World War. His second successor, Menahem-Mendl of Kotzk, went into seclusion in 1839, a century before the second conflagration involving entire peoples and continents.

Between the two, there was Rebbe Bunam, who in his own way was no less interesting than they. Interesting because he resembled neither. He was wise—profoundly wise—whereas they were extremists. They looked their part; not he. He didn't even look like a Rebbe. He dressed differently; in the manner of the "Germans," meaning: according to what was fashionable in the cities. Everything about him was elegant: his dress, his walk, his ways. Despite his Talmudic training and erudition, he earned his livelihood first as a wood merchant and later as a pharmacist. He is the "Merchant of Danzig" and the "Pharmacist of Pshiskhe" referred to in Hasidic literature. Names he himself invented—and kept to the end.

He was known as a traveler and lover of the picturesque, the bizarre. On his journeys through big cities, on business, he would visit strange places and meet . . . even stranger people. He played chess and cards; he debated with the emancipated and the atheists, the so-called enlightened; he played the guitar. Nor did he mind going to theatres and taverns—he enjoyed their atmosphere. Worse, he was even known to go to cabarets occasionally, for the purpose, of course, of bringing sinners back into the fold and unto the road toward salvation.

And yet, at the death of the "Jew," the orphaned disciples did not turn to one of his sons, but to the Merchant of Danzig. Why to him? Because he was more qualified than the others? Or because he had been the "Jew's" faithful companion? And his friend as well? Because he had followed him from Lublin? Or because in Pshiskhe the way was already being cleared for Menahem-Mendl of Kotzk? Could Rebbe Bunam have been nothing more, nothing else but a transition, a human bridge between two volcanoes? Or was this but another way for Pshiskhe to defy the establishment by saying: "Look! Our

Rebbe is a pharmacist and not the son of a famous Tzaddik! He doesn't even look like a Rebbe! See how appearances can be misleading!"

There could be truth in each of these hypotheses. The fact remains that Rebbe Bunam himself was surprised by his election: he neither sought nor wanted it; he was ... drafted. Even after he was nominated, he refused to "receive" Hasidim and behave like a Rebbe. Yet, in retrospect, he seems to have been the best candidate possible, and certainly the most qualified. He may have been less inspired than the other two, but he was their equal in inspiring others. And that, after all, is the secret and strength of the true Rebbe: to know how to inspire.

One of his disciples explained Rebbe Bunam's greatness: "Remember what happened to Elisha? Elisha was a simple shepherd who spoke to his cattle, not to humans. Then one day he met the Prophet Elijah and from then on he was another person: his soul had caught fire. Rebbe Bunam? You want to know about Rebbe Bunam? Simple. No matter how hardened, how icy your soul may be, at his touch it will burst into flames."

No wonder that countless young Hasidim came running to Pshiskhe. Just as they were to do later in Kotzk, newlyweds abandoned their wives, sons forsook their parents. Drawn by the call of a renewed Hasidism, they came with nothing but their thirst for fervor, truth and revolt. Pshiskhe became the magnet that attracted the intellectuals and the idealists, just as Kotzk did a few years later. Pshiskhe symbolized the courage to question, to try the experiment again by stripping away its blemishes and burdens. Hasidism in Pshiskhe was young and daring again, its enthusiasm was vital enough to overcome all obstacles and expose all taboos.

So strong was Pshiskhe's appeal to the young that the conservative leaders of the movement, determined to stem the current, decided to react publicly. The wedding in Ostila, famous in Hasidic literature, provided the opportunity. In the presence of some two hundred Tzaddikim, headed by the venerable Rebbe of Apt, Pshiskhe was put on trial. Much has been written about the wedding and the verbal joust that became more important than the wedding. Accusers and defenders outdid each other in eloquence, erudition and comparative Hasidic ideology. After hearing the arguments for and against, Avraham Yehoshua Heschel of Apt refused to condemn Pshiskhe. A wise decision: because of it, Hasidism can take its place among the rare movements that permit deviation and rebellion within. Pshiskhe, though opposed to traditional Hasidism, remained inside the movement.

What was the key message or idea of Pshiskhe? That the greatness and tragedy of man's condition lie in the very ambiguity of that condition. Man must believe that the entire universe was created for him alone, but also, that he is less than dust. Man is at the same time the corpse he will be and the carrier of life that he is, symbolizing, as long as he breathes, his own immortality. Man is vulnerable and weak—too weak to know the truth—yet he is also omnipotent, for his quest is its own ultimate justification.

Naturally, there are nuances; the "Jew" meant man when he spoke of the Jew; Rebbe Bunam meant the Jew when he spoke of man. Both men, and their successor in Kotzk even more, wanted man to believe that it is within his means to draw strength from the despair that is his lot. Since man is alone, he helps his fellow man and thereby breaks his own solitude.

Each of the three expressed himself in his own way: the "Jew" preferred sayings; Rebbe Bunam liked parables; and Menahem-Mendl of Kotzk chose silence.

Also: The "Jew" died young. The Kotzker Rebbe died alone, terribly alone. Rebbe Bunam died blind. Hearing his wife's sobbing, Rebbe Bunam said to her: "Why do you cry? Are you afraid? I am not. All my life I have done nothing but learn how to die."

Rebbe Bunam was a magnificent storyteller. Every one of his tales is a mixture of humor, melancholy and wisdom.

A funny story: "One day I felt like telling a story, or rather, I felt a story in me that wanted to be told. Except that I was afraid; it was what you would call a daring story. I felt that if I told it, my most ardent followers would stop calling me Rebbe. As for my enemies, they would know why they hated me. Yet I could not repress the story; it wanted to be told. So I told it. And to my great surprise, even my enemies began to admire me."

An image: "Sometimes it seems to me that every man is a solitary tree in the midst of the desert; and God has no one else in the whole world just as man has no one but God in the whole world."

A parable: A prince bought a pure-bred stallion, and to protect him from thieves, locked him into a stable built of stone. Its gate was bolted and guarded by an armed watchman. One night when he could not fall asleep, the prince went for a walk. He passed in front of the stable and thought that the watchman was looking perplexed. "Hey," he called to him, "what's on your mind?" — "There is this question that is bothering me: when you sink a nail into the wall, where does the mortar go?"

— "An important question," said the prince. "You do well to think about it." And he went home and back to bed. An hour later he still could not fall asleep. So he went down again, out to the yard and the watchman, who sat there with his head propped in his hands, meditating. "What now," said the prince, "what are you thinking about now?" — "Well, you see, it's like this: when you eat a bagel, what happens to the hole?" — "A profound question," said the prince. "You do well to concern yourself with it." And he went back to his quarters. He came down a third time, and for the third time the watchman seemed in a quandary. "Another question?" asked the prince. "Yes— and this is it: I tell myself that the stable is here, the walls are here and I am here—but the stallion, where in the world is he?"

A saying: "If God offered me the possibility of changing places with Abraham, I would refuse. God needs someone like Abraham, not a blind old fool like Bunam."

Usually, Rebbe Bunam explained his parables while making it clear that their true and deeper meaning defied explanation. "The secret of the secret cannot be divulged," he said.

A story: Once upon a time, there was a prince cleverer than most. One evening he stumbled upon a drunkard in the street and decided to teach him a lesson he would not forget. He had his men take him to the castle and put him to bed. On a chair next to his bed he had them lay out the robes of a bishop. And nothing else. Next morning, when the drunkard awoke, he couldn't remember where or who he was. The servants helped him put on his priestly robes and addressed him with the respect due a bishop. Which was fine, except that he didn't remember ever having been a bishop. Still, after a while, the first doubt crossed his mind: I may think that I am a drunken peasant who is dressed like a bishop, but what if it's the opposite? What if I am a bishop who thinks he is a drunken peasant? He decided to wait and see. For the moment he had nothing to lose. Only when the servants brought him a gold-encrusted prayer book, did he get frightened: now he would know the truth! If I can read, I am the bishop, he thought. If I can't, I am the drunkard. He opened the book and—couldn't read. Panic-stricken, he was on the verge of confessing everything, when a new doubt entered his mind: perhaps he was a bishop after all! The fact that he could not read was no real proof. After all, what guarantee was there that other bishops could?

The moral of the story? Man must not trust appearances. That is one of the dominant themes in the haunted universe of Pshiskhe. Another recurrent theme: that of the missed opportunity, the frustrated impulse. Man could—but does not—want. Or he wants only when it is too late. Then, and that is the worst of all maledictions, he forgets that he can.

Another tale, the saddest of all: Wanting to punish his son, the king sends him into distant exile. Suffering from hunger and cold, the prince waits to be recalled. The years go by; he has lost the very strength to wait for the royal pardon. Then, one day, the king sends him an emissary with full powers to grant the prince's every desire and wish. His message delivered, the emissary waits for the prince's instructions. Who asks him for a piece of bread and a warm coat, nothing else. He has forgotten that he is prince and that he could return to his father's palace.

In Pshiskhe, where there was no limit on the demands made upon oneself, man immunized man against oblivion.

.   .   .

"Oblivion is at the root of exile the way memory is at the root of redemption," the Baal Shem had said. But in Pshiskhe, ultimate redemption was of only marginal interest. One thought about the coming of the Messiah but one did nothing to bring about its advent prematurely. One worked on oneself rather than on God. The individual's goal was not to make the Messiah come but to go toward him, to make earth and the heart of man livable for man. The wait was going to be long? Never mind. There were enough things to be done in Pshiskhe; there was no hurry. Besides, the idea of messianic times was an alarming one. Reb Bunam gives this description of them: "In those days, the summer will be without heat, the winter without frost, the wise will have forgotten their wisdom and the Hasidim their fervor."

His successor went further. Menahem-Mendl of Kotzk understood that all these signs, all these evils could occur without necessarily heralding redemption. Thence his anguish: Could it be that there is no link between creation and Creator, between the eyes and what they see, between the dread of flight and that of reunion? Could it be that man is incapable of speaking of his suffering even to Him who inflicts it?

That is what Pshiskhe represents to the storyteller of today: gates opening upon the past and throwing an oppressive light upon the present, the eternal present, the treasure that makes us run from Cracow to Prague and from there to Rizhin and Sighet, when in fact it is nowhere to be found. For one among us—a Hasid of Pshiskhe? a child in Wizsnitz?—has already found and lost it. But he has not forgotten it, not yet.

MENAHEM-MENDL
OF KOTZK

Somewhere in central Europe, beyond the horizon, between Warsaw and Lublin, there was once upon a time a small village whose name made people dream and shiver: Kotzk.

The year is 1839.

It is winter. And snowing. Nestling close to one another, huts and cabins slowly vanish into the soundless night. The sky hangs low over deserted streets. The village is holding its breath; seen from the outside, it is a ghost village.

And yet, in a rustic wooden lodge, the most passionate, the most demanding disciples of Hasidism are readying themselves, on this Friday night, for the first of the Shabbat meals.

In the House of Study, seated around the rectangular table covered with the traditional white tablecloth, the Hasidim do not feel the biting cold. Their eyes are upon a tense, forbidding man: the Rebbe. They wait, as is their custom, for him to sanctify the wine and the bread. But the Rebbe's thoughts are elsewhere; he is in no hurry. Where is he? What is he doing? What could be on his mind on this peaceful evening that is like any other? He is struggling with his breath like a sick man; his eyes, staring at the candles before him, reflect an ancient though nameless anguish. The assembled guests are silent, oppressed; something about him makes them uneasy, frightens them. They sense an oncoming event: who knows what walls of what fortresses the Rebbe is about to overturn to clear the way for what storms? The silence is heavy with foreboding. No one dares move. Or even glance at his neighbor for reassurance. They wait for time to be torn open, for thoughts to be unveiled. And then the Rebbe—in his fifties but older-looking—his face fierce and terrifying, throws back his head and . . .

This is where the tale ends. Something happened; nobody knows what. One hundred and thirty years after the event, the mystery remains. Rather than testify for history, or at least chronicle, the witnesses seem to have vowed never to speak of anything related to the incident. None broke what seems to have been a conspiracy of silence to keep a secret whose meaning likely escaped them.

All we know is that secret there was. Something out of the ordinary happened in Kotzk that night; something incomprehensible, unspeakable. Hasidim refer to it still today, but only in carefully shrouded terms and only among themselves. Some speak of it as of an eclipse, others as of an ailment of obscure origins. Some suggest that on that evening the Rebbe chose, for reasons known to him alone, to surprise heaven and earth by refusing to serve as their link and justification.

Among the more or less fantastic versions circulating among Hasidim and their opponents, let us mention a few, if only to throw some light on the stage, the setting and, most of all, the central character.

After an interminable silence, says a Jewish Polish novelist, the Rebbe violated the Shabbat laws by reaching out to extinguish the Shabbat candles.

A second image: emerging from his meditation, the Rebbe

is said to have suddenly cried out against the scandal of the adversities seemingly inherent in Jewish history. He is said to have shouted: "Am I to conclude that *let Din velet Dayan,* that it is a history without judge and without justice?"

The third version is even more realistic: having learned of the new pogroms that were laying waste the Jewish communities of Poland and Russia, the Rebbe reportedly flew into a rage and pounded the table with his fist, roaring: "I demand that justice be done, I demand that the Supreme Legislator obey his own Laws!" As it happened, the passage in Scriptures to be read on that particular Shabbat related Esau's bartering away his rights as first-born to Jacob. And so he continued: "It is written in the Talmud that Esau later shed three tears, so much did he regret the bargain. And it is for these three tears that we continue to pay with our blood throughout our long exile. Well, how long are we to go on paying? Will it never end?" When he noticed the expressions of horror in the audience, he burst out with redoubled anger: "Why are you staring at me like that? Are you afraid? Of what? Of whom? I find this fear of yours repulsive, disgusting! You are nothing but liars, flatterers, cowards! Go away and leave me, do you hear me, I wish to be alone!"

Which one of these three versions—there are others—corresponds to truth? Again, nobody knows. However, one does know that all have the same ending: the Rebbe fainted and had to be carried to his quarters. Where he remained twenty years. Until his death.

After the incident, weeks and months went by during which he admitted no visitors, and showed no interest in what was happening outside. He followed services by peering through two holes drilled in his door for the purpose. When called to the Torah, he appeared muffled in his ritual shawl, disheveled and glassy-eyed, sowing panic as he passed. He hardly ate or slept, and refused to let himself be touched by doctors or comforted by friends. He no longer taught, nor did he participate in any work. He cared neither to give nor to receive. He showed no interest in any of the disciples who continued to flock to him from everywhere, drawn by the troubling mask he showed them. Sometimes, at night, one could see him hunched over the table, staring into space, a shadow among the sickly, timorous shadows cast by the yellowish flame of a flickering candle.

The Rebbe: Menahem-Mendl of Kotzk. Or, more simply: Mendl of Kotzk. The Master-against-his-will, the angry saint, the divine rebel. Among the thousands of Hasidic leaders, great and small, from the Baal Shem's time to the Holocaust, he is undeniably the most disconcerting, mysterious figure of all. Also the most tragic.

As with the others, there is a disparity between the man and his legend. But in his case, it is the personality that stands out, that marks. In his case, reality surpasses imagination. If there is in Hasidism a Master greater than the image he projects, an image undoubtedly rearranged and embellished, it is he.

The stories one tells about him, and they are many, barely situate him and throw but a feeble light on his personality; they do no more than hint. Every fragment contains him, but he is more than the sum of all fragments. He is the flame that draws the sparks, a free and powerful flame that rises and carries the world along. The more one talks about him, the deeper his mystery looms. Alive, people dared not look him in the face; dead, but strong in his legend, here he is still, judging us as if he were our contemporary.

He left no portrait, no personal possessions. It is as though he never existed. Whatever we know about him—his habits, his boundless projects, his sudden fits of anger, his calls and his silences—we learn from the rare companions and disciples whose presence he tolerated. It is said that he set his meditations to paper but that he destroyed the pages as quickly as he covered them; he burned at night what he wrote during the day.

One says of him what one said of his two predecessors: that he wished to condense all there is to say but cannot be said about man, his destiny and his passage on earth . . . into a single page. This page, by itself, was to constitute a work entitled: "The Book of Man." He wrote it every day only to tear it up as night fell.

"Do you know why I don't publish anything?" he asked a visitor. "I'll tell you why. Who would read me? Not the scientists, not the scholars; they know more than I do. To wish to read me, a man would have to feel that he knows less than I. Who might that be? A poor villager who works hard all week. When would he have the time to open a book? On Shabbat. When, at what time? Not on Friday night; he would be too tired. Saturday morning? Reserved for services. Following which, he comes home at midday, enjoys his meal, rushes through the customary songs and goes to lie down on his sofa, at peace with himself. Finally, he has a chance to glance at a book. He takes mine; he opens it. But he has eaten too much; he feels heavy. He gets drowsier by the minute; he falls asleep, and here is my volume falling from his hands. And is it for him —for that—that I should publish a book?"

On his deathbed he was still obsessed by the fear that his writings might survive him. Anxiously he questioned his old friend Yitzhak-Meir of Ger: "Have you searched everywhere? In all the hiding places? Are you sure that everything is burned? That everything is ashes?"

There remains only his oral teaching. And his legend.

A legend of fear and trembling, lacking the joy that is a characteristic of Hasidism. One listens to it and feels bitten, scorched by a black and living fire shielded by a night without dawn.

Unlike other Hasidic tales, those of Kotzk, about Kotzk, rarely make one smile. They do not amuse, they do not appease, they trouble the teller as much as the listener; both come away with the same uneasiness, almost a remorse at being alive, at feeling—or not feeling—trapped in a universe doomed to falsehood and decay. "It is written," he said, "that God looked over His work and found that it was good. Not I. I am more particular, more demanding than He. The world such as it is, I have no use for, except to blow my nose into it." To a disciple who complained about the imperfections and gaps in creation, he replied: "Could you do better? If so, what are you waiting for? Start working!" But he himself felt it was hardly worth the effort. "The world," he said, "deserves not even a groan." To him, it was inconceivable that man could see himself other than as a stranger—to his time, to his surroundings, a stranger to his fate. He said: "I don't belong here; this is not my place."

The tales, the sayings of the Kotzker Rebbe are easy to identify; impossible to mistake them for another's. They bear his mark, his scar. While those attributed to other Masters often seem interchangeable, his belong only to him. Indeed, they spring from a world which is a world all his own and in which one senses contained violence, dark and brutal powers, and the obsessions and conflicts of a man struggling with what negates yet attracts him, with what exalts yet mows him down: death, faith and the absolute. It is a world where man, despairing of his condition, deliberately, lucidly, chooses to probe deeply into his despair to seek, to hunt down a possibility of victory, however imprecise, however obscured by night.

Mendl of Kotzk wants man to be thirsty for truth, for the absolute, and never mind if he never reaches his goal and never mind if truth blinds and kills whoever discovers it, if the absolute takes revenge on whoever glimpses it. Faith? Faith is not all. There is the faith of the weak man who deceives himself. For Mendl of Kotzk, "Thou shalt not steal" meant: "Thou shalt not steal from thyself; not deceive thyself."

He notices a young student lost in thought, and asks him: "Do you remember the Talmud's advice: 'Whoever meets a wicked man needs only to lead him to the House of Study.' Ha! Did you actually think that by bringing him here, your task would be done? It isn't so. Every place has its wicked; the market and the House of Study each has its tempter. He is not that easily disposed of."

Faith then is not an absolute refuge. Even truth, the world of truth, is vulnerable to corruption. But then, where lies the solution? In total rejection of compromise. It may not be within man's power to find truth, but it is up to him to reject lies, hypocrisy and cheating. And to uproot the thief he clandestinely carries inside him. As far as Mendl of Kotzk is concerned, all the sins of the world weigh less than the conceit born of self-deception. Man does not lower himself by his failures but by the alibis he invokes. Rather perish than mutilate the truth; that is Kotzk. It is the merciless challenge of man looking squarely at himself. Who does not believe he is making a great gift to God when he performs a good deed. And who observes the Law for its own sake rather than to please anyone, not even

God. Result: whereas elsewhere one learns to serve God publicly and betray him in private, in Kotzk it was, if one may say so, the opposite. People claimed that it was easier to catch any other Hasid in flagrant sin than to catch a Hasid of Kotzk in flagrant obedience to the Torah.

A disciple tells him his woes: "I come from Rizhin. There, everything is simple, everything is clear. I prayed and I knew I was praying; I studied and I knew I was studying. Here in Kotzk everything is mixed up, confused; I suffer from it, Rebbe. Terribly. I am lost. Please help me so I can pray and study as before. Please help me to stop suffering." The Rebbe peers at his disciple in tears and asks: "And who ever told you that God is interested in your studies and your prayers? And what if He preferred your tears and your suffering?"

At this level, man is forced to choose between two extremes: reaching out to the stars or escaping toward death; savage truth or destructive illusion; ultimate reward or irrevocable malediction. It is one or the other; there can be no middle ground. Said the Rebbe of Kotzk: "The midde of the road is for horses." For man, the road to God is not a royal way but a solitary path situated very high or very low: "I stand with one foot in seventh heaven and with the other in the depths of the abyss." Compromise is for the weak; concessions for the cowards. "What I ask of you?" he told his disciples before going into seclusion. "Be strong! If that implies resisting fate, then you shall have to resist fate. If, in your search for truth, you must stand up to God, well, so be it."

One Simhat Torah eve, the Rebbe watched his faithful dance holding the scrolls of the Law. "That's not the way to dance!" he commented, looking angry. To please him, they started over again, this time with more fire. "No," he said, annoyed, "that's not how one dances." After several more failures, the Hasidim froze into an attitude of waiting. And the Rebbe exploded: "Imagine yourselves on a mountain peak, on a razor's edge, and now: dance, dance, I tell you!"

Difficult? No matter! Who says that to be a man means to keep one's balance? Who says that to be a Jew is to accept oneself and submit? "Let the heart fly into pieces," he roared, "let the shoulders come unhinged, let heaven and earth collapse, but man must not stray from his path!" Obstacles are unimportant. On the contrary, the more of them, the greater the merits of trying. Little does it matter if, going from discovery to discovery, one comes up against an unknown God, a God who does not compromise; one must continue one's quest, and nothing else counts. Thus it is not really surprising that Mendl of Kotzk should have praised the unsuspected qualities of a Pharaoh; he knew, that one, how to defy even God! "What a fellow," the Rebbe marveled, "he didn't cringe as soon as the blows started falling; he persevered!" What is important is to accept the challenge, to fight the battle; what is important is to choose an opponent more powerful than oneself.

Jacob did it. He fought the angel all night. Victorious, he sent him away at dawn. That was a mistake. He should have guessed the angel would come back more than once, in more than one disguise, perhaps even disguised as Jacob. Except that Jacob, in the meantime, had become Israel, who one night dared confront God and associate his mystery and name to His.

All his life Mendl of Kotzk continued this struggle with the angel and night. Alone. Alone against man, alone against heaven, against generations of dead ancestors and ancestral traditions that weigh on every memory.

That is why, in all the tales relating to him, what is stressed is the question rather than the answer, the thirst rather than what quenches it, the quest rather than the goal. What counts is the action, and never mind if it is desperate. What counts is what is missing, and never mind if it is never found. For the Rebbe of Kotzk, man is the lonely fighter who, beyond a certain point, expects nothing further from anybody: "The Messiah will come and there will be nobody left to redeem."

Surely, the exemplary wrath of Kotzk, born in Pshiskhe, went against the course charted by the Baal Shem and his companions. The song of the Baal Shem was stifled in Kotzk, transformed into a call of warning and despair.

Like the "Jew," like Rebbe Bunam, Mendl of Kotzk is a Rebbe unlike other Rebbes, opposed to other Rebbes. The goal he sets for himself and the means he uses turn him into a magnet and his school into a hotbed of agitation.

He rebels against anything that is established and revered, he strikes out at all the taboos of the movement. In his opinion, one speaks too much of love and perfection; one uses words that are too big too often. The most pure, the most beautiful concepts, for being repeated too frequently and too smugly, lose their meaning, their vigor, their weight of silence. He, Mendl of Kotzk, decides to save Hasidism by redefining its objectives.

Ambitious, arrogant, he wishes to go beyond his limits; he considers himself the Baal Shem's equal. "The Baal Shem never said there would never be greater than he!" Nor is he content merely to spread his teachings. He has nothing but contempt for those who take the beaten paths, for those who yield to habit; to imitate another or oneself is equally debasing. His ambition? To open unexplored roads, become a forerunner, a pioneer himself, throw over customs, social conventions, unmask the cheaters, review the progress already made and expose its traps and its illusions. Failing this, the movement would flounder and lose its substance.

He turns impudence into a virtue. Blind faith irritates him as much as mediocrity. "In hell," he says, "one prays better than in paradise." For the worshippers crowding the Tzaddikim's anterooms, he has nothing but contempt. "Ten Just Men," he says, "were able to save Sodom, the city of sin. But ten sages would not enlighten an assembly of fools. Worse: a thousand fools would turn a sage into just another fool." Appeals to caution have no effect on him; there is no recalling him to order; he is not to be intimidated. Pressure incites him only to further action. The more he is attacked, the less vulnerable he considers himself. Awe-inspiring, contemptuous of love, he pushes ahead, no risk too great for him. And too bad for those who fail to understand him.

And so, with him, the sanctuary is set ablaze. Flames that perhaps are heralding other conflagrations on two continents. A Europe fragmented by the lightning of wars, wonders about its future and rejects its past. Nations change their faces, their destinies. Revolution in France, revolution in America. Napoleon reshapes the universe, kings fall, others extend their powers. History stirs and makes men shudder; it even makes them think. Thus Kotzk is neither coincidence nor anomaly. The Rebbe's groping search, filled with existential anguish, progresses in a solitude culminating in delirium. For him, anxiety and solitude recover their rights in Hasidism.

Who is Menahem-Mendl of Kotzk? Born in Goray in 1787, this glazier's son marries at fourteen, receiving a dowry of one thousand ducats. A year later, unhappy with his orderly, predictable life, he breaks with his father—an ardent and notorious adversary of Hasidism—and joins the Seer of Lublin, whom he eventually leaves to follow the Jew of Pshiskhe.

"In my town, long ago, there was an old man who told stories; I loved to listen to him. He would tell what he liked and what he knew, and I would remember what I needed. That is how I became a Hasid," Rebbe Mendl reminisced.

At the death of the "Jew," he remains with the "Jew"'s spiritual heir, Rebbe Bunam, and eventually succeeds him. He is then forty years old. At first, he resides in Tomashov and then in Kotzk, where at the age of seventy-two, almost blind, he departs as though disgusted with life.

A life lived under the sign of revolt against his father, then against his first Master and, in the end, against his own admirers. With the passing years, his rebellion gains in audacity and intensity; he aims it at all of creation and sometimes even beyond.

Already in Lublin and in Pshiskhe he is conspicuous among the other disciples, constantly swimming against the current. He is nicknamed "Mendl the Dark," so somber, withdrawn and gruff is he. He never takes part in the collective activities of the court. He speaks little, prefers not to be spoken to. His knowledge and prestige as a Talmudic scholar are such that he is left to do as he pleases. He is free to live in seclusion. He is considered strange, but the opinions of others leave him indifferent. Cloistered within himself, his contacts with the outer world are rare. Compliments bore him, social amenities exasperate him. Pious tears and noisy lamentations arouse in him a disdain he is not loath to display. The Seer, who keeps an eye on his favorite students, finds it necessary to have a word with him. He starts by commending him for his work, for his dedication, for the progress made in all areas, then he enjoins him to be more sociable: "Be careful, Mendl, your path leads to melancholy; it is dangerous, it is unhealthy!" Mendl is outraged. That the Seer should give him a lecture, all right. But that he should compliment him or speak of risks is unacceptable. Does he think Mendl can be impressed or frightened? Mendl has no use for a Master who protects his disciples instead of lacerating their souls! He moves on to Pshiskhe without taking his leave from the Seer.

In Pshiskhe, where he has come to find himself a Master, he also meets companions: Rebbe Bunam, Rebbe Henokh, Rebbe Hersh, and Rebbe Yitzhak-Meir, future Rebbe of Ger.

This is how the latter came to take a liking to him: it was on New Year. During *Minha* services. The whole assembly was praying with fervor. Only Mendl, standing motionless in a corner by himself, prayed without moving his lips. This reticence, this implicit refusal, attracted Yitzhak-Meir's attention. He became, and remained, Mendl's friend.

Mendl, a frantic non-conformist, has his own way of saying his prayers. His way is to remain silent. He is the only one to refuse when asked to recite psalms for the dying Seer. "The cry one holds back is more powerful," he said later. Also: "Certain experiences may be transmitted by language, others—more profound—by silence; and then there are those that cannot be transmitted, not even by silence." Never mind. Who says that experiences are made to be shared? They must be lived. That's all. And who says that truth is made to be revealed? It must be sought. That's all. Assuming it is concealed in melancholy, is that any reason to seek elsewhere?

Here we are back at the key word of Kotzk: truth. The best-kept secret in creation, it counts for more than life and for as much as faith, and perhaps more than faith. In Kotzk, truth

becomes obsession. It takes precedence over everything, shifts
everything around. Even prayer, even study. And certainly joy,
ecstasy and peace of mind. Man was created not to know happiness but truth. To discover it, one must start anew; everything must be reviewed. Man, chosen by God, must choose Him
in turn. All ready-made answers, all seemingly unalterable certainties serve only to provide a good conscience to those who
like to sleep and live peaceably. To avoid spending a lifetime
tracking down truth, one pretends to have found it. But, so one
says in Kotzk, revelation itself, once it has become a habit and
a front, becomes suspect. The Rebbe would trade all the riches
of the world for one grain of truth. Riches? What riches?
The word makes him sick. So does the sight of money. Everything that shines nauseates him. Honors? He despises them for
others and even more for himself. Thus it is not surprising that
the very functions of rabbi provoke in him a fierce resistance;
he is too much of an individualist to accept the notion that a
man, whatever his title, could resolve the problems of his fellow
man. You cannot live, you cannot fulfill yourself by proxy; no
one can seek in your place. The thief in you is underhanded, he
hides inside you, he *is* you; you must dig deep to root him out.
No one will dig in your place. No one will lay claim to truth in
your stead, in your name. No one will be your intermediary,
just as you cannot be another's. Your relationship with truth is
your affair and no one else's. And so, Mendl the Dark refuses
the position of rabbi. He sees himself rather in the role of anti-
rabbi. But even his resistance has limits; in spite of his protests,
Mendl finally gives in to his companions' wishes; after Rebbe
Bunam's death he ascends the throne.

More precisely: his friend Yitzhak-Meir gives up the crown
in his favor. The Hasidim would have preferred Yitzhak-Meir,
who is closer to them, more accessible. They respect Mendl the

Dark but he confuses them. They do not understand him nor do they understand the uneasiness they feel in his presence.

The two friends spent a whole night in a tavern, discussing, trying to convince one another to take charge of Pshiskhe's souls and thus assure the school's continuity. No part of their conversation has come down to us; chronicle has recorded none of their arguments. All that is known is the outcome.

Named to succeed Rebbe Bunam, the young Menahem-Mendl settled down in Tomashov for two years, undoubtedly the two most beautiful years of his life; everything still seemed possible to him.

Bursting with enthusiasm, energy and boundless imagination, he turned his court into a laboratory for new ideas, into an experimental center for a renascent Hasidism. People said: "The spark kindled in Pshiskhe is now ablaze in Tomashov." The flowery speakers, the miracle-makers, were to be found elsewhere. Tomashov was dominated by a far more exalted need; that of knowledge, of truth. The Rebbe did not deal in the supernatural, nor did he promise paradise and pardon; his faithful did not lapse into beatitude in his presence. Together, in one common impulse, they explored, they sought; Hasidism had become an adventure once more.

Young people were flocking to Tomashov from every corner of the land; it was becoming the capital of youth. At times one could witness odd scenes: mothers, abandoned wives, besieging the Rebbe's house, begging him to return their sons or husbands to them. To no avail. Every being, said the Rebbe, owes his life to three authors: father, mother and God. And God's share in man has priority. Besides, even if he had relented, his students would have refused to leave him. One does not leave a place, a community where every moment is an experience; one does not leave a man who lets you share in something unique: a liberation of the universe in terms of the individual.

In the battle of the generations, the Rebbe came out the winner. The young followed him. Enchanted, they asked nothing more than that he let them link their destiny to his. The parents wept and stormed in vain; the sons remained in Tomashov. With the Rebbe who, like an older brother, almost like a comrade, instilled in them his ideas and thirst for renewal. They danced, they sang, they studied together; they shared joys and discoveries, failures and longings; they lived in a kind of kibbutz. Joint assets, communal kitchen. Equality extended even to the House of Study; nobody enjoyed special rights or privileges. Often the Rebbe would walk the fields and forests with them, and there, in direct contact with nature, he would speak to them of his projects, his ambitions. And, following the Baal Shem's example, he would share his dreams with them.

Dreams to make one's head spin; romantic perhaps, but surely poignant. Captivating, unreal dreams, turning around an obsession: if he were to succeed in recruiting a spiritual elite, he could change the world.

It was in Tomashov that these theories began to take shape. Let them bring him ten courageous men, strong and pure—free of all lies—and they would tame, they would master fate. "If I had a few companions [three hundred?] ready to climb the roof of the universe with me, coiffed with sauerkraut and girded with straw, to shout that God is God, victory would be certain!"

A striking image, more fiery than poetic, which shows his peculiar concept of his relations with the absolute and with his allies. From the latter he demanded total allegiance. *Emuna*, on his lips, meant not faith but loyalty. Whoever wished to join him had to forget all terrestrial concerns and bonds. One cannot at the same time covet the pleasures of the senses and carve oneself a place in the beyond; one cannot at the same time crave the essence and the accessory, the being and the superfluous. The absolute tolerates no fragmentation, no rival.

Tomashov took the place of Pshiskhe, Mezeritch and Medzebozh. Whoever entered, stayed. Stimulated to the limits of his capacity, the Hasid felt himself to be privileged. "Know this," wrote Yitzhak-Meir to Henokh of Alexander, "just as there was lightning and thunder at Sinai, there now is lightning in Tomashov." And Rebbe Mendl, without false modesty, made this remark to his intimates: "I shall tell you who I am. There was the Great Maggid of Mezeritch, there was Shmelke of Nikolsburg, there was Elimelekh of Lizensk, there was the Seer of Lublin, there was the holy 'Jew' of Pshiskhe and there was Rebbe Bunam. I am the seventh, the sum, the substance: I am Shabbat."

But the prelude of Tomashov came to an abrupt end. The local rabbi had his misgivings about the feverish activities of the Hasidim; they eluded his authority. The relationship soon became poisoned. Rebbe Mendl decided it would be best to move. To Kotzk, a small town—population: 1652 Jews, 1270 Christians. In no time at all it became famous.

Why Kotzk? Because there the Rebbe had a devoted admirer in the person of the local rabbi—which simplified matters greatly. Legend, however, provides a more picturesque explanation: the Rebbe and his faithful were wandering from village to village, nowhere finding a hospitable place to settle down. In Kotzk they were welcomed by flying stones. "Well now, this is a good omen," the Rebbe is said to have commented, "here at least the people are not indifferent."

• • •

During the next ten years the Rebbe worked on himself and his disciples as though they were metaphysical raw material, elaborating his concept of man projected into the universe between God and death.

He said: "God sends souls down to earth and then brings them back by making them climb ladders. Thence men's preoccupation: souls upon souls, all in pursuit of ladders. Some give up; they throw themselves toward heaven, and fall. Never mind. They will try again."

Falls did not discourage him. He seemed drawn to, hypnotized by, the abyss. The idea that he might find an answer, that he might glimpse a certainty at the end of his voyage, only increased his anguish.

To his friend Yitzhak-Mcir, he said: "When he cursed the serpent, God condemned him to slither on the ground and feed on dust. What a strange malediction! The serpent will never be hungry, is that a malediction? Yes, it is, and a dreadful one at that!"

A need that could be satisfied, a thirst that could be quenched were of no interest to him. A God whose intentions he would understand could not suit him. To Rebbe Yaakov of Radzimin, who told him that the purpose of man was to work for the perfection of his soul, he replied disdainfully: "No, no, it wouldn't be worth it. The purpose of man is to raise the sky." To raise it until it becomes unattainable. Rather look at a sky way up high, lost in the clouds, than see it in the mud, at your feet.

Easier said than done. Stated the Kotzker: "It is easier to extract Israel from exile than exile from Israel." The problem is that men want to live in this world as much as in the other.

"Since God is God, let Him come down from His throne. Let him visit the huts, the hearts in distress. There are children to be fed, to be clothed, there is the wife to take care of, the creditor to placate; there is the head that is bursting."

Confronted with worshippers who saw in him a rabbi like all the others, here to help them carry their burdens, the Rebbe cried out: "What do they want from me? Why do they harass me? How am I to make them understand that it is not my task to fill their stomachs and appease their sleep?"

A man began to sob: "I am a widower and poor; I have seven hungry children at home." — The Rebbe shook his head: "What do you want me to do? Comfort you? I won't do it. It's too much for me. Ask God: let Him comfort you."

"Pray for me," a Hasid begged him. "Things are going badly, I need help; intercede on my behalf." — And the Rebbe answered him harshly: "Are you too sick to say your own prayers?" — "I don't know how." — "What? You don't know? *That* is your true problem!" And he dismissed him.

One night he awakened his friend Hersh Tomashover. There he stood, a candle in his hand, saying: "Look, here in my heart there is such pain, such terrible pain, and they, out there, think of nothing else but haunting me with their foolishness and foibles."

The old intimacy and comradery between Master and disciples that had existed in Tomashov is gone. Disillusioned and bitter, the Rebbe detaches himself more and more from his followers. The extraordinary Rebbe is burdened with disciples who are ordinary Hasidim. They irritate him and he shows it. He becomes impatient, intolerant, more unrelenting than ever.

These people, riveted to their bodies, annoy him; he thinks they do it on purpose. Their timorous servility makes him nasty. He sees everything as being petty, derisive: "Whoever believes in miracles is an imbecile, whoever does not is an atheist," he says.

Impossible to do the right thing. He states something and promptly denies it. Not content to revel in paradox, he drives it to paroxysm. He demands erudition but does not hesitate to mock it; he stresses the importance of preparations for services, but services themselves are dispatched almost absent-mindedly. The external signs of joy repel him, but he does not appreciate those who think to "buy" God with tears. He aspires to wrest man from his all too human condition, yet at the same time he declares that sanctity itself must be human. Man who addresses God in a familiar way incurs His displeasure as much as man who treats Him as a stranger.

Of course, the more strangely he behaves, the more his prestige grows. This displeases him. In the other Hasidic courts he is criticized, denounced; he rejoices. He finds his disciples' praise much more embarrassing. He feels stifled, he would like to be free, break his chains, but his faithful are in his way. He is convinced of it: they are holding him back. He would give anything to see them go. Let them go, let them turn against him. But they do not. On the contrary, their numbers increase. This living knot, tense with contradictions, clearly is in touch with invisible forces. They admire him, they would lift him to the clouds. Fortunately, he is on his guard. He gives free rein to his rage: "Long ago, in my youth, when I could still see inside myself, all these people did not dare approach this closely!" The more he screams, the more they crowd his doorstep. He wins men by the fear he inspires.

From now on, in Kotzk, one lives in awe and fear. And in

misery as well. (Letter from the Rebbe to his friend Yitzhak-Meir: "If you have had no news from us, it is because we lack the money for stamps.")

In Kotzk one does not speak; one roars or one keeps quiet. One spends one's time fighting, cheating desire; one does the opposite of what one feels like doing. One eats when one is not hungry, one does without water when one is thirsty. One prays either later or earlier than is customary. The Rebbe says: "When one feels like shouting and doesn't, that is when one truly shouts." A convalescing Rebbe David is questioned by his father: "You thought you were going to die?" — Yes, that was what he had thought. — "And what did you feel?" — "The need to recite the *Sh'ma Israel* to proclaim my faith in God." — "And did you do it?" — No, the son had checked himself. — "Very good," cries the Rebbe of Kotzk, "you are a true Hasid!"

Silence in Kotzk is so heavy, so dense that it tears the nights. One doesn't dream, one is delirious. One doesn't walk, one runs. One walks a tightrope, and it is he, the Rebbe, who holds both ends. He is present in all eyes, in all thoughts; he paralyzes. One runs after him, but he flees. Sometimes he awakens a faithful and tells him: "Go away, I am the Master here." And the other bursts into sobs. It is enough for him to look into someone's eyes for the other to faint. "Why do you address God by calling him Father?" he scolds a young man. "Who told you He is your father? Did He? If you want Him to be, you must force Him!" Another time he stops a disciple: "Do you know where God resides?" And as the other gapes in astonishment, the Rebbe continues: "I'll tell you: He resides where He is allowed to enter."

With his questions, his unpredictable outbursts of anger, he terrorizes people; as soon as he appears, they feel guilty. Guilty of weakness, of cowardice. "Faces, faces, you all have faces," he cries one night, "but is there one, just one, that could compare itself to God's?" Created in God's image, man owes it to himself to resemble Him, to be whole like Him. Says he: "I prefer a total miscreant to a Jew who is only half Jewish." And his also these harsh, harrowing words: "If I am and You are because I am myself and You are Yourself, then I am I and You are You; but if I am because You are, then I am not I and You are not You."

His words are repeated over and over; they are endowed with special meanings. One hesitates between the desire to understand and the fear of violating an interdiction. In the end, even his friends are at a loss. Without explanation, he will praise someone he publicly insulted the day before. His wife is sick; he does not leave her bedside for weeks. His son gets married: it takes a great deal of persuasion to make him attend the wedding.

Another contradiction: he who has but contempt for earthly matters becomes interested in politics. He offers his support to the Polish national revolution against the Russian occupant. He signs proclamations and appeals, lends his name to collect funds. The Poles are subdued, crushed. And the Rebbe, threatened with arrest by the Russians, changes his name: Halperin becomes Morgenstern.

A change which in no way affects his fate. He remains the rebel he was. He only goes deeper into the shadows that crowd his universe. Some of his disciples, among them Mordhai-Yosseph of Izhbitze, begin to balk: "He is going too far; we need a human being, not a seraph, to lead the way." The Rebbe senses the growing opposition, but does not condescend to take offense. And that is when the mysterious incident, mentioned earlier, takes place. The break occurs. "Broken are the tablets of the Law," exclaims Mordhai-Yosseph, the dissidents' leader. And like his Master had done earlier, he leaves, taking along a large number of disciples. Wounded in his pride, the Rebbe does not hide his resentment. He who had hoped to found an elite was losing his best men, and for what petty reasons! Because he did not show enough concern for their daily bread! His disappointment is doubly bitter.

A few faithful remain, men of distinction all: Yitzhak-Meir, Yehiel-Meir of Gostinin, the Gaon of Sokhatchov and Yitzhak of Worke. But the Rebbe is inconsolable. Perhaps he loved those who left him in spite of what they had done. They resembled him, they dared defy him, even him.

And, in a little while, some of the dissidents return; he chases them away: "Why did you come back? To see me? Am I a chimney sweep that you should stare at me like that?"

Withdrawn, cantankerous, his eyes reddened from lack of sleep, his beard unkempt, speaking in abrupt sentences, the Rebbe aspires to nothing but silence and solitude. "There is nobody I want to see," he tells his faithful friend Hersh Tomashover. "Tell them to leave me alone; use a cane if you must." Another time: "I shall throw myself on these beggars like a wounded bear separated from his brood."

From this period there remain, recorded helter-skelter by chronicle, a cry of anguish, a story, a parable. The same shudder runs through them all.

A parable: The Midrash tells the episode of the traveler who loses his way in the forest. He sees a castle in flames. It's an empty castle, thinks the traveler. Suddenly he hears a voice crying: "Help, help me, I am the owner of the castle!" And the Rebbe repeats: "The castle is ablaze, the forest is burning, and the owner cries for help; what does it mean? That the castle is not empty and that there is an owner!"

And the Rebbe began to tremble and all those present trembled with him.

An offering: Yitzhak of Worke, one of the rare disciples that the Rebbe of Kotzk continued to receive after he went into seclusion, greeted him on that certain day the way he always did: "Peace upon you, Rebbe." — "Don't say that! You hear me? Don't call me Rebbe, I am something else. You want to know who I am? A goat, yes, a goat! You don't believe me? Well, then listen to the story of the holy goat, which is the story of an offering.

"Once upon a time there was a Jew who lost his snuffbox. He searched everywhere, for it meant a lot to him. And then he was too poor to buy himself a new one. When he could not find it anywhere, he began to cry. While walking and searching, he cried and cried. Until he suddenly realized he was in the middle of a forest. And in this forest he came upon the strangest creature, and the most generous as well: a goat. A holy goat, who roamed the roads of time and of the universe waiting for midnight. And every midnight he touched the heavens with his immense horns, awakening the stars and inspiring them to sing the glory of that which is eternal. 'Why are you so sad?' the goat asked. And the Jew told him the truth; that he had lost his snuffbox. — 'Is that all?' the goat asked. 'Nothing could be simpler, it is foolish to cry; I'll help you. Do you have a knife? Yes? Good; take it out. And now, cut yourself a piece of horn and make yourself a snuffbox.'

"The Jew didn't have to be told twice. When he came back to the village the people marveled; his tobacco had the smell of paradise. He was harried with questions until he admitted that

251

it was not the tobacco but the snuffbox. In the end, he had to tell them the whole story. No sooner had he finished, than the entire village population ran for their knives and into the forest, where they did indeed find the most amiable and saintly goat in the world. And they began to cut his horns, which became smaller and smaller by the minute until they disappeared altogether. And so, that same night, the goat was no longer able to touch the sky to wake up the stars and make them sing; he could only look at them from far away, with longing and a little remorse . . . That is why I forbid you to call me Rebbe, do you hear me?"

A visit: One night the Rebbe walked up to Feivel the Watchman, who was asleep: "*He* was here, did you hear him?" Taken aback, afraid to vex the Master, Feivel stammered: "Yes, I heard him." He didn't know whom the Rebbe meant, but he could not keep himself from trembling. And the Rebbe went on musing: "He came, he said what he had to say, he left again. My ears can still perceive the sound of his steps but his voice no longer reaches me."

"Some of the things he said I understood only forty years later," said the Gaon Avraham of Sokhatchov. Forty years? Three times forty.

A stranger to his own generation, Mendl of Kotzk seems to belong to ours; he could be our contemporary. His anger is our anger, our revolts reflect his.

Yet the figure remains obscure, unexplained. It cannot be helped. Kotzk cannot be explained; with some luck, it can be told. For Kotzk, within the Hasidic movement, is an experience transmitted from being to being, lips closed and eyes meeting eyes. A question that continues, unreconciled with either time or life, Kotzk is neither philosophy nor social system; Kotzk is a narrow and solitary road whose beginning touches its end; a road where silence enters the word and tears it apart the way the eye tears apart what it sees. Kotzk means throwing off despair through despair. Kotzk means prison become sanctuary.

Let us come back to our starting point, that fateful and harrowing Shabbat when the Rebbe, pushed to the limit of his endurance, chose to protest against the scandal of history.

Why did he withdraw from man? What did he want to say, and to whom, in his solitude and silence? What enemy was he hiding from? And which one was he pursuing?

Many texts suggest that his seclusion, from a certain point on, was imposed upon him. Sequestration? Possibly. It was necessary to protect both the Rebbe and his Hasidim; he was spreading panic. Who can measure the effect on a disciple of seeing his Master in the throes of depression? Better to limit their contacts.

But scholars seem to agree that in the beginning, the Rebbe's isolation was of his own choosing. He fled crowds for fear that they would absorb him, that his being would be swallowed by theirs. And then he clung fiercely, jealously, to his secret. He even said it: "Once revealed, every secret is diminished." In order to receive the Law, Moses had to climb the mountain alone.

Did Mendl of Kotzk blaspheme? It hardly matters. The fact is that noted religious personalities—the Rebbe of Ger, the Gaon of Sokhatchov, the Rebbe of Worke—remained loyal to him to the end. They had undoubtedly accepted the fact that while he could speak to God in ways different from their own, he nevertheless asserted their common faith.

Perhaps his break with society corresponded to a disillusionment on another level. Could he have become aware of the change that had occurred in him? Earlier he had been afraid never to discover truth; now he was afraid that he had already discovered it. Therefore, there was no solution; whether man turns to one side or the other, he still encounters fear. The link between man and God, between man and his fellow man? Fear. God wants to be feared rather than loved. And Mendl of Kotzk protests: "If that is life, I don't want it; I'll go through it as a stranger. If that is man, what is the good of saving him?"

Another hypothesis: Could he have foreseen that one hundred years after his retreat another fire would set the continent ablaze, and that its first victims would be Jewish men and women abandoned by God and by all mankind? Could it be that from that moment on he planned to fight fire with fire—attempting to prepare us, demanding that we be strong, intransigent, capable of resisting evil no matter what form it takes, the comfort of faith included; capable of resisting even God and the hope in God?

Be that as it may, since Menahem-Mendl of Kotzk, we know that man can become drunk on God, that man can offer Him his soul and his reason as well. That man can become mad of God, on God.

His last words were: "At last I shall see Him face to face."

We don't know—nor will we ever know—whether these words expressed an ancient fear or a renewed defiance. In the final analysis, Mendl of Kotzk will have had a dialogue with one single Being. And the story of Kotzk is the story of that dialogue—a story that burns as burns the castle, as burns the forest. But thanks to Kotzk, we hear a voice and we know that the castle is not empty, that history is not deserted; somebody is there and he is calling us.

. . . H AVING REACHED THE END *of his*
first pilgrimage to the sources of Hasidic experience, the
narrator feels a need to explain himself briefly; if only to define
the meaning and motivation of his undertaking.

Obviously, his purpose was not to create a scholarly work
of critical analysis. Nor does he claim the role of either his-
torian or philosopher; the only role that suits him is the one,
less presumptuous though more limited, of storyteller who
transmits what was given to him, as faithfully as possible, yet
lending it his own voice and intonation and sometimes his
wonder or simply: his fervor.

Here then is a volume that could have been composed or
structured in a different way; this Master rather than that, one
more legend added to so many others.

For the teller of these tales has chosen his subjects following
fancy rather than reason, in the course of various lectures
given here and there in France and the United States. He might
have chosen to outline the theories or sociological and theologi-
cal implications of Hasidism. Instead, he was seduced by the
idea of bringing back to life some of the characters that peopled
his universe, the universe of his childhood. They fascinate and
haunt him still, ever more. For the Hasidic movement that

preached brotherhood and reconciliation became the altar upon which an entire people was immolated. Sometimes the child in me tells me that the world did not deserve this Law, this love, this spirit and this song that accompany man on his lonely road. The world did not deserve the fables the Hasidim told them; that is why they were the first to be caught and swept away in the turmoil.

These Hasidim, whose fate my grandfather shared in life as in death, were part of my world. I responded to their simplicity, their love of beauty. They knew how to worship. And trust. They had mastered the art of giving and receiving. Of sharing and taking part. In their communities, no beggar ever went hungry on Shabbat. In spite of their poverty, their misery, they asked nothing of others. And were endlessly surprised by and grateful for the smallest expression of warmth, of generosity. Therefore, they could not survive in a society ruled by cold cruelty, a cruelty both impersonal and absurd.

Why is there a renewal of interest in them today? Is it that man feels guilty? Does their death weigh on his conscience? Perhaps. But there is something else: he is moved and troubled by their message, its loss irrevocably linked to his own inability to believe and persevere. "God is prayer," said Rebbe Pinhas of Koretz. And never has modern man been more closed to prayer.

It must also be pointed out that all the conditions that existed in the eighteenth century, when Hasidism came into being, prevail again today. Physical and emotional insecurity, fallen idols, the scourge of violence. Where can one go, where can one hide? "Hell exists and it is of this world," said Rebbe Nahman, "but none dares speak of it." Wrong. Today everyone dares. Never before has mankind known such anguish. Such ugliness. Man walks the moon but his soul remains riveted to

256

earth. Once upon a time it was the opposite. Despairing of the present, man seeks beauty in legends. Like the Hasid long ago.

In his universe, beggars are princes; the mute are sages. Endowed with special powers, vagabonds roam the earth and change it. Such is the nature of Hasidism: the accent is placed on presence and also on transformation. In Hasidism, everything is possible, everything becomes possible by the mere presence of someone who knows how to listen, to love and give of himself. The essence of a Hasidic legend? An attempt to humanize fate.

And so the story that I have tried to tell here has been told more than once, by more than one person. It is always the same, and I, in turn, do nothing but transmit.

A needless repetition? No. Repetition, in Judaism, can assume a creative role. Of Eliezer Ben-Hyrkenos it was said that he never pronounced a word he had not heard from his Master. Strange compliment. Could Rabbi Eliezer have invented nothing, composed nothing? On the contrary: he did much. Still, it was by repeating the teachings that linked him to Moses and through him to God, that he contributed to Jewish thought and destiny. To transmit is more important than to innovate. Every question a disciple will ask his Master, and that until the end of time, Moses already knew. Yet, we must ask the questions and make them ours by repeating them. In Hebrew, the word massora, tradition, comes from the verb limsor, to transmit. In our history, this need to communicate, to share, comes close to being an obsession.

Of course, all experiences cannot be transmitted by the word. There are those that must be transmitted from being to being, by a whisper or a glance, or—and why not—through laughter. Rebbe Henokh of Alexander knew that when his Master, Rebbe Mendl of Kotzk, told him funny stories, he was actually lamenting the destruction of the Temple in Jerusalem. And when, at the conclusion of Shabbat, I listened to the old men speak of their respective Rebbes, I closed my eyes to see what they were seeing.

The Baal Shem, the Maggid, Levi-Yitzhak, Israel of Rizhin; now it is my turn to show them the way I saw them as a child, as I see them still. They are subjective, incomplete, these portraits, with their share of unavoidable repetitions, errors and gaps. They may well say more about the narrator than about his characters. Perhaps he only told the tales of Nahman of Bratzlav or Mendl of Kotzk to show how they influenced his own attitude toward language and what it conceals, toward man, his truth and his solitude.

Perhaps he spoke of Levi-Yitzhak of Berditchev only to claim his heritage. And of Zusia of Onipol only to acknowledge what he owes him, what he owes all these Rebbes of another era who have remained his Masters. The omission of certain illustrious figures is due only to chance, nothing else. Shneur-Zalmen of Ladi, Haim of Tzanz, Yitzhak-Meir of Ger, Meir of Premishlan, Naftali-Hersh of Ropshitz, Mendl of Kossov, Moshe of Ujhely; each one of them founded a school, each is a source of enrichment. The teller of tales hopes to show this later; this is but the beginning of his pilgrimage. If the priorities seem arbitrary, it is because they are dictated by his childhood. In his town, for instance, one spoke more of Rizhin than of Ger, one felt closer to the Baal Shem than to his commentators. Thus his choice stems from criteria no one else is obliged to accept. He takes what he needs and leaves the rest for another time. If he favors a particular legend over another, it does not mean that it is any truer but only that he heard this one and not the other. If a certain tale is attributed to two, three or five different Masters, it becomes his gift to the one he loves most. Nor will he be the first to do this; every Hasid does it, and has done it since the Baal Shem. Why, then, shouldn't he?

All the more since—in his role of storyteller, and that is the essential point—he has but one motivation: to tell of himself while telling of others. He wishes neither to teach nor to convince, but to close gaps and create new bonds. Nor does he try to explain what was or even what is; he only tries to wrest from death certain prayers, certain faces, by appealing to the imagination and the nostalgia that make man listen when his story is told.

BACKGROUND
NOTES

AGGADA: Parables, commentaries, legends, proverbs and fables, most often deriving from Biblical texts, expounding on their complexities and constituting one of the aspects of Talmud and Midrash. Whereas Halakah enjoins conformity by tracing guidelines to a way of life, Aggada, less severe and less coercive, and even at times and as circumstances require, mischievous or poetic, awakens thought, meditation or prayer, and brings into focus the foundations of a system of ethics and faith.

BAAL SHEM (literally Master of the Name): Title attributed since the Middle Ages to men who know the true name of beings and things, recognize their secret and can act upon them, through them. By naming the forces, such a man masters them; his knowledge is power. Were he to use this power to attain immediate or profane gains, he would be nothing more than a miracle-maker. But if he chooses to bring the names closer to the Name, and unite beings and things with God, he becomes Master of the Good Name, Baal Shem Tov.

BEIT MIDRASH (literally "House of Study"): In order not to interrupt meditation and discussion on the sacred Word, the rabbinical academies chose to remain there for services rather than move to the Beit Knesseth, the assembly house (synagogue). The two "Houses" often became one, or at least were made to adjoin, with services extending into study and study culminating in prayer. "At the hour of prayer and study" is a frequently recurring expression in Hasidic texts.

According to Aggada, the first Beit Midrash was founded by Sem on the morrow of the Deluge. When Isaac was freed of his bonds and left the altar, that is where he retired to study.

DAYAN: Judge of the rabbinical tribunal, arbiter.

DIN: Judgment, legal decision; *midat hadin:* divine rigor and severity.

FRANK, JACOB (1726–1791): Last of the "great" would-be Messiahs. A disciple of Shabtai Tzvi, he tried to "rehabilitate" Christianity for the Jews, ultimately converting amid great pomp in the Warsaw cathedral with Emperor Augustus III as his godfather. Later he spent thirteen years in prison for heresy. Retired to the Rhineland with his daughter Eve, famous for her beauty, he taught and practiced the "rehabilitation" of sexuality by unrestrained indulgence in its every form.

GAON OF VILNA, or Rabbi Elijah ben Salomon Zalman (1720–1797): The most exalted rabbinical figure of Eastern European Jewry, a man of outstanding moral stature and quasi-encyclopedic learning. The unchallenged Master of Halakah, he also had a profound knowledge of Kabbala. Leader of the Mitnagdim, he vehemently opposed the Hasidic movement and vigorously fought its expansion in Lithuania.

HALAKAH (literally: walk, way, rule): That which in Talmud and rabbinical literature concerns itself with the ritual, social and economic life of the community and the individual. Like the texts of Aggada, with which they overlap, the texts of Halakah are generally based on Biblical exegesis. They constitute the basis of an ample body of laws regulating every aspect of the life of a practicing Jew.

HASID (literally: fervent, pious): One who acts out of love, with tenderness. Derived from *hesed*, grace, one of God's attributes complementing *din*, strict justice. God's grace calls forth the fervor, the piety of man, his love for God and all His creatures.

In the Psalms, Hasid (plural, Hasidim) often denotes the "faithful," the "lover of God." In the Talmud (Pirkhe Aboth, V, 13–16), Hasid is "he who says: what is mine is yours and what is yours is yours; he who is slow to anger and quick to relent; he who enjoys giving and likes others to give"—and again, "he who, even before he prays, turns his heart to God—for at least one hour" (Ber. 30b)—and even "the Hasidim among the Gentiles will have their share in the world to come" (Toss. Sanh. 13; Mishne Torah, Melakhim 11).

In the second century B.C. a Jewish sect, the Hasidim or Assideans, "valiant men whose hearts were bound to the Law," fought with the Maccabees against Antiochus Epiphanus. But refusing all compromise on religious law and unwilling to become involved in politics, they broke away from the Hasmonean dynasty after victory had been achieved. The Talmud refers to them as "the Hasidim of yore."

In the thirteenth century of the Common Era, there flourished in the Rhineland an important school called the Hasidim of Ashkenaz, the "Holy Men of Germany"; they created a trend of thought that found wide acceptance. Their major work, the *Sefer Hasidim,* the "Book of the Devout," rooted in Jewish mystical tradition, stresses the majesty of God but also the mystery of oneness, elaborating a veritable philosophy of history and man's relationship to man, emphasizing the importance of silent piety, of prayer, and of a system of ethics based on renunciation of earthly matters, spiritual serenity, total love of one's fellow man culminating in the expression of the fear and the love of God in "the joy that scorches the heart."

HILLEL AND SHAMMAI, respectively president and vice-president of the Sanhedrin—in the first century B.C. They are the last and best known of the "couples" of rabbis whose opinions challenge and complete one another. The "School of Shammai," more concerned with principles and ultimate goals, was the more severe, the more rigorous of the two; the "House of Hillel," mindful of the lessons of the past, leaned toward a gentler approach.

KAVANA (literally: intention): Spiritual concentration on prayer or the religious act to prepare for *devekut—*

compliance with the Divine Will. The Talmud stresses
the need of directing one's thoughts toward God, not
only while praying but also while obeying the Commandments. The "mystics" of the Middle Ages, and later the
Hasidim, insisted on this form of contemplation, and
composed *Kavanoth,* "prayers—or poems—of intention," to prepare and assist in the transition into ritual
service.

LAMED VAVNIK: "The world," says the Talmud, "must not
contain fewer than thirty-six Just Men who have been
allowed to contemplate the Divine Presence. It is thanks
to them that the world subsists. Popular imagination
took hold of these Lamed Vavnik (the numerical value
of the letters *lamed* and *vav* is thirty-six), gave them a
background of poverty and obscurity and described
them as leading hidden lives, revealing their qualities
and powers only in cases of need, when the survival of
the community, the people, or the world is at stake.

LURIA, ISAAC, also referred to as the "Ari," the "Holy Lion
of Safed" (1534–1572): He was born in Jerusalem,
lived in Cairo and died in Safed; one of the most mysterious, complex and popular Masters of Kabbala. His
strictly oral teachings owe their dissemination to notes
taken by his disciple Hayim Vital. His thoughts on
Tzimtzum (the withdrawal of God into Himself to leave
room for human groping and error); on the *Shevirat
Hakelim,* the "broken vessels" of Primary Light whose
sparks subsist even in the infernal regions; on the
Tikkun (the "bridging" of gaps, the in-gathering of
sparks, "restoration" as a historical objective); on the

Messiah in chains awaiting the redemption of our every
deed, all strongly influenced Hasidism.

MEZUZAH (literally: doorpost): A small tubular case, usually
of metal or wood, containing a tightly rolled piece of
parchment inscribed with verses 4–9 of Deut. 6 and
13–21 of Deut. 11 on one side, and *Shaddai* (a name
applied to God) on the other, the latter visible through
an aperture in the case. The mezuzah is traditionally
attached to the right doorpost of the Jewish home. The
great philosopher-legislator of the Middle Ages, Moses
ben Maimon (Maimonides), expressed its meaning
this way:

"By the commandment of the mezuzah, man is reminded, when entering or departing, of God's Oneness,
and is stirred into love for Him. He is awakened from
his slumber and from his vain worldly thoughts to the
knowledge that no thing endures in eternity like knowledge of the 'Rock of the World.' This contemplation
brings him back to himself and leads him unto the right
path."

MIDRASH: From a Hebrew verb meaning to expound, to
interpret, to deduce; specifically to expound the precepts and ethical dicta of Scriptures; in fact, a large body
of Talmudic literature that developed during the Tan-
naic and Amoraic periods (second century of the
Common Era).

MITNAGDIM (literally: adversaries): They opposed the "new
Hasidic sect," judging it revolutionary, dangerous, heretic.

SHABTAI-TZVI (1626–1676): The most prestigious of the false Messiahs. Born in Smyrna, well versed in Talmud and practical Kabbala, he wandered from Salonika to Jerusalem, enticing crowds and attracting wrath, teaching a doctrine in which are evident elements of the school of Luria. In 1665 he proclaimed himself Messiah. The news spread like wildfire and aroused indescribable enthusiasm and exultation in the Jewish world; people everywhere prayed for "our Master, the Anointed of the Lord"; some even sold their property, expecting an imminent miraculous departure for the Holy Land. In 1666 he expressed the wish to meet the Sultan so as to request recognition of his sovereignty over the Land of Israel. Instead he found himself in prison. Then, one day, the Sultan summoned him; we don't know what took place, except that soon thereafter Shabtai-Tzvi converted to Islam—only to be exiled to Albania, where he ended his days in obscurity.

Yet the most fervent among his disciples saw in his conversion but another step in a divine pattern; his cult subsisted until the twentieth century in the East, and at least one hundred years in the West, where he provoked controversies and suspicions, heresy and excommunications.

SH'MA ISRAEL (literally: Hear O Israel): A liturgical prayer, prominent in Jewish history and tradition, recited daily at evening and morning services, "you will say them when you lie down and when you rise" (verse 7, Deut. 6); it brings together three passages of the Pentateuch, all expressing Israel's ardent faith in and love of God.

The important place it holds in Jewish consciousness has made it into a veritable "profession of faith" that is repeated by the dying man and the martyr.

SHIMON BAR-YOHAI (second century of the Common Era): Famous Master whose teachings are frequently quoted and expounded in the Talmud. He was condemned to death for having criticized the Roman occupiers but succeeded in escaping. With his son, he took shelter in a cave, where he spent thirteen years. There are numerous legends woven around this period in his life: it was said that he explored the mysteries of Kabbala during his reclusion and laid the foundations of the Zohar. To this day, there are considerable numbers of faithful who visit his grave in Meron, near Safed, on the thirty-third day after Passover, the anniversary of his death.

TANYA: The basic work of the HaBaD movement within Hasidism which produced the school of Lubavitch. Authored by the founder of HaBaD, Rebbe Shneur-Zalmen of Ladi (1747–1813), the Tanya consists of two parts: the first shows the way to "those who are neither perfect Just Men nor evil outcasts," in other words those who may, through study, prayer and meditation, attain the love of God; the second, the "Book of Unity and Faith," is a commentary on the *Sh'ma.*

TZADDIK: Just Man, ideal of moral, social and religious perfection, he is a man "who lives by his faith," and to whom God responds. In the Hasidic movement the Tzaddik rapidly became an institution, but though a "spiritual model," when exposed to temptation, he was not always able to resist, going as far as to proclaim himself intermediary between his disciples and God, presiding over veritable courts and founding dynasties.

YOHANAN BEN-ZAKKAI, also called Rabban, our Master: One of the key figures in the elaboration of the Talmud. In order to protect the continuity of studies, he fled a Jerusalem occuped by Vespasian and founded the Academy of Yavneh, which succeeded the Sanhedrin and guaranteed the survival of the tradition. After the destruction of the Temple, Rabbi Yohanan Ben-Zakkai compiled all that was known of sacrificial ritual, down to the smallest details, in expectation of Messianic restoration. At the same time he stressed the important place held, in the absence of the Temple, and to this day, by study of the holy texts and the synagogal cult.

ZOHAR: The "Book of Splendor," principal work of Kabbala, esoteric commentary on the Pentateuch, traditionally attributed to Rabbi Shimon Bar-Yohai.

SYNCHRONOLOGY

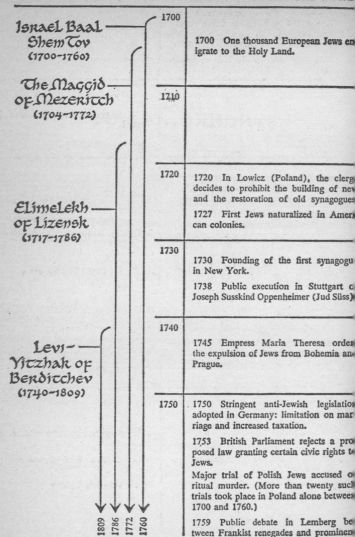

Israel Baal Shem Tov (1700–1760)

The Maggid of Mezeritch (1704–1772)

Elimelekh of Lizensk (1717–1786)

Levi-Yitzhak of Berditchev (1740–1809)

1700

1710

1720

1730

1740

1750

1700   One thousand European Jews em igrate to the Holy Land.

1720   In Lowicz (Poland), the clerg decides to prohibit the building of nev and the restoration of old synagogues

1727   First Jews naturalized in Ameri can colonies.

1730   Founding of the first synagogu in New York.

1738   Public execution in Stuttgart c Joseph Susskind Oppenheimer (Jud Süss)

1745   Empress Maria Theresa order the expulsion of Jews from Bohemia an Prague.

1750   Stringent anti-Jewish legislatio adopted in Germany: limitation on mar riage and increased taxation.

1753   British Parliament rejects a pro posed law granting certain civic rights t Jews.

Major trial of Polish Jews accused o ritual murder. (More than twenty suc trials took place in Poland alone betwee 1700 and 1760.)

1759   Public debate in Lemberg be tween Frankist renegades and prominen rabbis.

1809   1786   1772   1760

IN THE WORLD AT LARGE	IN THE ARTS
1700–1721 The "Great Northern War." Russia, led by Peter the Great, Poland and Denmark fight against Charles XII of Sweden for supremacy in the Baltic. 1701–1714 War of the Spanish Succession.	
	1715 Pope translates the *Iliad* into English.
	1726 Swift's *Gulliver's Travels*.
1733–1735 War of the Polish Succession.	1733 J.S. Bach's B-Minor Mass.
1740–1748 War of the Austrian Succession.	1740 Hume's *Treatise on Human Nature*. 1742 Handel's *Messiah*. 1748 Montesquieu's *Spirit of the Laws*.
1756–1763 Seven Years' War. Russia, Austria, France and others against Prussia and Great Britain.	1759 Inauguration of the British Museum. —— Haydn's First Symphony performed. —— Voltaire's *Candide*.

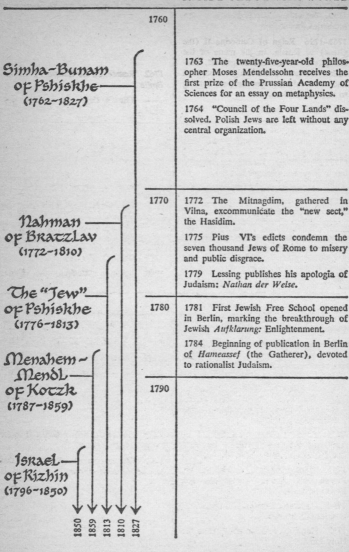

Simha-Bunam of Pshiskhe (1762–1827)

Nahman of Bratzlav (1772–1810)

The "Jew" of Pshiskhe (1776–1813)

Menahem-Mendl of Kotzk (1787–1859)

Israel of Rizhin (1796–1850)

1760

1763 The twenty-five-year-old philosopher Moses Mendelssohn receives the first prize of the Prussian Academy of Sciences for an essay on metaphysics.

1764 "Council of the Four Lands" dissolved. Polish Jews are left without any central organization.

1770

1772 The Mitnagdim, gathered in Vilna, excommunicate the "new sect," the Hasidim.

1775 Pius VI's edicts condemn the seven thousand Jews of Rome to misery and public disgrace.

1779 Lessing publishes his apologia of Judaism: *Nathan der Weise*.

1780

1781 First Jewish Free School opened in Berlin, marking the breakthrough of Jewish *Aufklarung*: Enlightenment.

1784 Beginning of publication in Berlin of *Hameassef* (the Gatherer), devoted to rationalist Judaism.

1790

1850 1859 1813 1810 1827

IN THE WORLD AT LARGE	IN THE ARTS
1760 Beginnings (in England) of the Industrial Revolution. 1762–1796 Reign of Catherine II (the Great) of Russia. In the name of the Enlightenment she encourages art, education and letters, and instigates political and social reforms—yet she does nothing to abolish serfdom. 1764–1795 Reign of Stanislas II (Poniatowski), last king of Poland. The country is dismembered by Russia, Austria and Prussia during the first (1772), the second (1793) and the third (1795) partitions. Having no country left to govern, he resigns in 1795.	1762 Rousseau's *Le Contrat Social* and *Émile* —— Gluck's *Orfeo ed Euridice* performed.
1772 First partition of Poland. 1775–1783 American war for independence. 1778–1779 War of the Bavarian Succession.	1771 First publication of the Encyclopaedia Britannica. 1772 Diderot publishes last volume of *Encyclopédie*. 1774 Goethe's *Werther*. 1779 Lessing's *Nathan der Weise*.
1789–1799 The French Revolution.	1781 Kant's *Critique of Pure Reason*. 1785 Mozart's *Marriage of Figaro*.
1793 Second partition of Poland. 1793–1794 The Reign of Terror. Robespierre massacres opposition, Marie Antoinette is guillotined. 1794 Polish national uprising led by Thaddeus Kosciusko crushed by combined Russian and Prussian armies. 1795 Third partition of Poland. Russia, Prussia and Austria absorb the last Polish territories. 1796 Napoleon Bonaparte embarks on a series of victories. 1799 Napoleon and his army reach the Holy Land.	1790 Goya's *Caprichos*, works of social satire. Goethe's *Faust*. 1797 Chateaubriand's *Essays on Old and Modern Revolutions*.

1800

**Nahman
of
Bratzlav**
(1772–1810)

1810

**The "Jew"
of
Pshiskhe**
(1776–1813)

1812 Napoleon's invasion of Russia
brings about the emancipation of its
Jews.

1815 Pius VII reinstitutes the Inquisi-
tion. The constitution of Poland—finally
formulated—denies civic rights to Jews.

1819 Beginning of movement "Wissen-
schaft des Judentum's" in Germany; it
will expand to all of Western Europe.

**Simha-
Bunam
of Pshiskhe**
(1762–1827)

1820

1824 Mass persecutions of Jews in Russia.

1830

**Israel
of Rizhin**
(1796–1850)

1840

1840 Jews accused of ritual murder in
Damascus.

1842 More persecutions of Russian
Jews; their children are forced into military service for twenty-five-year stretches.

1845 Jews are expelled from Basel.

1847 A Jew becomes a member of the
British Parliament: Baron Lionel of
Rothschild.

**Menahem-
Mendl
of Kotzk**
(1787–1859)

1850

IN THE WORLD AT LARGE	IN THE ARTS
	1800 Schiller's *Marie Stuart*.
	1807 Byron publishes his first poems; Fichte, his *Sermons to the German Nation*; Hegel, his *Phenomenology of the Mind*.
	1808 Beethoven's Pastoral Symphony.
1812 Napoleon invades Russia.	
1813 Battle of Leipzig—Napoleon defeated.	
1815 Waterloo. Napoleon definitively defeated and exiled.	
1814–1815 Congress of Vienna ends wars of Napoleonic era.	
1815 The Holy Alliance is signed by all European rulers except the King of England, the Pope and the Sultan. Alexander I is the most active sponsor of this agreement, which allies Christian principles with politics and which generally represents a reactionary policy against liberal ideas.	
1825–1855 Reign of Nicholas I of Russia is marked by autocracy and repression of all liberal tendencies.	1820 Keats publishes his major poems, the *Odes*; Shelley, his *Prometheus Unbound*.
	1827 Heine's *Das Buch der Lieder*.
	1830 Victor Hugo's *Hernani*.
	1831 Stendhal's *Le Rouge et le Noir*.
	1838 Dickens' *Oliver Twist*.
	1843 Kierkegaard's *Fear and Trembling*.
1848 Revolutions in Austria, Prussia, Hungary, Italy, Prague . . . all of Europe is in an uproar.	1849 Dostoevsky arrested for his political activities, condemned to death, but pardoned by the Tsar and sent to prison.
	Tolstoi tries to establish a school for peasants at Yasnaia Polyana, his family's estate.
	1850 Balzac's *La Comédie Humaine*.
	1859 Darwin's *Origin of the Species*.

AUTHOR'S NOTE

The main chapters in this volume are based on lectures delivered at the Sorbonne in Paris and at the 92nd Street "Y" in New York. The latter would not have been undertaken had it not been for the initiative of Lily Edelman, Director of Adult Education of B'nai B'rith, the cooperation of William Kolodney, former Educational Director of the 92nd Street "Y," and the dedication of Herbert Reiman, also of B'nai B'rith.

My thanks to Professor Gerson D. Cohen for his valuable suggestions during the preparation of the Synchronology, and to Professor Abraham J. Heschel, my gratitude for sharing with me his own insight on Mendl of Kotzk.

The tales and sayings are translated from the original Yiddish and Hebrew texts, the languages used by the Hasidic Masters and their disciples. Their names and the names of their towns are spelled—arbitrarily—to approximate the way they were pronounced by the Hasidim I knew.

ABOUT THE AUTHOR

Elie Wiesel was born in 1928 in the town of Sighet in Transylvania. He was still a child when he was taken from his home and sent first to the Auschwitz concentration camp and then to Buchenwald. After the holocaust he was brought to Paris, where he lived and worked as a journalist and a writer. He has been an American citizen for some years, and he and his wife live in New York City for most of the year, spending the balance in Paris and Israel.

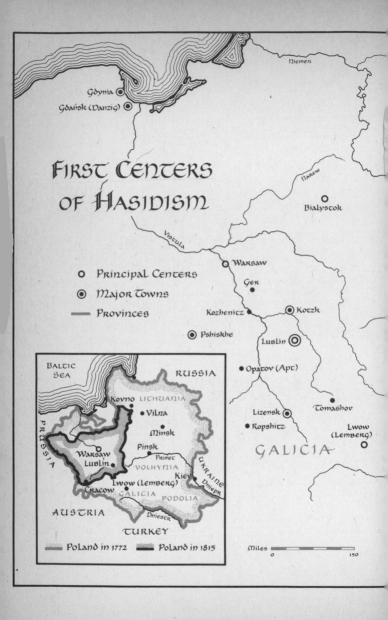

FIRST CENTERS
OF HASIDISM

- ○   Principal Centers
- ◉   Major Towns
- ━━   Provinces

Gdynia

Gdansk (Danzig)

Niemen

Narew

Bialystok

Vistula

Warsaw

Ger

Kozhenitz

Kotzk

Pshiskhe

Lublin

Opatov (Apt)

Lizensk

Tomashov

Ropshitz

Lwow (Lemberg)

GALICIA

BALTIC
SEA

RUSSIA

Kovno

LITHUANIA

PRUSSIA

Vilna

Minsk

Pinsk

Pripet

Warsaw

Lublin

VOLHYNIA

Kiev

UKRAINE

Lwow (Lemberg)

Dnieper

Cracow

GALICIA

PODOLIA

AUSTRIA

Dniester

TURKEY

▨ Poland in 1772   ▩ Poland in 1815

Miles

0

150

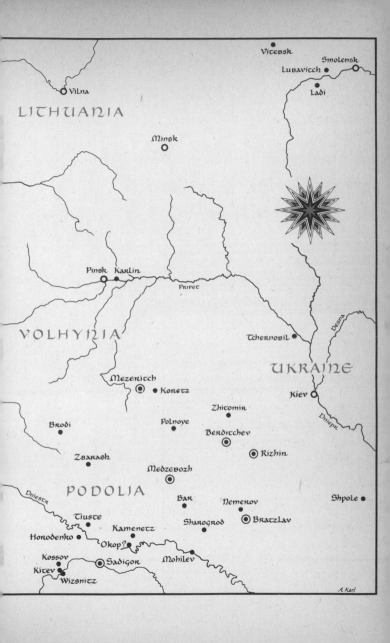

Vitebsk

Lubavitch Smolensk

Vilna Ladi

LITHUANIA

Minsk

Pinsk Karlin

Pripet

VOLHYNIA

Tchernobil

UKRAINE

Mezeritch

Konetz

Kiev

Zhitomir

Brodi Polnoye

Berditchev

Dniepr

Zbarash

Rizhin

Medzebozh

PODOLIA

Bar Nemerov Shpole

Dniester

Tluste

Sharogrod Bratzlav

Kamenetz

Horodenko

Okop?

Kossov Mohilev

Kitev Sadigor

Wiznitz

A. Karl

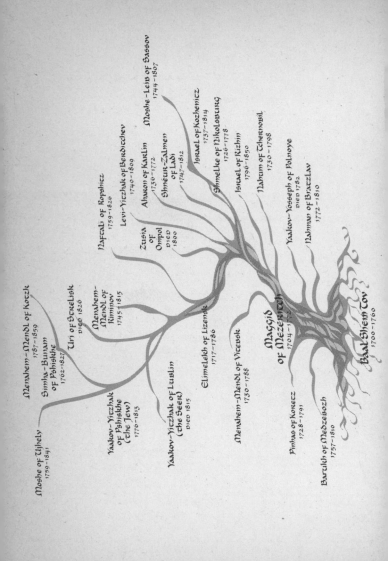

Moshe of Ujhely
1759–1841

Menahem–Mendl of Kotzk
1787–1859

Simha–Bunam
of Pshiskhe
1762–1827

Uri of Strelisk
died 1826

Menahem–
Mendl of
Rimanov
1745–1815

Yaakov-Yitzhak
of Pshiskhe
(the Jew)
1770–1813

Yaakov-Yitzhak of Lublin
(the Seer)
died 1815

Elimelekh of Lizensk
1717–1786

Menahem–Mendl of Vitebsk
1730–1788

Pinhas of Koretz
1728–1791

Barukh of Medzebozh
1757–1810

Maggid
of Mezeritch
1704–1772

Nafcali of Ropshitz
1759–1820

Levi-Yitzhak of Berdichev
1740–1809

Zusia
of
Onipol
died
1800

Aharon of Karlin
1730–1772

Shneur-Zalmen
of Ladi
1747–1812

Israel of Kozhenitz
1737–1814

Shmelke of Nikolsburg
1726–1778

Israel of Rizhin
1796–1850

Nahum of Tchernobil
1730–1798

Yaakov-Yosseph of Polnoye
died 1782

Nahman of Bratzlav
1772–1810

Moshe-Leib of Sassov
1749–1807

Baal-Shem-Tov
1700–1760